CW01636873

ELGIN
FROM OLD PHOTOGRAPHS

JENNY MAIN

AMBERLEY

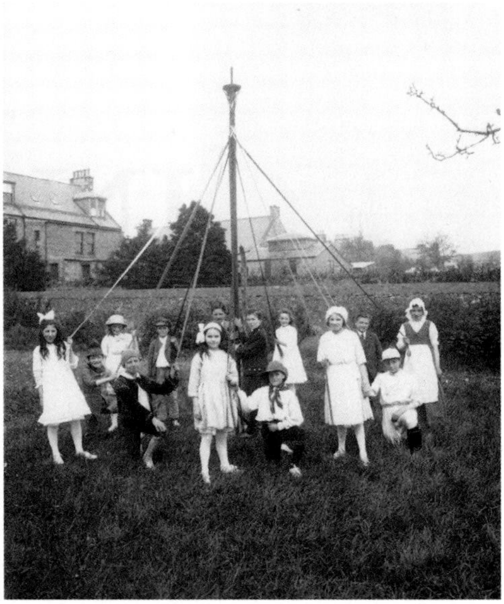

First published 1996
This edition published 2009

Copyright © Jenny Main, 2009

Amberley Publishing
Cirencester Road, Chalford,
Stroud, Gloucestershire, GL6 8PE

Dedicated to all of George's friends

All rights reserved. No part of this book may be reprinted or reproduced or utilised in any form or by any electronic, mechanical or other means, now known or hereafter invented, including photocopying and recording, or in any information storage or retrieval system, without the permission in writing from the Publishers.

British Library Cataloguing in Publication Data.
A catalogue record for this book is available from the British Library.

ISBN 978-1-84868-443-0

Typesetting and origination by Amberley Publishing
Printed in Great Britain

CONTENTS

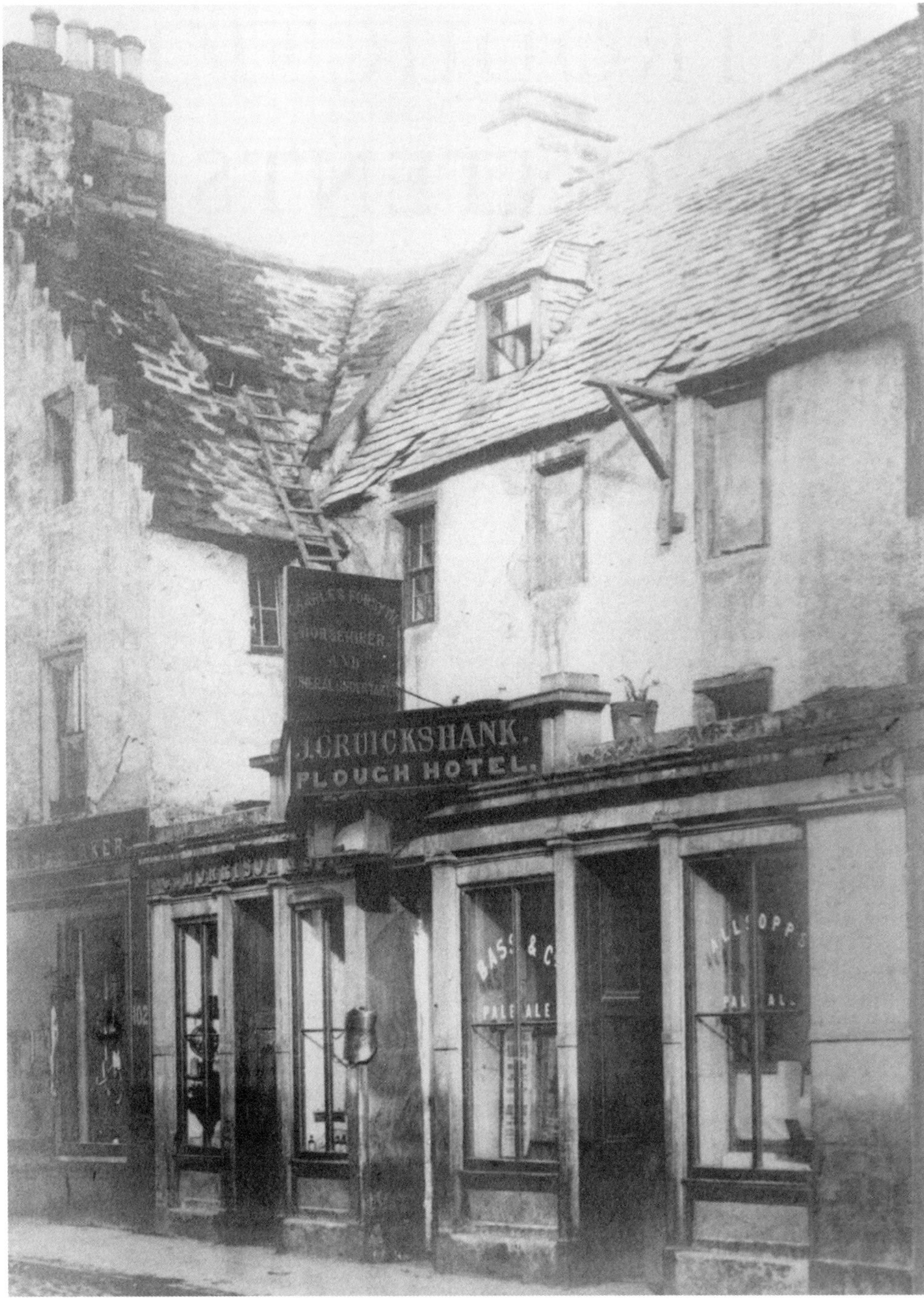

Where it all started: The Palace Buildings replaced the Plough Hotel at the end of the last century and Studio Tyrell began its photographic business there. Most of the glass negatives reproduced in this book, dating between 1884 and 1920, were discovered in the Old Studio in 1971 and salvaged by Tony Spring when he took over the business at that time.

Introduction

Millions of years ago when reptiles roamed the earth they left footprints in the muddy soil. Some died in the mud and their footprints and skeletons were preserved in the layers of rock that were to become the sandstone beds of Moray. Dinosaurs came and went; the earth changed and climatic upheavals sculpted the landscape. As the ice finally retreated mankind began to explore further north. The coastline and straths of the north-east of Scotland were roamed by nomads who left little tangible evidence of their existence, apart from tiny flints such as those found at Culbin. In a climate warmer than that of today, Neolithic farmers arrived and changed the landscape. Forests of scrub oak, hazel, juniper and birch were cleared with stone or flint-head axes to provide grazing for animals, to grow crops and to provide wood. These folk left behind burial mounds, flints and a few shards of pottery.

Later immigrants from the Continent buried their dead in stone cists. One such man, covered in hairy ox-hide and with a bronze dagger, was found in what is now the Bishopmill area. Mounds and cairns were built. Earthworks, henges such as Quarrywood, and stone circles reveal the existence of an increasingly complex and organized society.

From 1000 BC the climate gradually worsened and crop-raising became more difficult in upland areas. The invaders who ushered in the Iron Age left behind gold torques and jewellery and substantial stone forts. Their building skills were inherited by the Picts who continued to develop and cultivate the area, fighting, farming and trading far afield. Skilfully carved Pictish stones illustrate their many capabilities.

The rivers from the great hills fed the lands of the Laich. The sea provided an efficient means of travel and communication between the tribes of Picts and the peoples of the Continent and Scandinavia. The intrepid Romans left evidence of their presence in the area too. Travellers brought back new artefacts, ideas and religion. Celtic people infiltrated from the West and Moray continued to develop in importance. Elgin Castle was in existence in 1040 when King Duncan allegedly died there after being wounded by Macbeth.

The influence of the Church increased and in 1224 a proper cathedral church was established in Elgin. Its construction required many skilled workers and craftsmen, and the trades of Elgin formed themselves into corporations as the town grew in both size and stature.

In 1226 Edward I took up residence in the castle at Ladyhill for several days while accepting submission from the Scottish nobles. Edward's army of 35,000 men camped outside the castle and it was joined by the retinues of the submitting Scots. Morayshire must have been a prosperous place to support such numbers - no matter how reluctantly.

In 1390 the notorious Wolf of Badenoch burnt the town and the cathedral. Extensive repairs resulted in what was considered to be the most beautiful of all the cathedrals erected in Scotland. Written records give some insight into the life of those times. Political and religious turmoil followed the Reformation and by the end of the seventeenth century Moray had survived civil wars and famine. Craft guilds - hammermen, glovers, tailors, shoemakers, weavers and squarewrights - gradually obtained greater political influence in the town. Foreign trade increased and flourished. Ale was exported to Holland, Norway and the Baltic Sea ports until the heavy export and import duties imposed after 1707 resulted in the gradual decline of brewing. Linen and fine cambric were woven from flax grown and spun in the Laich of Duffus, and much was exported to the Continent.

By the early nineteenth century educated men found time to investigate the environment of Moray and correspond with eminent scientists of the day. Fossil remains of fish, ancient reptiles, a dinosaur and fossilized footprints were discovered in the sandstone quarries around Elgin. In 1836 the Elgin and Morayshire Scientific Association was formed, which eventually became the Moray Society. In 1842 the Elgin Museum was built to house the growing collections. The fossils, flints, tools, jewellery, pottery and mysterious carved stone balls provided a link to Moray's previous inhabitants. The intricate patterns on the Pictish stones, the powerful images of the carved bulls housed in the museum, and the scenes of hawking pictured on the stone now located in the cathedral grounds all give an insight into the lives of the Pictish people who lived and loved around Elgin.

There is no shortage of written records of life in the recent past. Newspaper articles from the nineteenth century reveal a lively social life for some townsfolk, with lengthy descriptions of fancy-dress balls and social occasions held in the great town houses. They also report the failure of the potato crop in 1846 and the subsequent Moray meal riots. Late in the century photography became a burgeoning art form and, for the first time, it was possible to record people, places and events as well as daily life. In 1971 when Tony Spring took over the Tyrell photographic studio in Elgin he discovered boxes of old glass negatives dating back to the end of the nineteenth century. Sadly many of them had been damaged in the belief that they were of no interest. Luckily Tony was able to rescue some and he donated these to the Elgin Museum when he retired in 1995. These glass negatives form the bulk of the photographs in this book and show us the people of the past who, under the influences of their forbears, helped form the Elgin of today.

This book is not an attempt to provide a cohesive record of the history of Elgin. It is merely a random selection, as in a family album. Unnamed faces may seem familiar, or a family resemblance recognized. There may be lively discussions about the exact location and function of places and buildings, and differing opinions about the improvements or lack of them. Elgin has changed considerably from the town of 4,000 souls at the beginning of the nineteenth century. Thanks to the art of the camera we are among the first generations who can look back more than a century and see how it was.

Jenny Main

Section One

The Heart of the Town: St Giles

The original St Giles' Church was built forty years before the cathedral, and has been the heart of the town ever since. The woodwork of the original building was destroyed by the Wolf of Badenoch in 1390, but later local troubles left it unscathed, and by the Reformation in 1560 it was still intact. After the Reformation the officiating priests disappeared and the private altars belonging to the magistrates and the incorporated trades were removed. Following a service in 1679 the roof fell in and, at a cost of £4,000 Scots, the building was restored to the form of a Greek cross. In 1700 the north and south aisles were removed in order to widen the street. The old building was finally demolished in 1826.

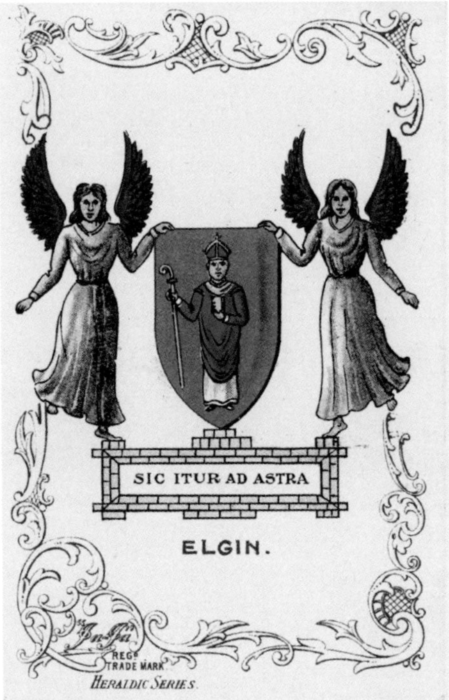

The coat of arms was granted to Elgin in 1678. The Latin motto can be translated, 'Thus we aspire to the stars'. In 1996 a petition was granted to have the coat of arms restored, ensuring that this historical link with the past was maintained.

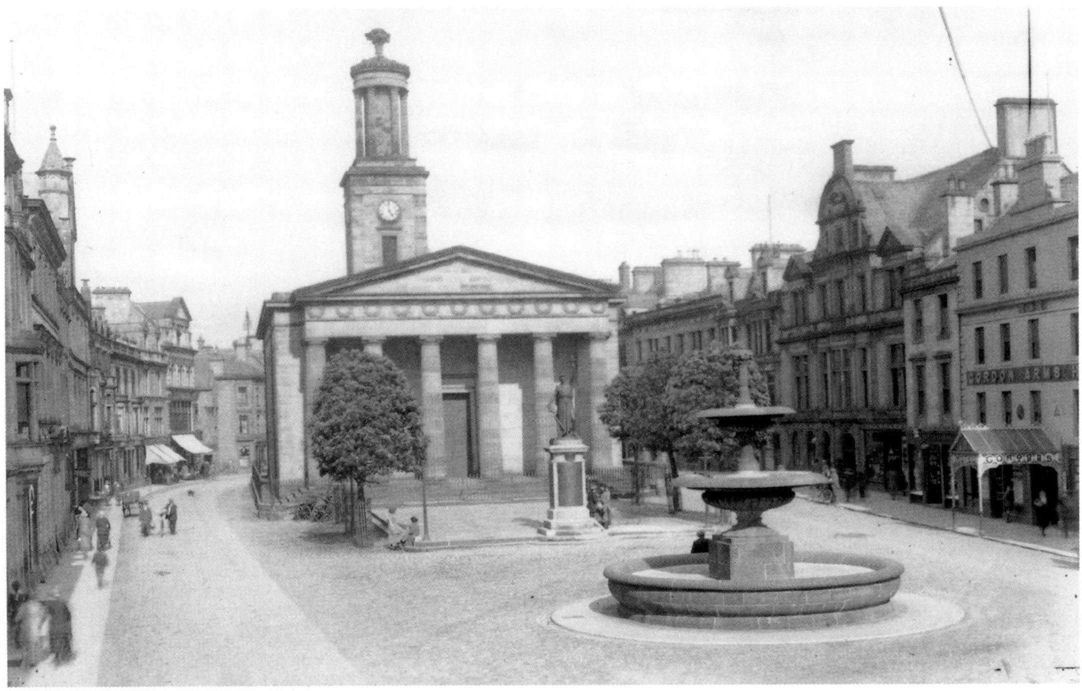

In 1826 the original St Giles' Church was considered dangerous and was demolished. The new building, designed by Archibald Simpson in the style of a Greek temple, cost £8,700. The foundation stone was laid by Sir Archibald Dunbar in 1827.

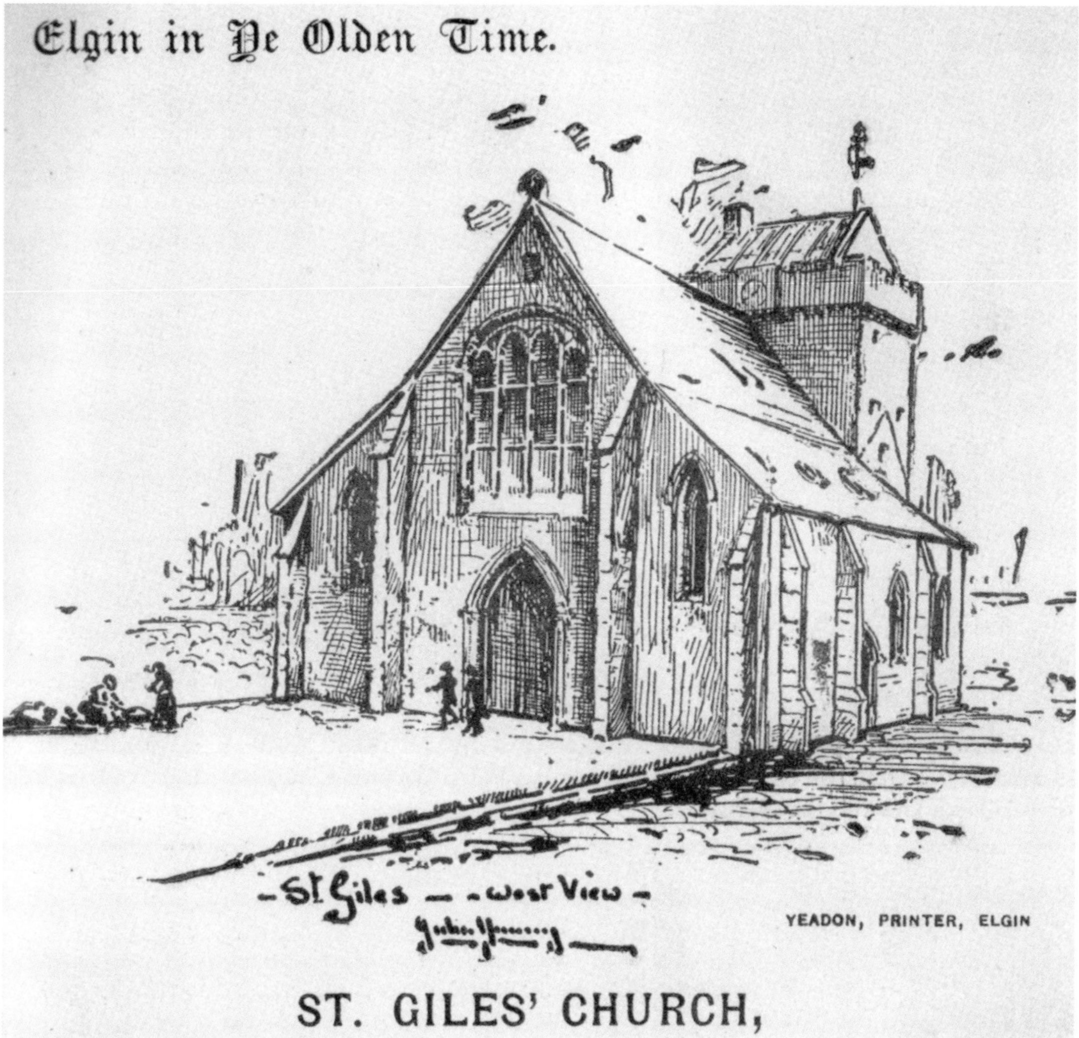

Drawing of St Giles' Church, built between 1180 and 1200. St Giles had many churches named after him. His legendary protection of the weak against the rich and powerful endeared him to the struggling burghs of the eleventh century. From a very early period the area surrounding the church was used as a burial ground. A Pictish slab, known as the Elgin pillar, was discovered there and is now situated in the cathedral grounds. The practice of using the church grounds as a burial area was discontinued in the first half of the seventeenth century. When old St Giles' Church was demolished many remains were found under the floor. Some were transferred to the cathedral, others were used as top-dressing on local pastures. Many of the flagstones covering graves were used to form pavements.

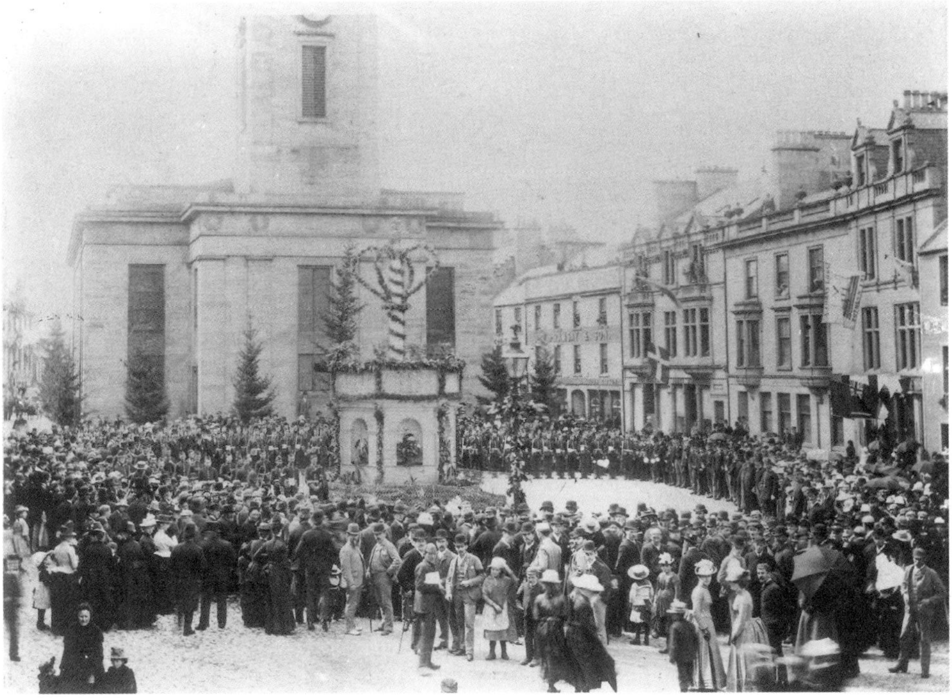

Celebrations in 1889. Elgin celebrated when the eminent local landowner, Alexander Duff, Duke of Fife, married Queen Victoria's granddaughter, Princess Louise.

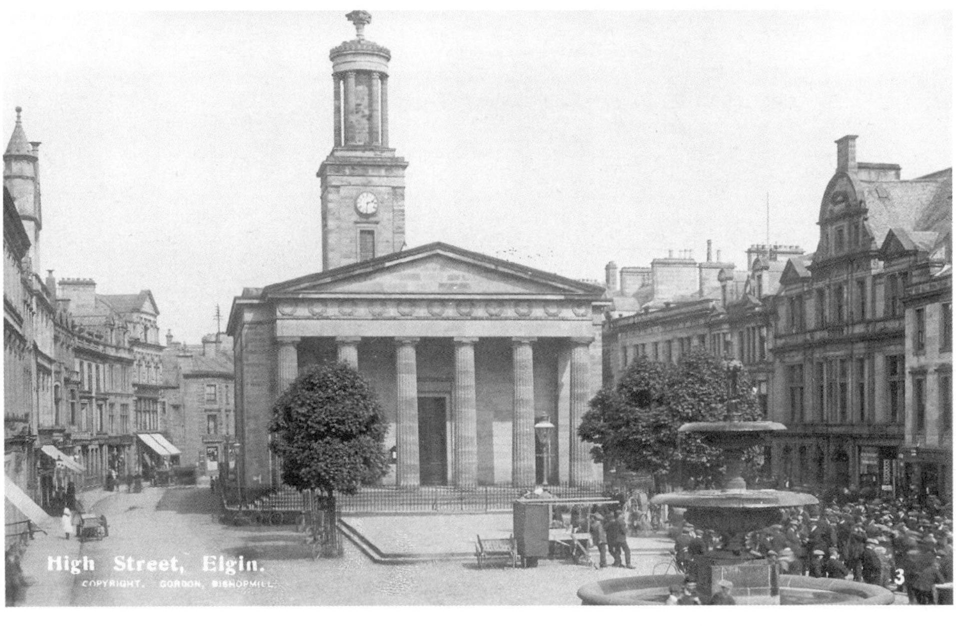

The absence of the war memorial suggests that this photograph was taken before 1921. In 1692 the Scottish Parliament abolished the practice of markets in churchyards and the Plainstones were the venue for the Friday corn market and feeing markets. The new market was built in 1851 between Batchen Street and High Street.

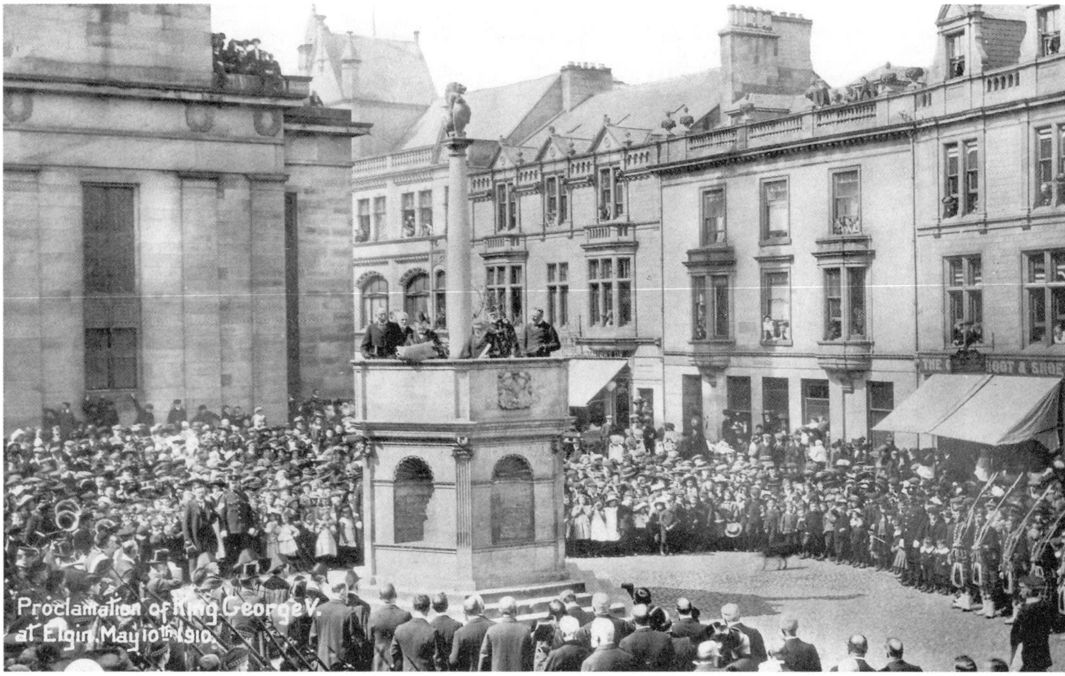

The proclamation of King George V in 1910. In those days the public enjoyed pomp and ceremony — bands and parades were not yet associated with war.

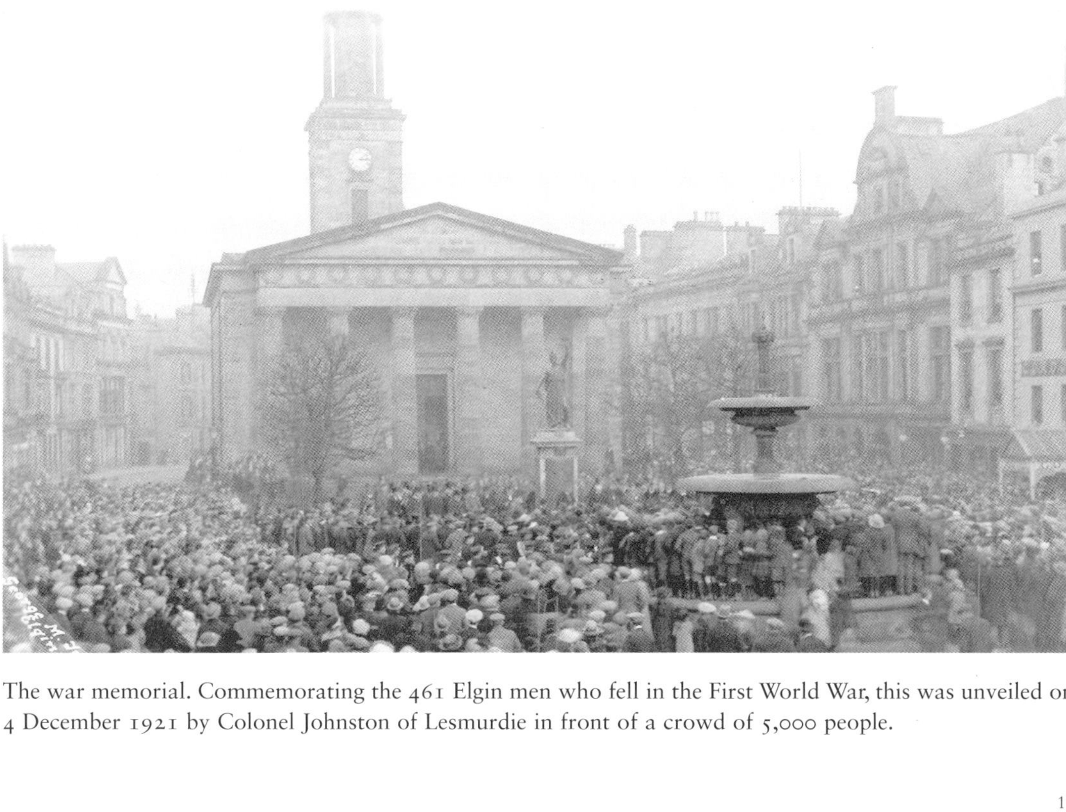

The war memorial. Commemorating the 461 Elgin men who fell in the First World War, this was unveiled on 4 December 1921 by Colonel Johnston of Lesmurdie in front of a crowd of 5,000 people.

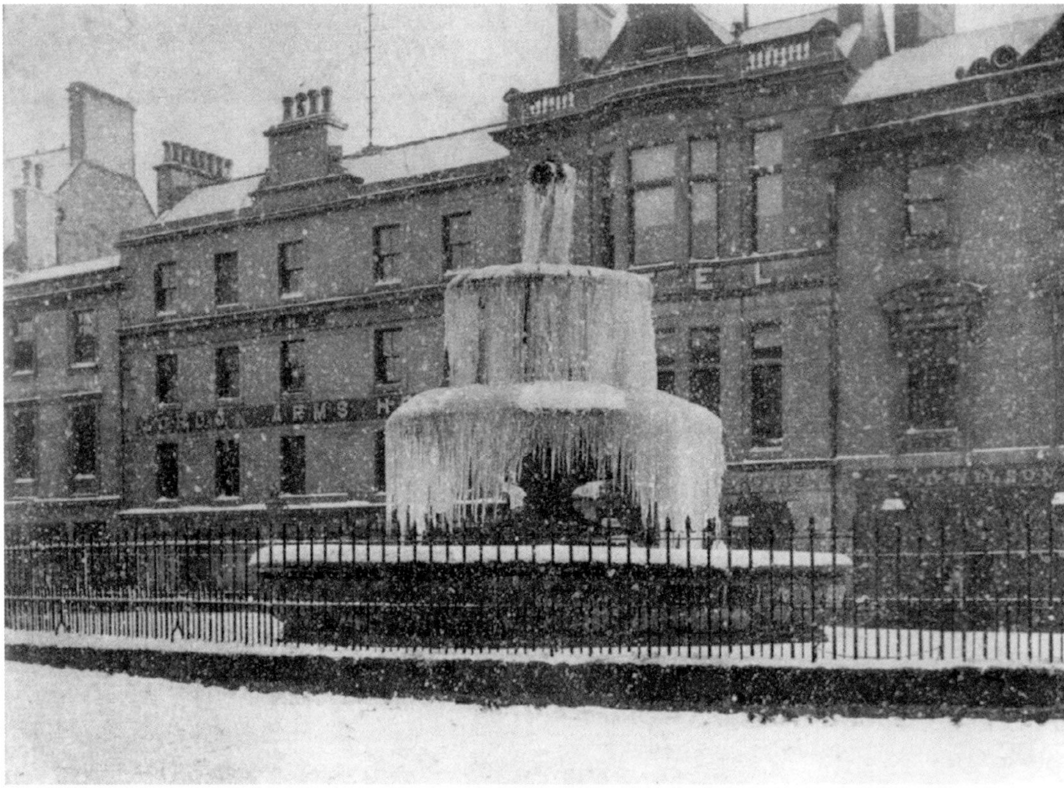

The fountain was designed in a Grecian style by Thomas Mackenzie and erected in 1846 on the site of the old tolbooth and council house of the burgh. It is seen here frozen over during one of the particularly harsh winters at the turn of the century.

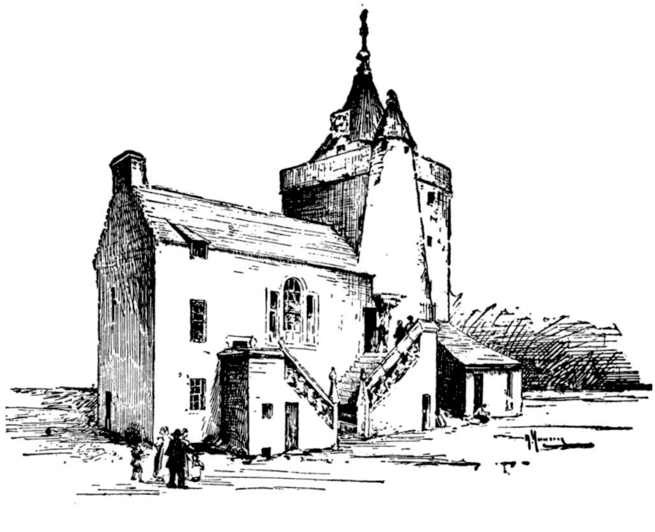

The tolbooth became the place for confining debtors and defaulters. Several tolbooth buildings occupied this site over the years, the stones from St Giles' kirkyard wall were used in their construction. At the south side was a 'meal house' built in 1736 after a harvest failure. The tolbooth and council house were demolished in 1843.

SECTION TWO

HAIKING ROUND THE HIGH STREET

The buildings around the town centre have changed a lot over the years. The numerous hotels and inns have been replaced by shops, which in their turn have changed in shape and function, reflecting the priorities, tastes and pace of the times.

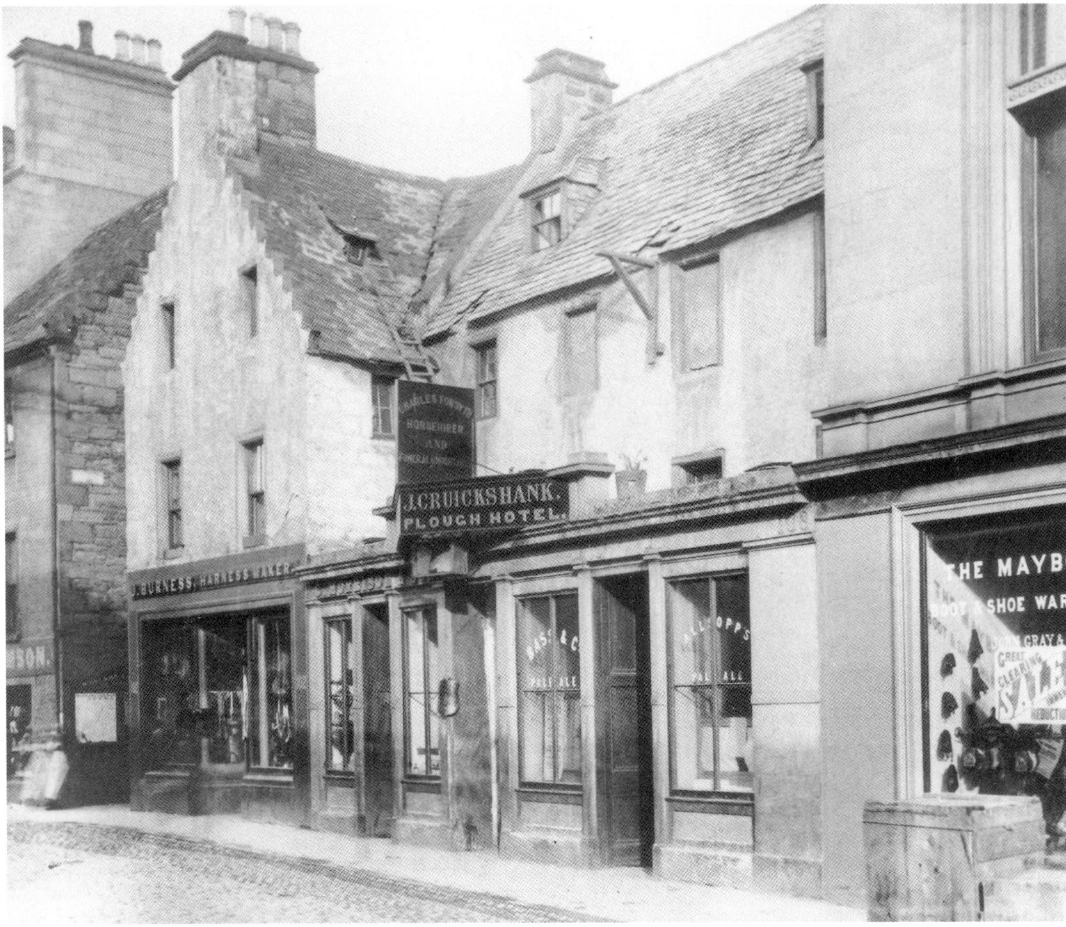

The Plough Hotel, 106 High Street. About a century ago the old Plough Inn was replaced by the short lived Palace Hotel, the garage of which opened on to South Street. Beams from the front of the old Plough Inn were incorporated into the new building. The Palace buildings housed what was to become Studio Tyrell. This was a photographic business founded by George Tyrell, who took many of the older photographs in this book.

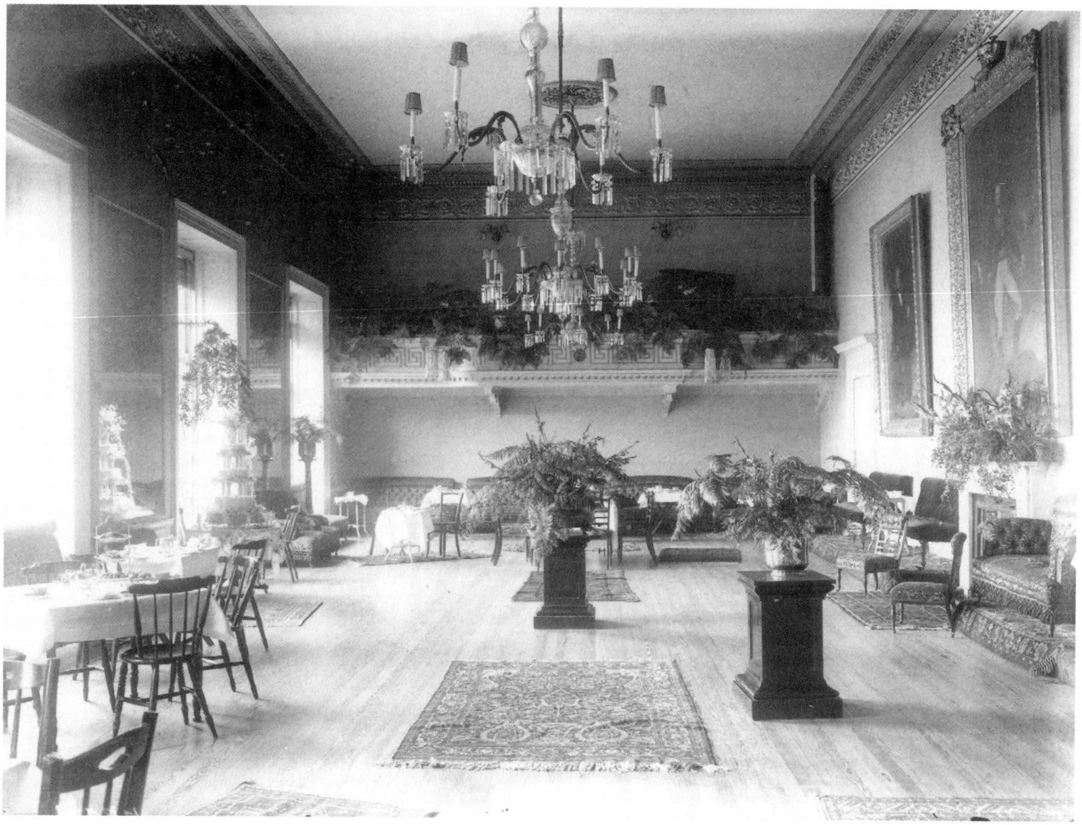

Inside the Assembly Rooms. North Street was formed when the old Calder mansion was demolished. The original Calder house had belonged to a physician and was thought to be haunted by a female apparition. She may have been one of his patients, who was seen pattering up and down the stairs demanding the return of her 'liver and lights'. The Assembly Rooms were constructed on this site in 1822 by the Trinity Lodge of Freemasons for their own use and that of 'the nobility and gentry of the county and the town'. The sprung dance floor was renowned. Workers from the nearby White Horse 'smiddy' would assess the numbers of folk dancing and adjust the floor tension accordingly. The underprivileged who never saw the Assembly Rooms in their glory can admire the present building, erected in 1970.

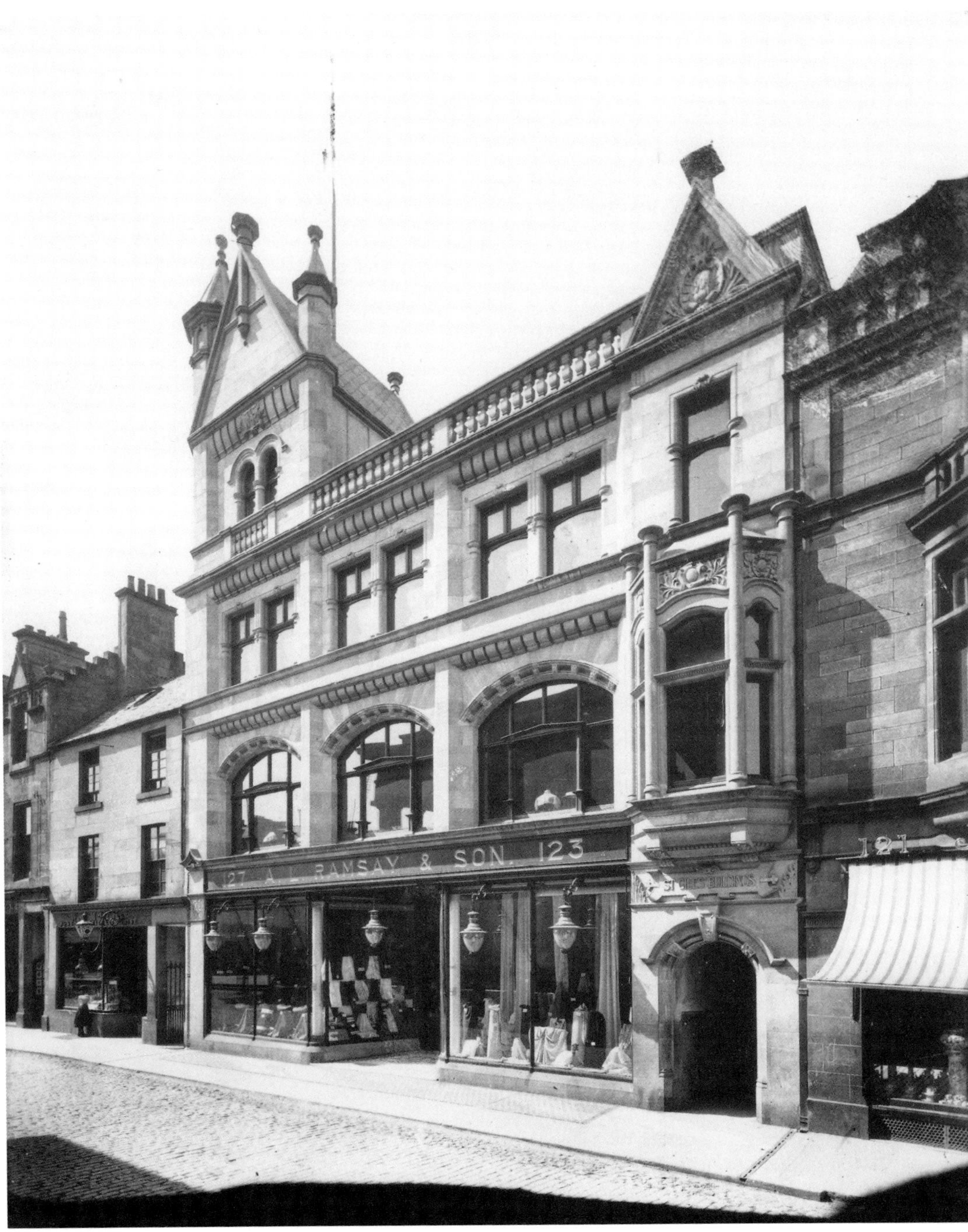

A. L. Ramsay started his business in 1845 and was joined by his son William, who became a partner in 1869. This magnificent building was erected as a drapery store in 1904 and later became Benzie and Miller. Eventually the building was taken over by Arnotts, a department store whose demise is still much regretted.

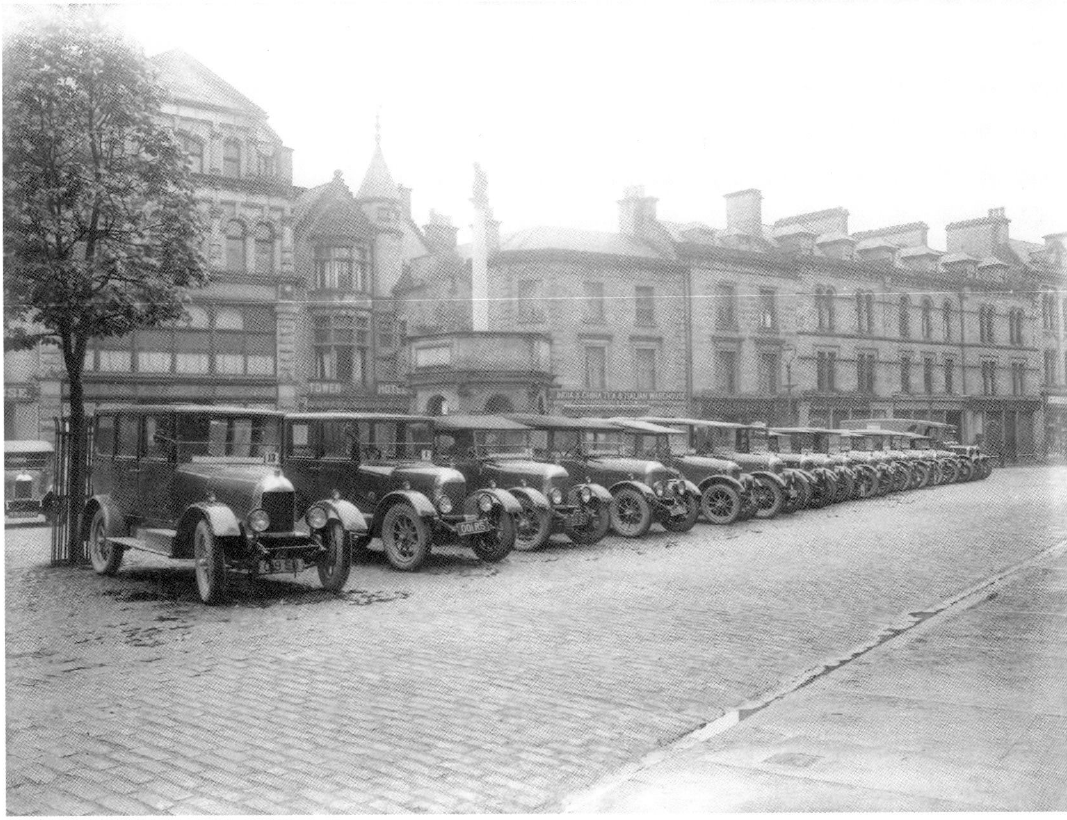

An impressive line of cars around the Muckle Cross. There was a cross as early as 1365 in the market place and it is believed to have stood a little to the west of this cross. The present one is a replica of that erected in the time of Charles I, which was demolished in 1792 when it had become ruinous. It is possible that the Pictish slab, now situated in the cathedral grounds, was the original market cross.

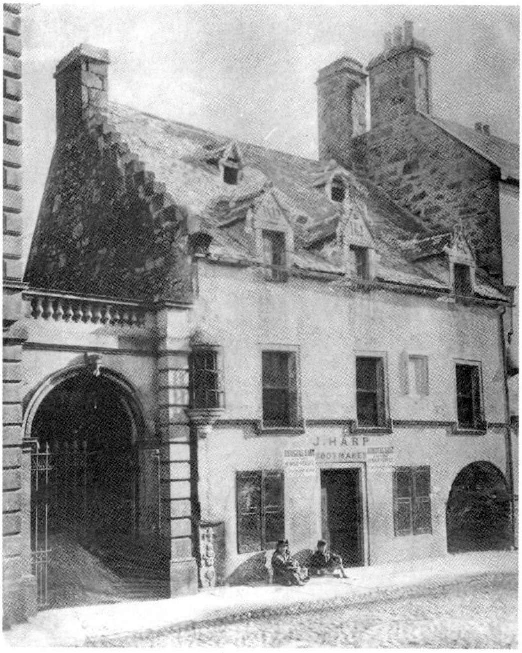

Ritchie's House, 147-9 High Street. Possibly dating back to 1619, this building came into the possession of John Ritchie towards the end of the eighteenth century. His descendants left it to endow a fund, known as the Ritchie Fund, for the poor persons of Elgin.

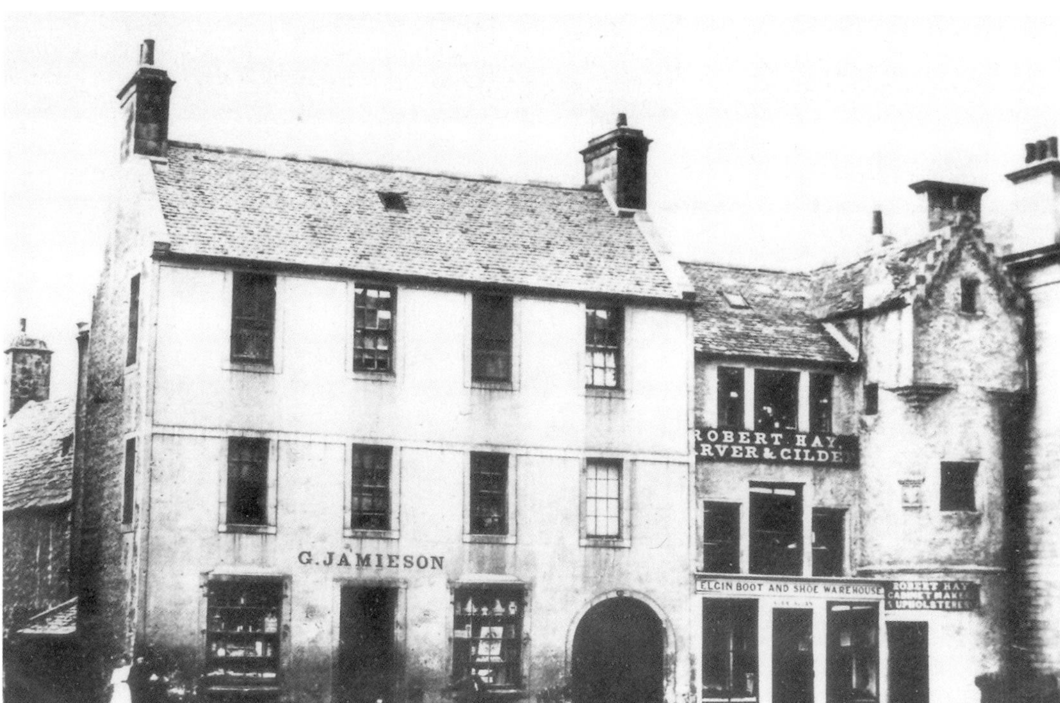

The Tower Hotel. Traditionally this building, dating back to the thirteenth century, had belonged to the Knights of St John. Later, Isaac Forsyth established a bookselling business there, followed in 1789 by the first circulating library in the north.

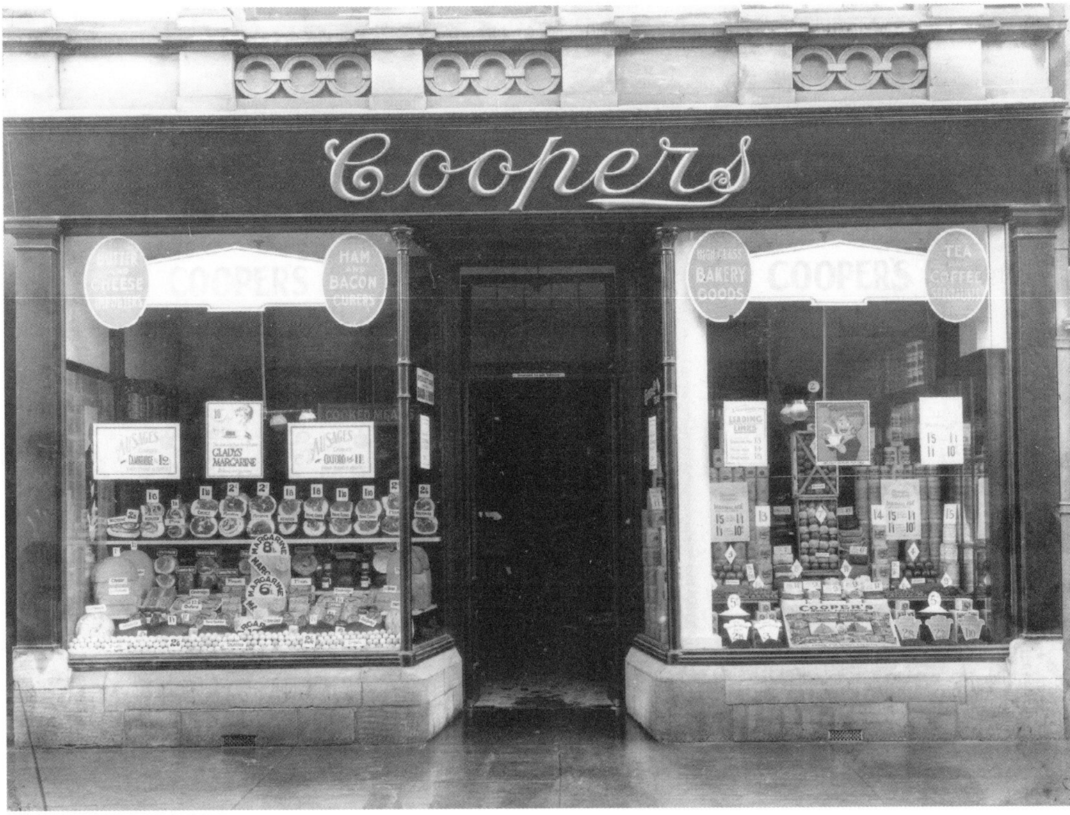

Coopers window. Opposite St Giles', the smell of coffee and ham pervaded the interior of Coopers shop, which eventually became William Lows and then, years later, the Lite Bite Café.

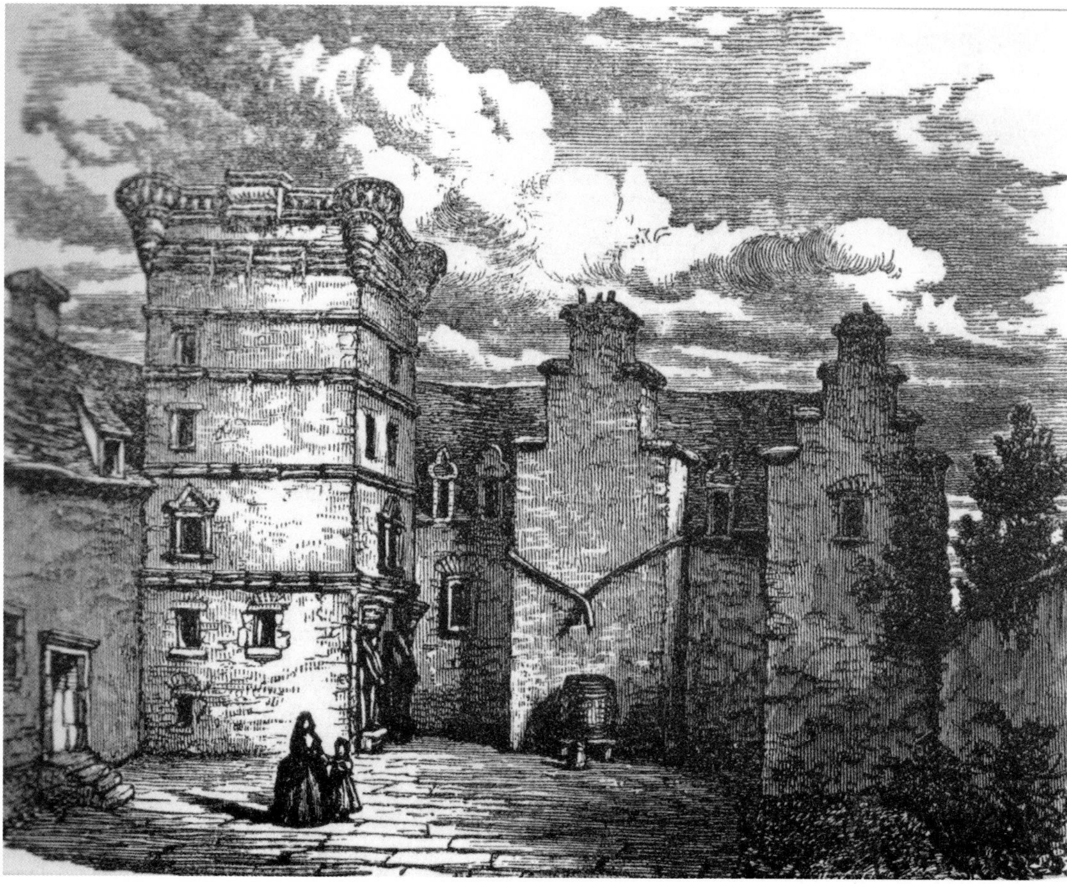

Thunderton House was the royal residence after the castle on Ladyhill became ruinous. Known as the Great Lodging, or 'The King's House', it was surrounded by gardens and orchards stretching from the tolbooth to the foot of Ladyhill and had a bowling green. It was the residence of the Earls of Moray when they came to town to administer justice. In 1455 it passed to the Dunbars, then to the Sutherlands of Duffus, who had two carved stone 'savages' on either side of the door. These were the supporters on their coat of arms and the carvings can now be found in the Elgin Museum. Prince Charles Edward Stuart stayed here prior to the battle of Culloden and his ghost is said to haunt the building.

Section Three

Cathedrals and Kirks

Since its consecration on the site of old Holy Trinity Church, the cathedral, called 'the Lantern of the North', has been the centre for growth and development in Elgin. Without the cathedral the town would not have attracted the craftsmen, scholars and merchants responsible for its creation and who helped make Elgin a seat of culture. The cathedral grounds contained six manses, as well as the Bishop's Palace, and these formed a distinct community once the gates were shut. In 1914 there were ten different churches in Elgin, the result of a number of complex developments and schisms in the religious life of Moray.

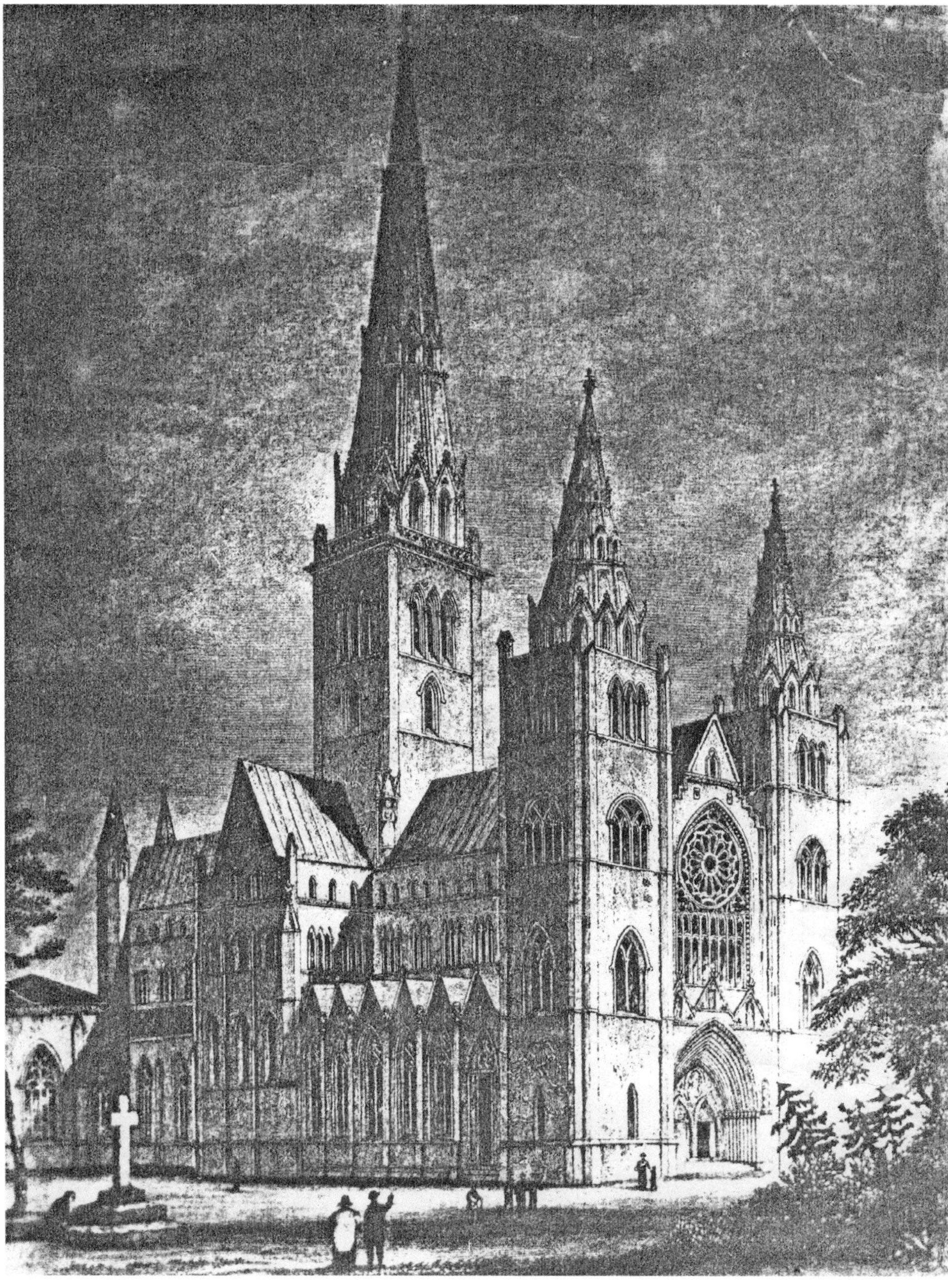

Elgin Cathedral. Even allowing for some exaggeration the cathedral was a magnificently impressive building, second only to St Andrew's in importance. The design is a simpler and smaller version of the great medieval cathedrals of northern France, and there were many alterations over the centuries. In May 1390 the Wolf of Badenoch with his 'Wyld Wykkyd Heland-men' burnt the town of Elgin, the Church of St Giles, the Maison Dieu, eighteen manses of the canons and chaplains and the cathedral, with all the books, charters and valuables within. Seventy years of continuous work were needed to repair the damage. The surrounding graveyard contains many graves removed from the old St Giles' graveyard.

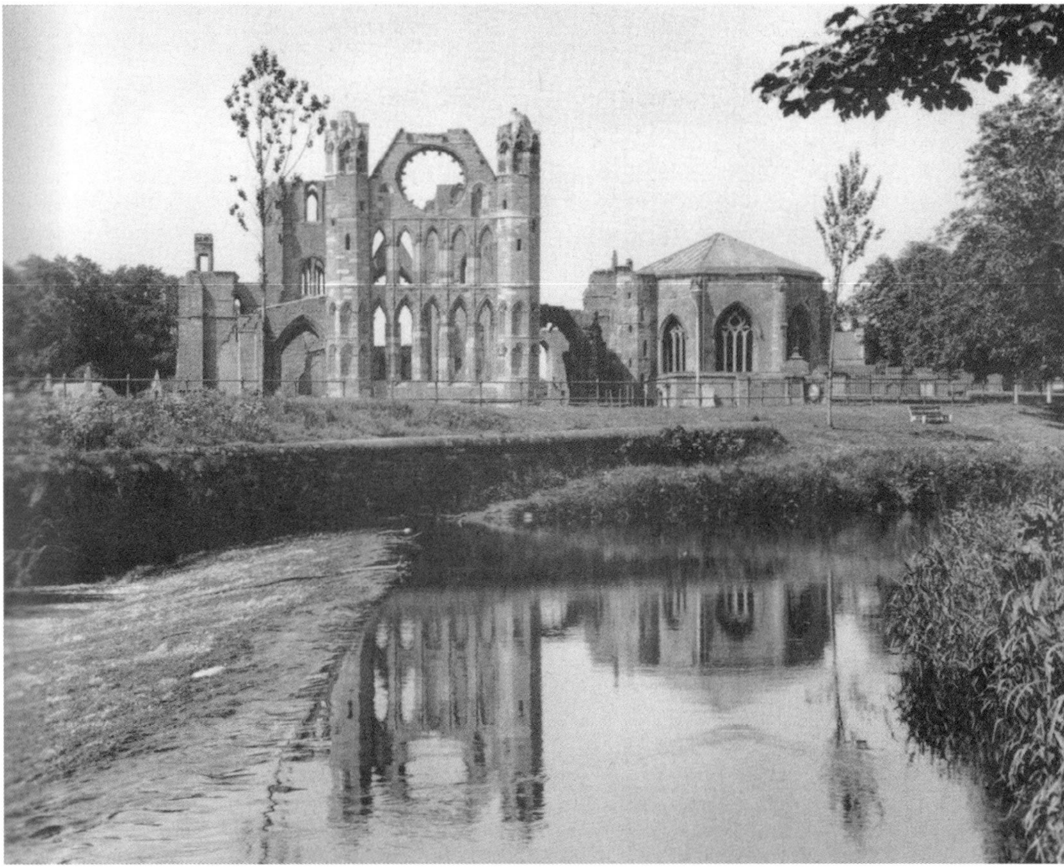

In 1567, after the Reformation, the lead was removed from the cathedral roof. Wind and weather gradually eroded the building, although Catholics used to secretly worship there until 1714. The incorporated trades held meetings in the Chapter House for several years from 1671 onwards. In 1825 John Shanks was employed to look after the neglected ruins. He removed 2,866 barrow-loads of rubbish, dumping them in the nearby deep pool known as the Order Pot. So the prophesy of Thomas the Rhymer was fulfilled - 'The Order Pot and the Lassie grey, Shall sweep the Chan'ry Kirk away'.

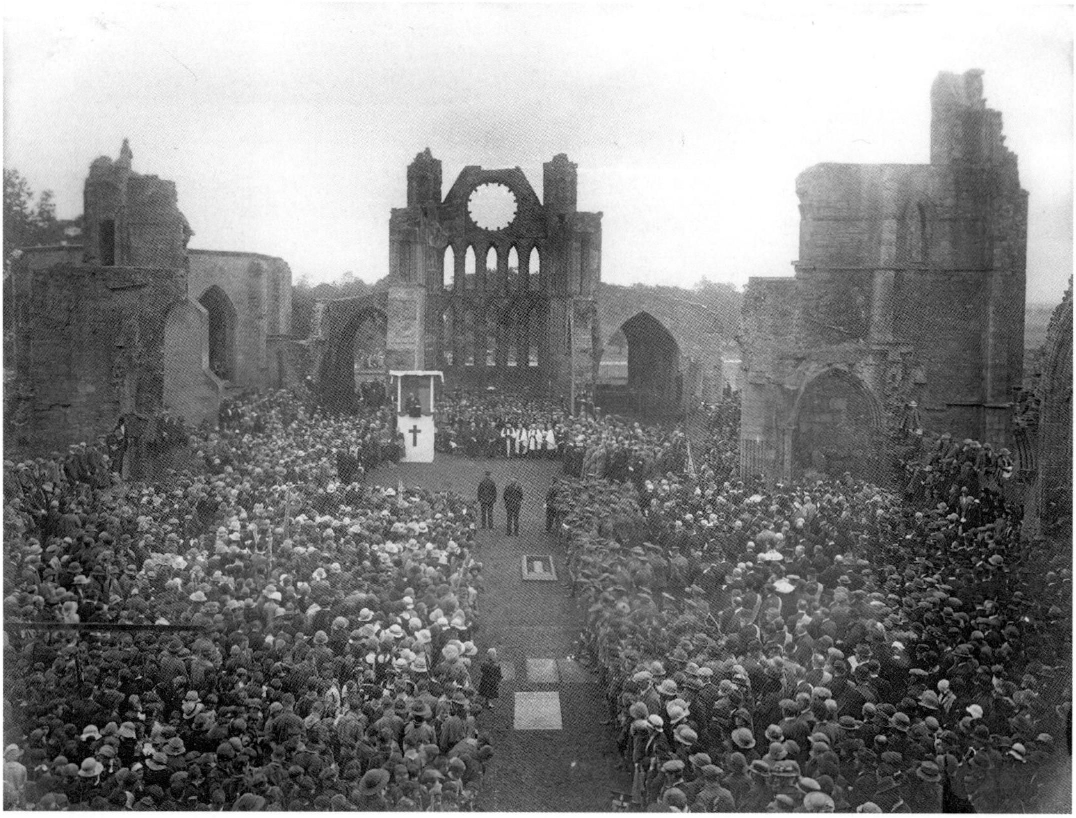

The original ceremony, with processions and banners, translating the cathedral from Spynie to Holy Trinity took place on a brilliant sunny day, 15 July 1224. In 1924 the ceremony seen here was held to mark the foundation of Elgin Cathedral 700 years previously. Having been left to ruin and decay for centuries, the cathedral was considered a piece of Romish vanity, and the central tower fell in 1711. The ruins were used as a quarry. After so much neglect the people of Elgin eventually came to appreciate the cathedral and to celebrate its unique contribution to the life of the town.

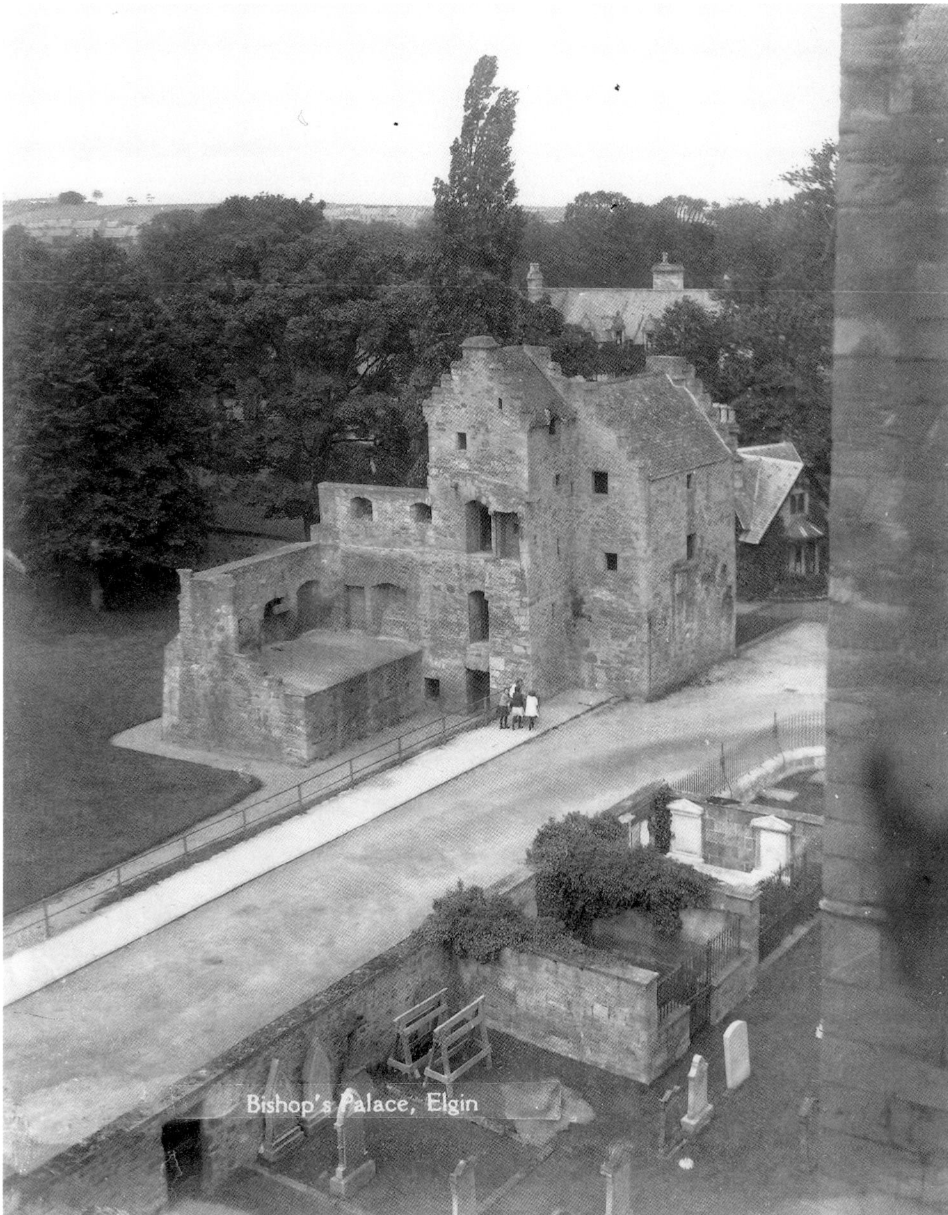

Known as the Bishop's Palace, the building is in fact the Precentor's Manse and was a lodging of the Precentor or a Canon of the Catherdral Chapter. It is thought that some of the present remains could date back to the rebuilding of the cathedral precincts around 1406, although most of the east wing which remains is dated 1557. There were more than twenty manses within the cathedral precincts. This view would appear to have been taken at the beginning of this century.

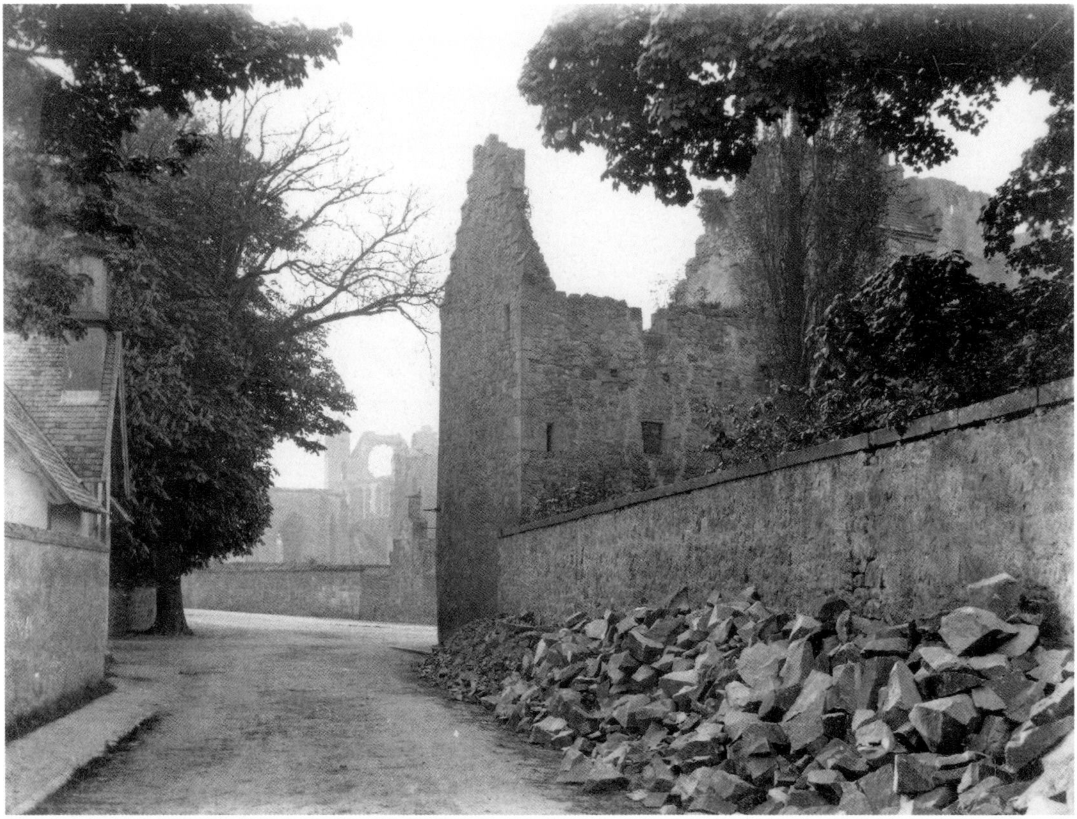

The Bishop's Palace. With the cathedral in the distance this is a different view of the Bishop's Palace, or Precentor's Manse. It occupied eighty-six square feet and was inhabited until the end of the eighteenth century. After the Reformation it was known as Dunfermline House, being the property of the First Lord of Dunfermline. It was purchased by the Duke of Gordon in 1730 and the roof was removed at the end of the century. A later owner, the Earl of Seafield, was prevented from pulling down the building in 1851 and the square tower, corbelled turret and east gable were saved. The remaining building was gifted to the town in 1884 by the Countess-Dowager of Seafield. In 1891 most of the south wing collapsed.

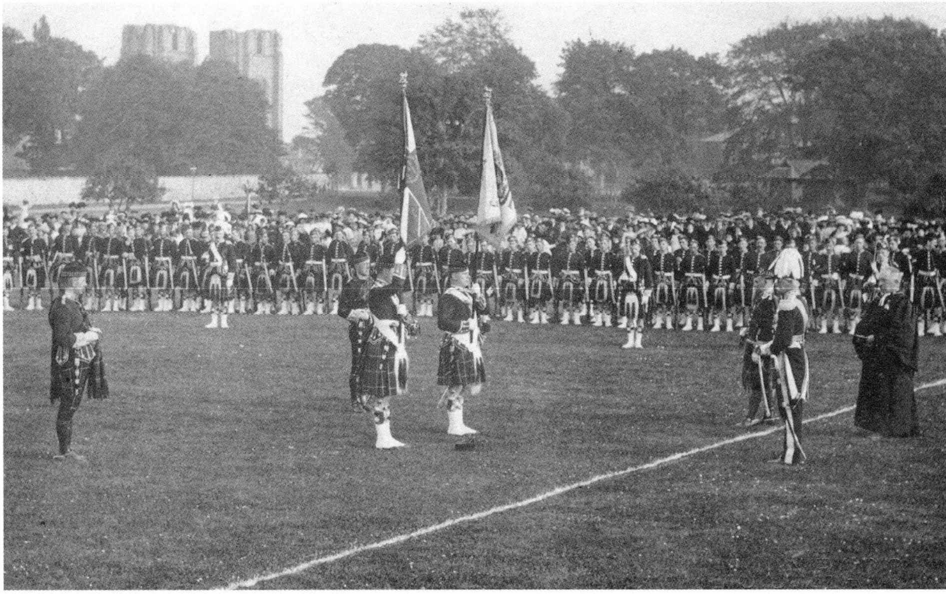

Presenting the colours, 18 September 1909. His Grace the Duke of Richmond and Gordon KG, presenting the new colours gifted by Sir George A. Cooper, Bart., to the 6th (Morayshire) Battalion Seaforth Highlanders in the Cooper Park.

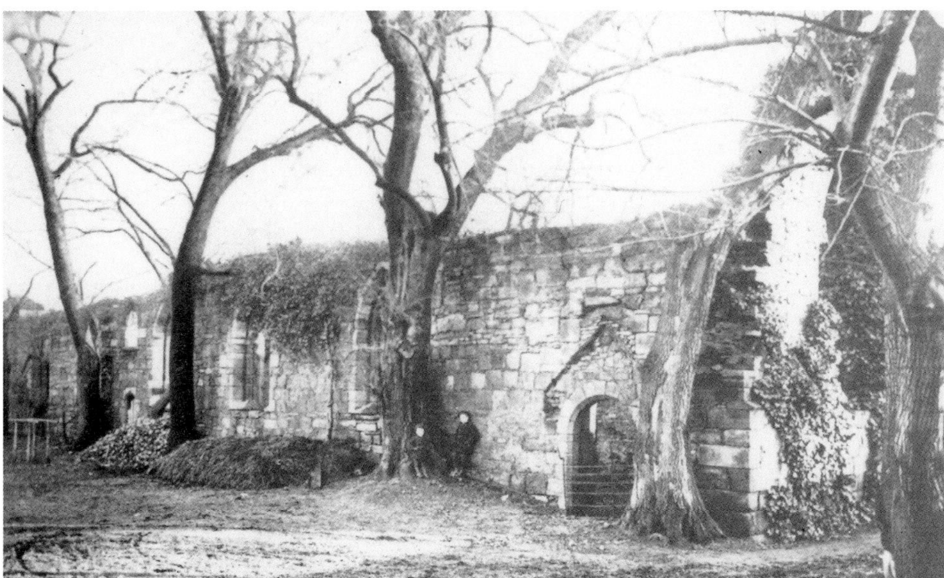

Greyfriars Convent fell into secular hands after the Reformation and the buildings went to ruin. The church was eventually purchased by the Sisters of Mercy in 1891, and five years later it was restored and mass was celebrated there for the first time since the Reformation in September 1898.

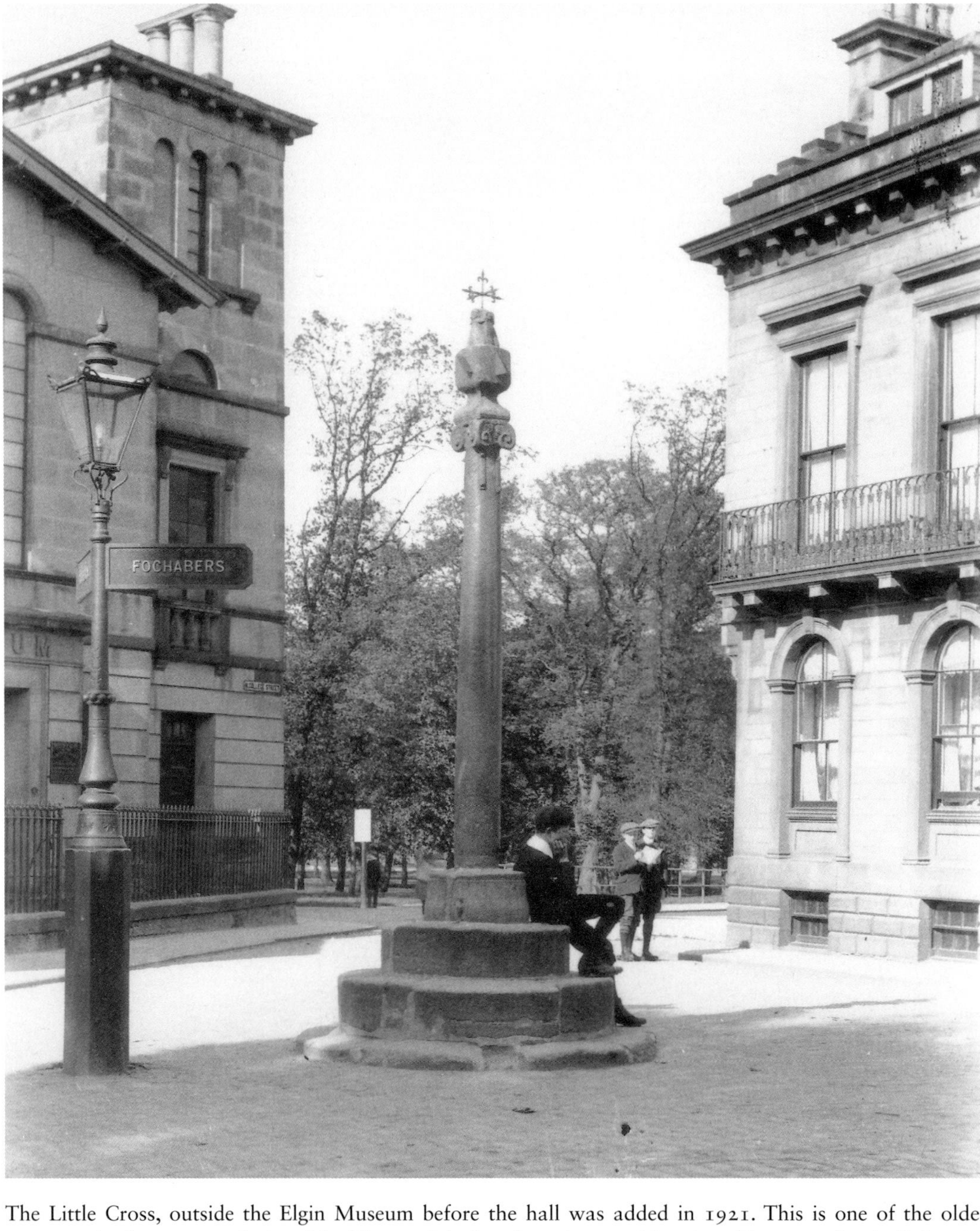

The Little Cross, outside the Elgin Museum before the hall was added in 1921. This is one of the oldest museums in the country, designed by Thomas Mackenzie and opened in 1843. The extension built in 1896 was designed by his grandson, Marshall Mackenzie. The Little Cross marked the western end of the cathedral enclosure and was erected by Alexander Macdonald as part of his penance after he 'spulzied' the cathedral in 1402. In the closing years of the sixteenth century Little Cross was a place for punishment, being the site of the town jougs (a pillory). Prisoners were marched the length of the High Street and were preceded by the town drum (now in the museum) before being locked in.

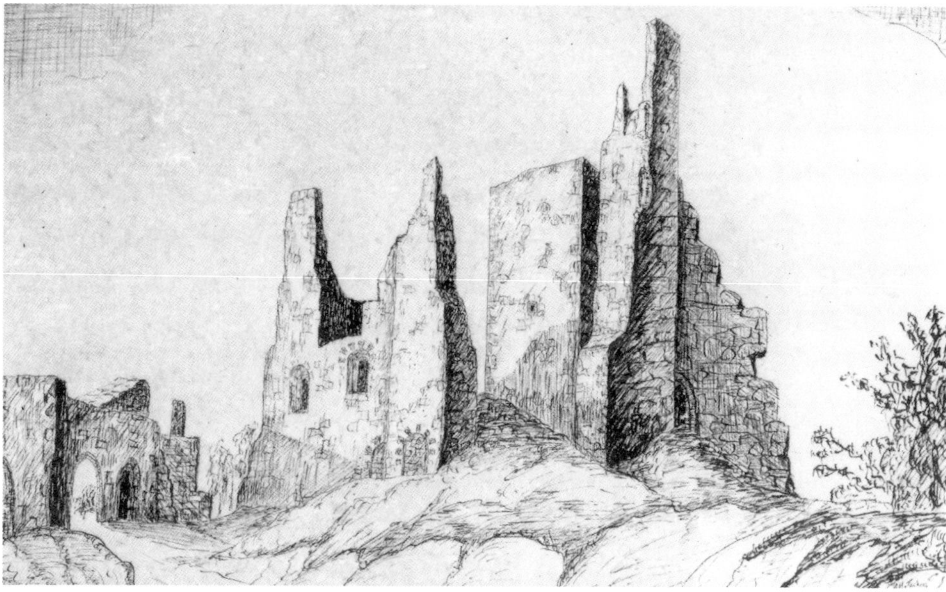

The hospital of Maison Dieu was founded by Bishop Andrew of Moray in the thirteenth century, near the 'brook of Taok' (the Tyock burn) and the Leper House. It was considered equal in grandeur to the architecture of the cathedral. It was destroyed by the Wolf of Badenoch, but later rebuilt. It fell into ruin after the Reformation and all the materials were carted away. This is a rare record, an old sketch illustrating the size of the ruins. All that is left is the name Maison Dieu Road.

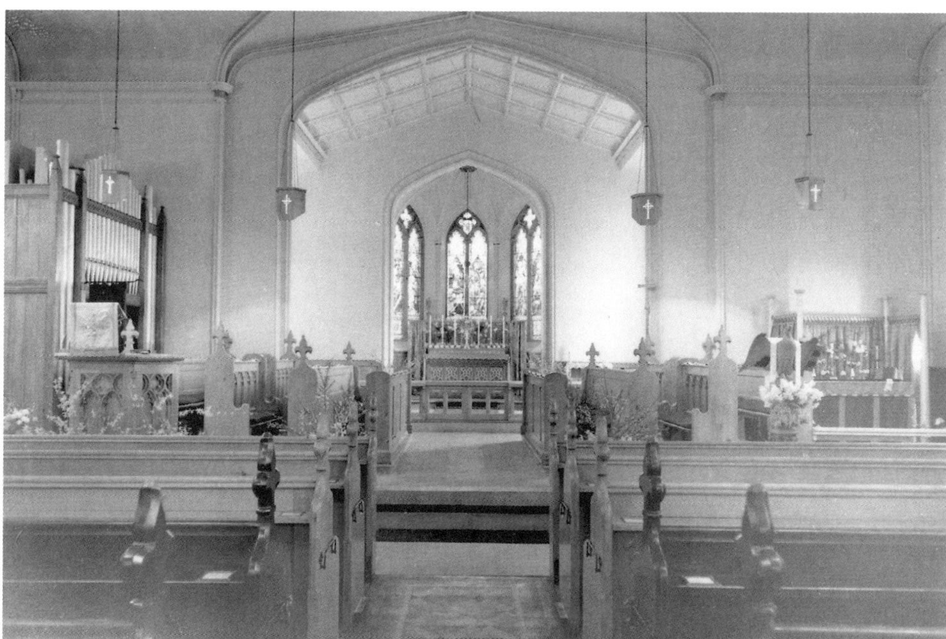

The Gothic-style Holy Trinity Episcopal Church was built in 1826, following the opening of North Street.

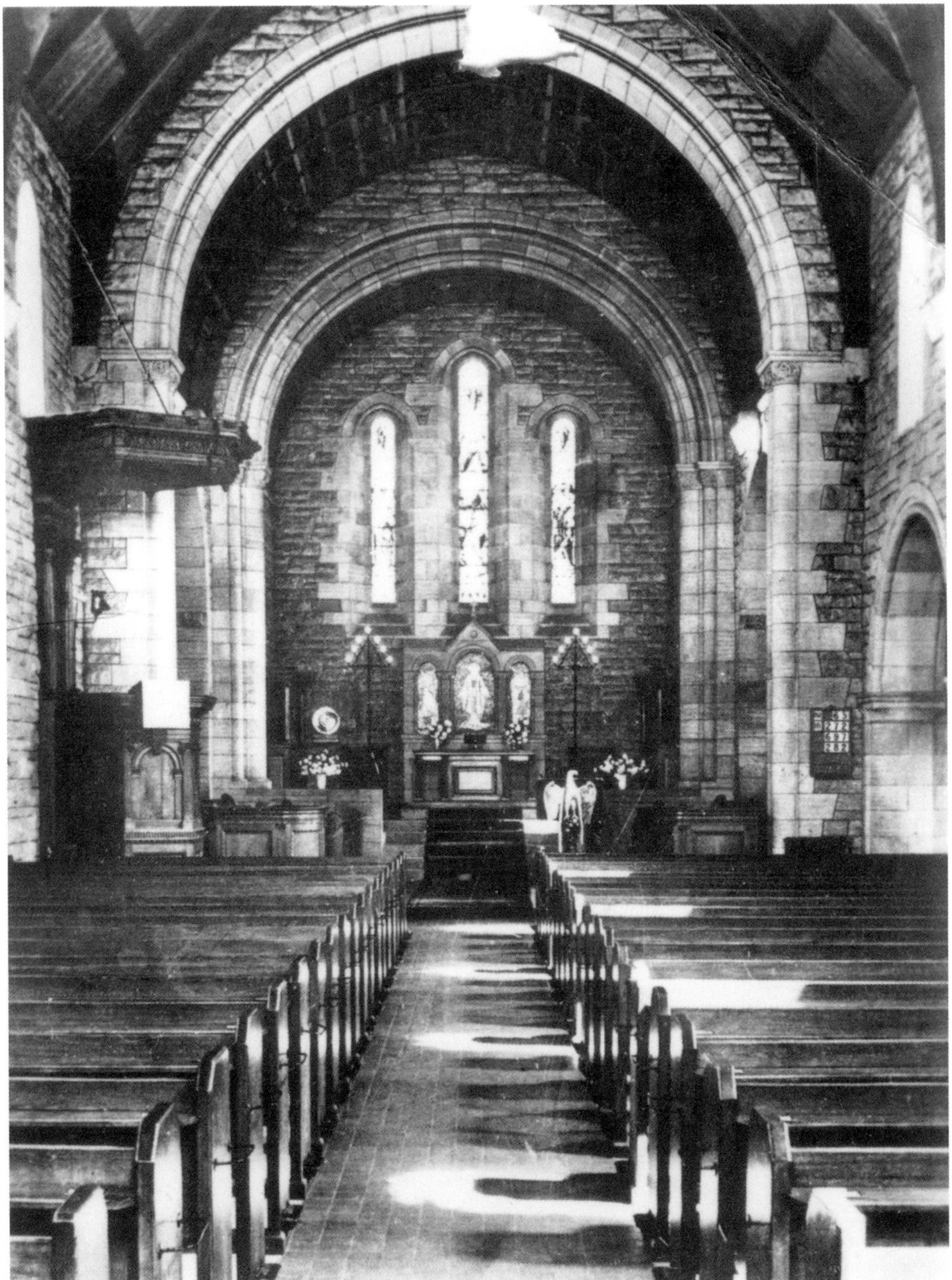

St Columbas's Church was erected in 1906 in the Norman style. The old oak pulpit, seen on the left, is elaborately carved and bears the date 1684. It was removed from the old St Giles' kirk in 1826, when that building was taken down, and was bought by the Earl of Fife for £5. It was preserved at Pluscarden Priory Church until gifted by the Duke of Fife to the Elgin Kirk Session when the estate was sold.

Section Four

Some Special Buildings

Before the architectural 'improvements' of recent years, Elgin possessed some magnificent and grandiose buildings — proof of the self-confidence and flourishing growth of the town. Many of these grand buildings live on only in folk memory, while others are submerged by new developments. The old town hall was a very grandiose affair — the turrets were topped with statuettes of men with spears, and the projecting keystones bore the sculptured heads of Apollo, Vulcan and Ceres. The keystone of the porch arch featured the figure of St Giles, with the head of Minerva below it.

TOWN HALL, ELGIN

ENORMOUS ATTRACTION!

Monday & Tuesday, Jan. 7th & 8th, 1889

FOR TWO NIGHTS ONLY

JOHN TULLY

(Lessee and Manager, Theatre Royal, Coatbridge),

Has the honour to announce that he has made arrangements for the appearance here of

MISS

EDITH BLANCHE

THE CHARMING YOUNG LEADING ACTRESS

(Late of Drury Lane, Novelty, and Vaudeville Theatres, London),

Supported by her own Powerful Company.

First Production here of the two Latest London Successes,

MR BARNES OF NEW YORK

AND

THE MYSTERY OF A HANSOM CAB

Received everywhere with Unbounded Enthusiasm.

Doors Open 7.30; Commence at Eight; Carriages at 10.30.

PRICES—2s, 1s, and 6d.

Seats can now be secured at Messrs J. & J. A. WATSON,
159 High Street, Elgin.

A programme from the old town hall, 1889. This building was a hive of civic and cultural activity. Before other entertainments were developed, many dances, theatre productions, festivals and concerts took place in the large hall, which could seat 1,000 people.

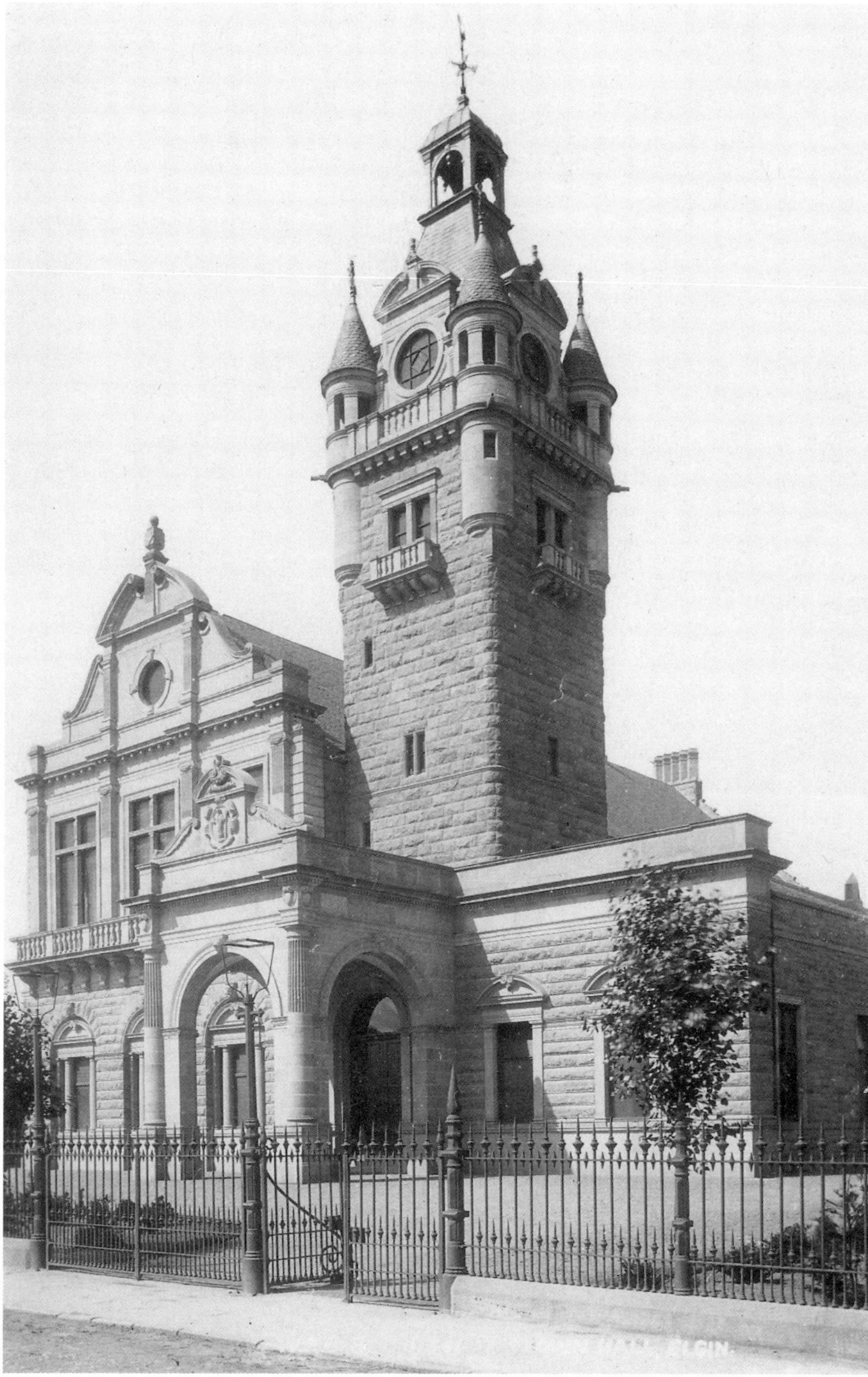

The town hall. This unusual building was designed by A. Marshall Mackenzie in the Jacobean style. The foundation stone was laid in 1884 and the building was formally opened with a full masonic ceremony by the Earle of Fife in 1885. A commemorative medal was presented to each of the 1,300 schoolchildren of the burgh.

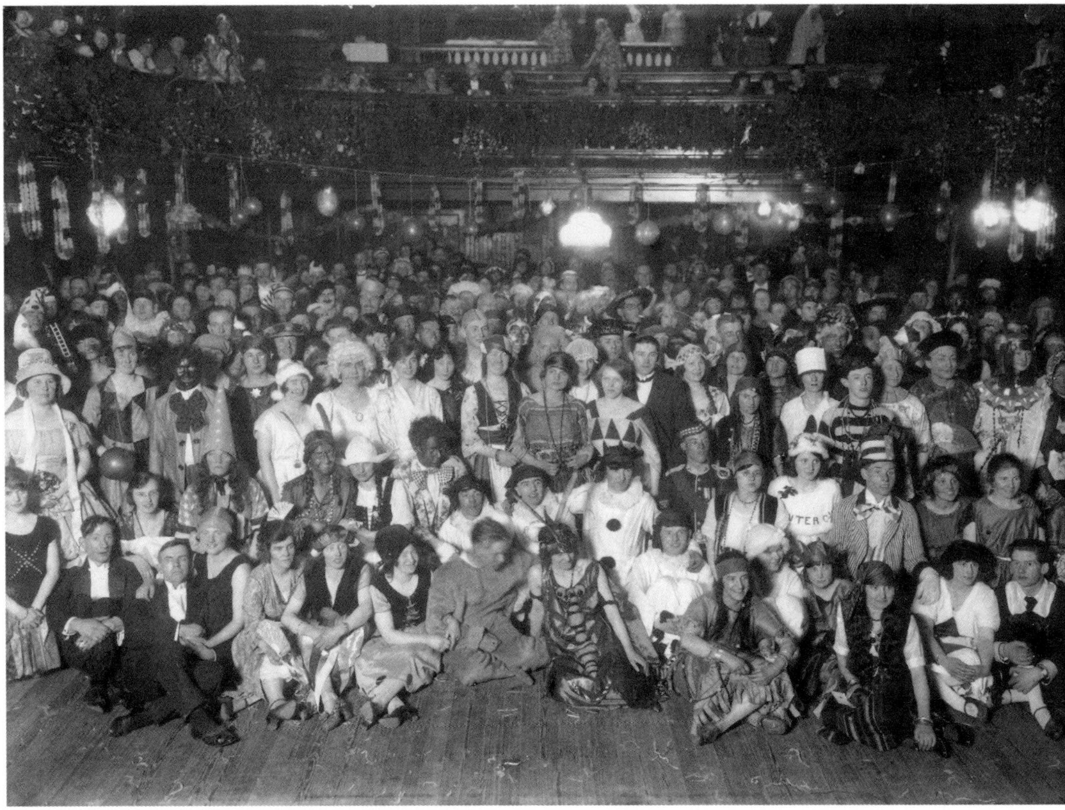

A party in the old town hall in 1926. The main entrance to the building was at the base of the tower, and opening from the vestibule were the cloakrooms and gallery staircases. The grand corridor was 80 ft long. Adjacent to the corridor were the caretaker's apartments and a small supper room measuring 60 ft by 30 ft. The main hall was 127 ft by 50 ft, and was 48 ft high, with excellent stage facilities.

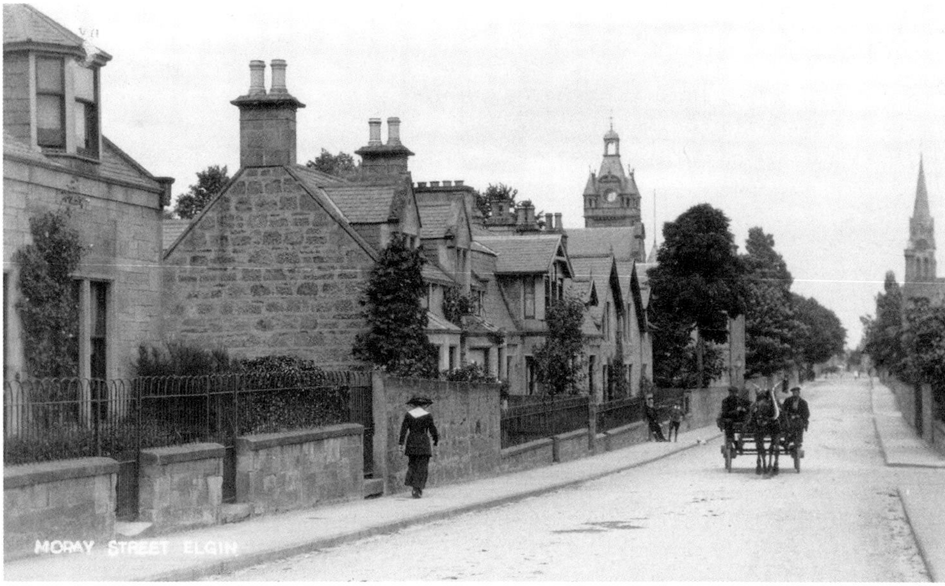

Moray Street. The town hall building was impressive viewed from any angle, if a little ornate.

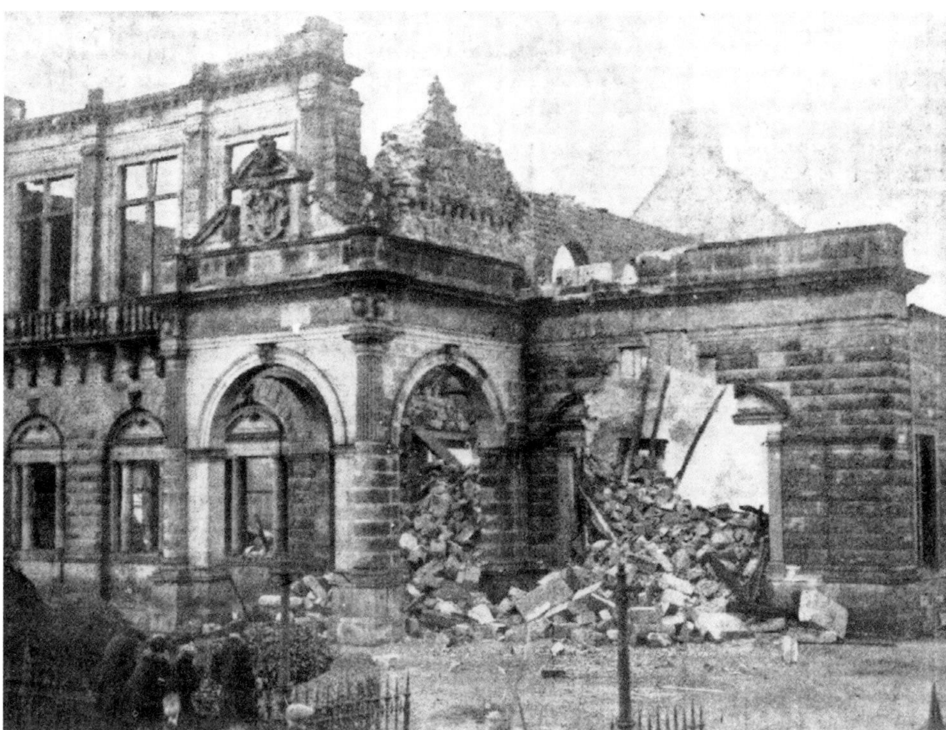

The burnt ruins of the old town hall. A fire started in the afternoon of 11 December 1939 and reduced it to rubble within a few hours. Local rumours blame the start of the fire on soldiers who were billeted there at the time. The new police station now occupies the site that saw so many social events.

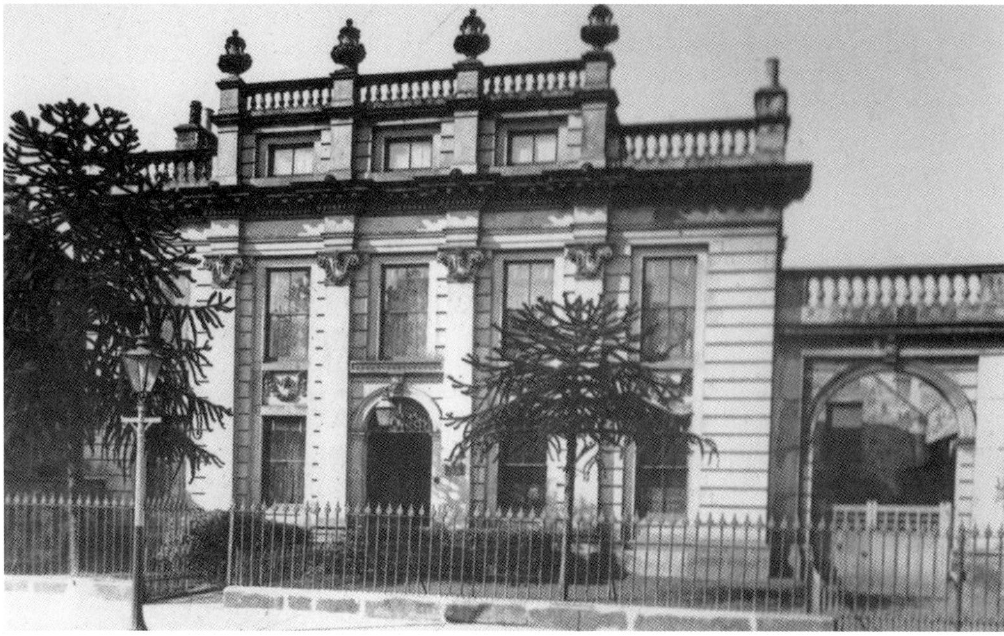

The progressive 'improvements' at 209 High Street. Once the home of General Anderson, it was bought by the Commercial Bank and in 1853 the highly ornamental front was added. It also contained the office of the town clerk. When Hugh McIsaac, the senior solicitor at Stewart & McIsaac, became town clerk in 1885 the firm's law offices moved to the building too. He was created honorary sheriff-substitute. The building was replaced in 1971. Four elaborate carved stone capitols from the building were recovered from a council dump in 2008.

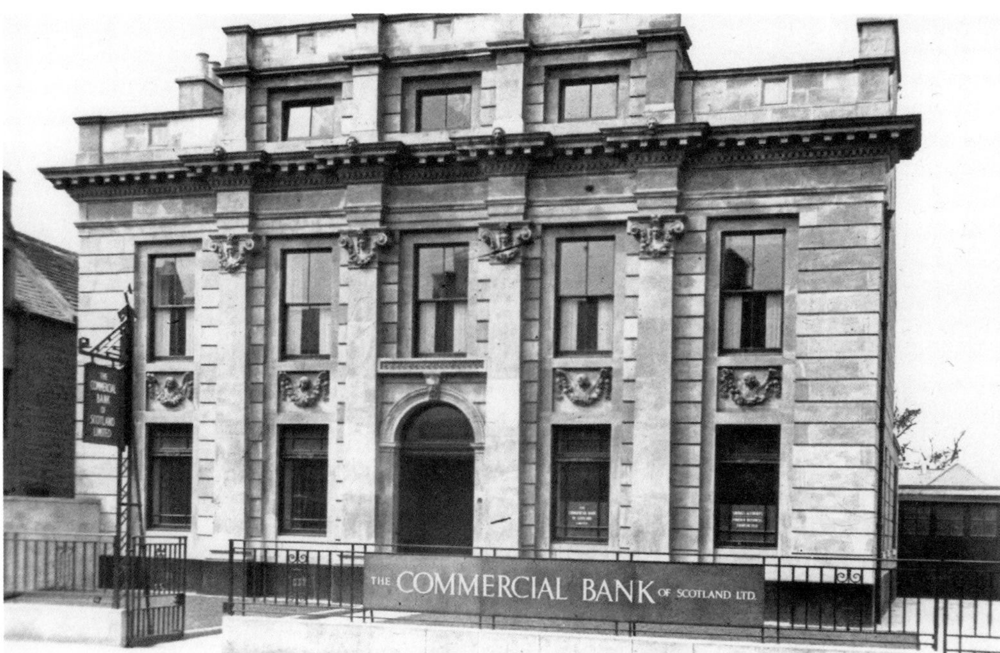

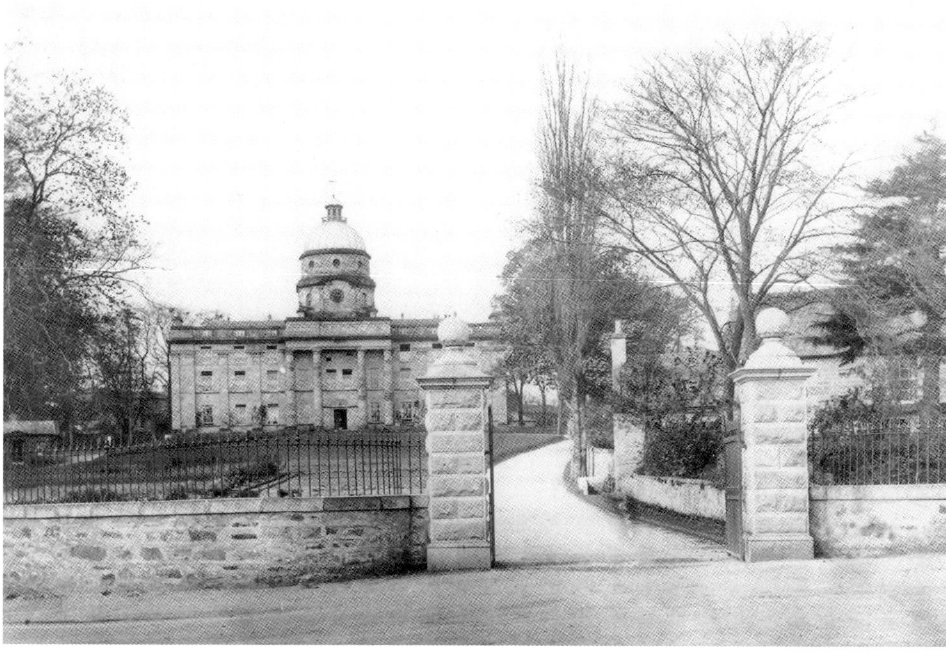

Dr Gray's Hospital. This was built with an endowment by Dr Alexander Gray, a native of Elgin who made his fortune with the Honourable East India Company. His philanthropy was tempered with the wish to ensure his wife did not benefit from his money. The infirmary was opened in 1819 on the site of Snuff Croft and a new wing added in 1939. Patients from the adjoining Bilbohall psychiatric hospital helped tend the gardens and orchards in the grounds.

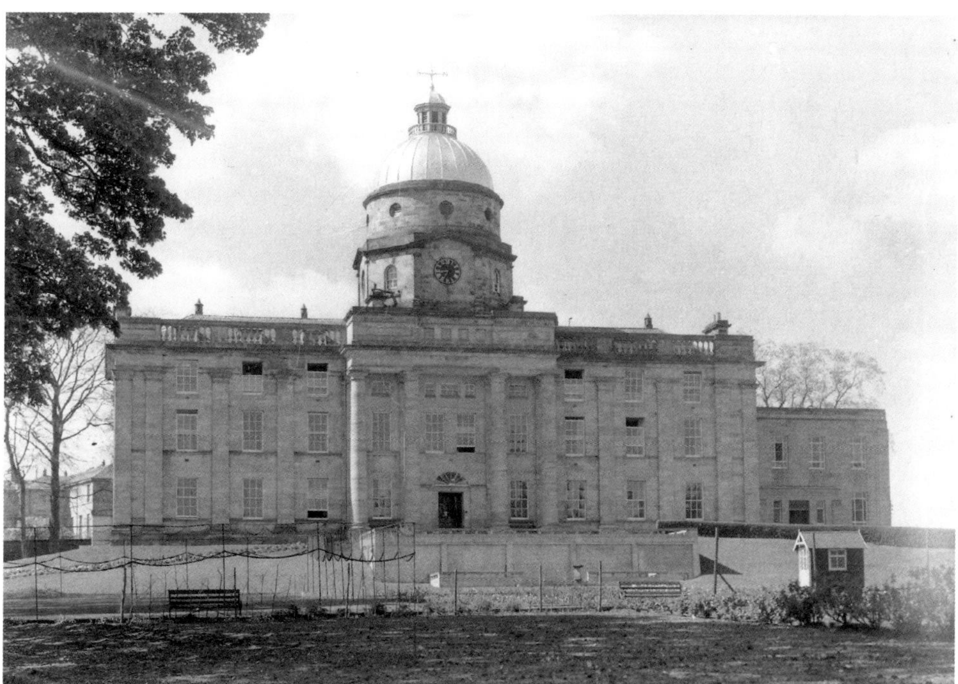

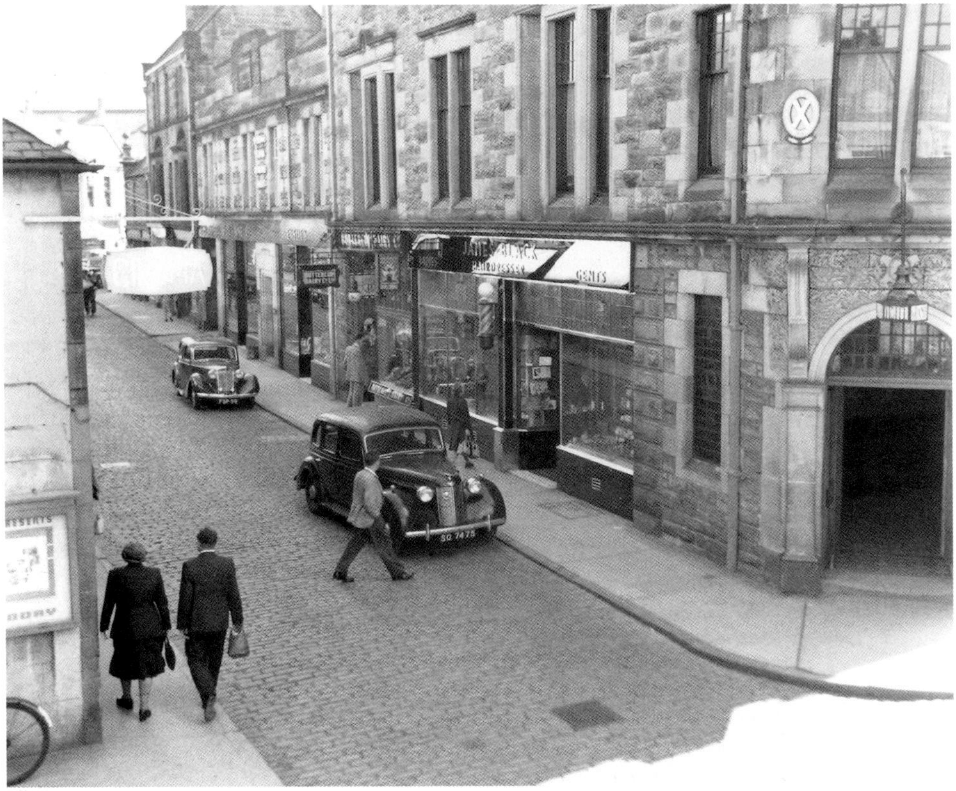

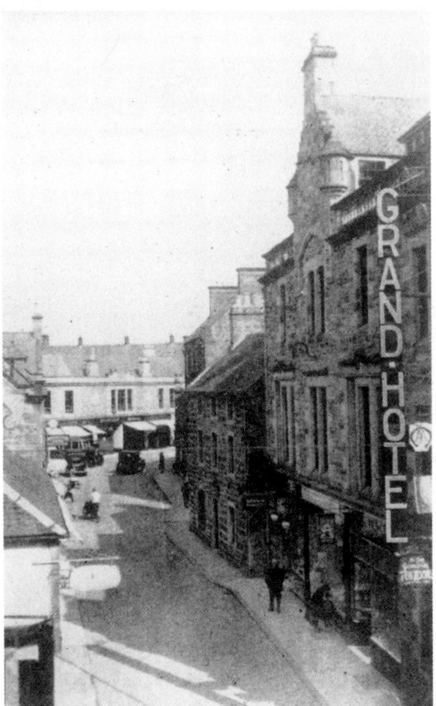

The Eagle Inn site, top picture, was one of the last of the old hostelries to have stabling opposite. The car SO7475 was owned by Sandy Mutch. In 1937 South Street was widened and the Argyle buildings erected. The Grand Hotel next door was the first public building in Elgin to have neon lights. It was built for Alexander Austin, the baker, in 1898 on the site of the Royal Oak Inn. The Royal Oak sign was discovered in a flea market in Edinburgh — it was bought for £20 and returned to the Elgin Museum in the late 1960's.

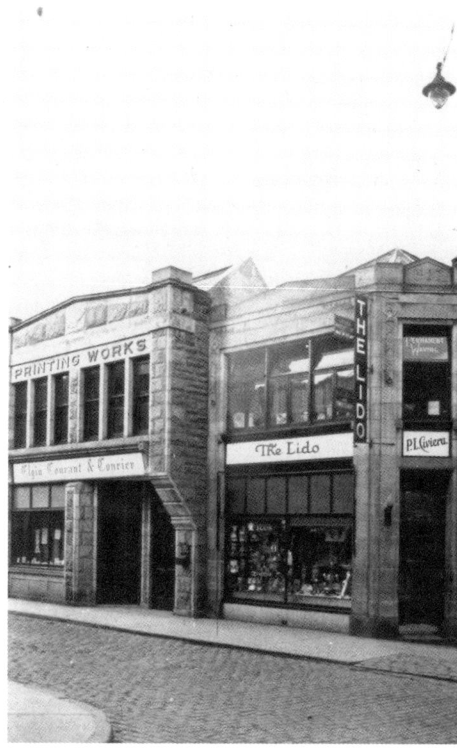

The Lido Café with Art Deco parapet, pediment and carvings. It was opened in 1926 and boasted a soda fountain and a jazz band known as the Lido Four. The café was well patronized by crowds going to the nearby Picture House.

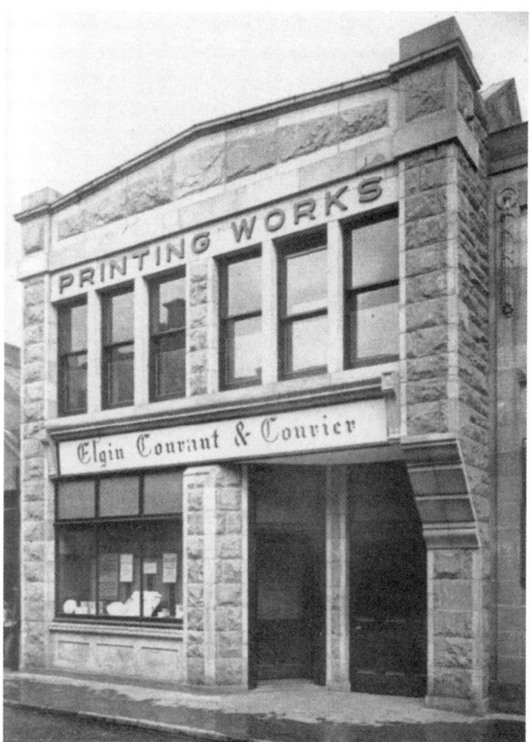

The *Courant* office. The first Moray newspaper, the *Courier*, was published in 1827. It failed, but the *Courant* was started in 1834. In 1843 the *Courier* was revived and in 1874 the two were amalgamated.

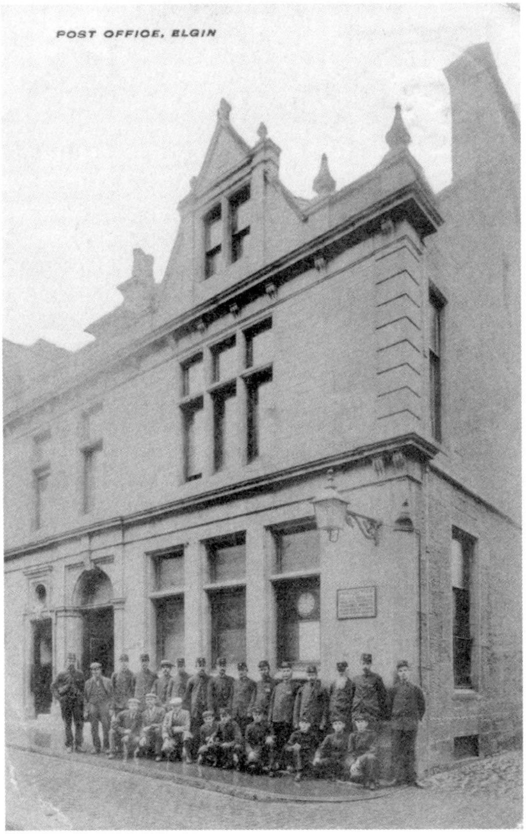

The old post office. First located in Commerce Street in 1860 within the Commercial Buildings, the post office moved across the street in 1894. It was extended in 1909 and was in use until 1963 when the new, purpose-built post office was located at the west end of the High Street. The top picture would have been taken at the turn of this century; the lower picture appears to be some fifty years later.

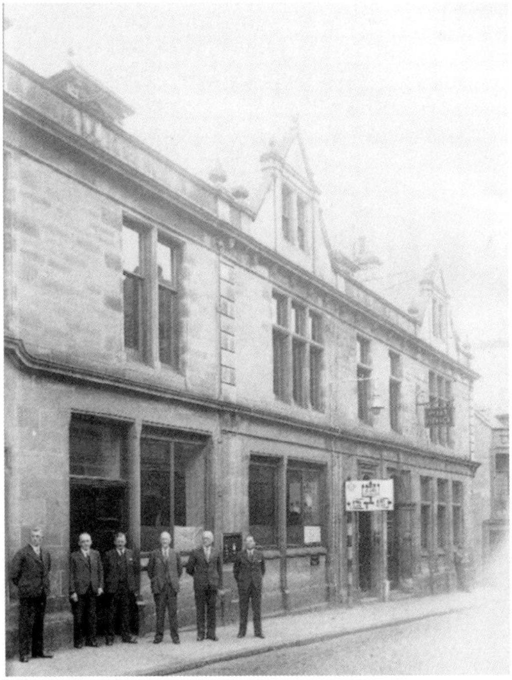

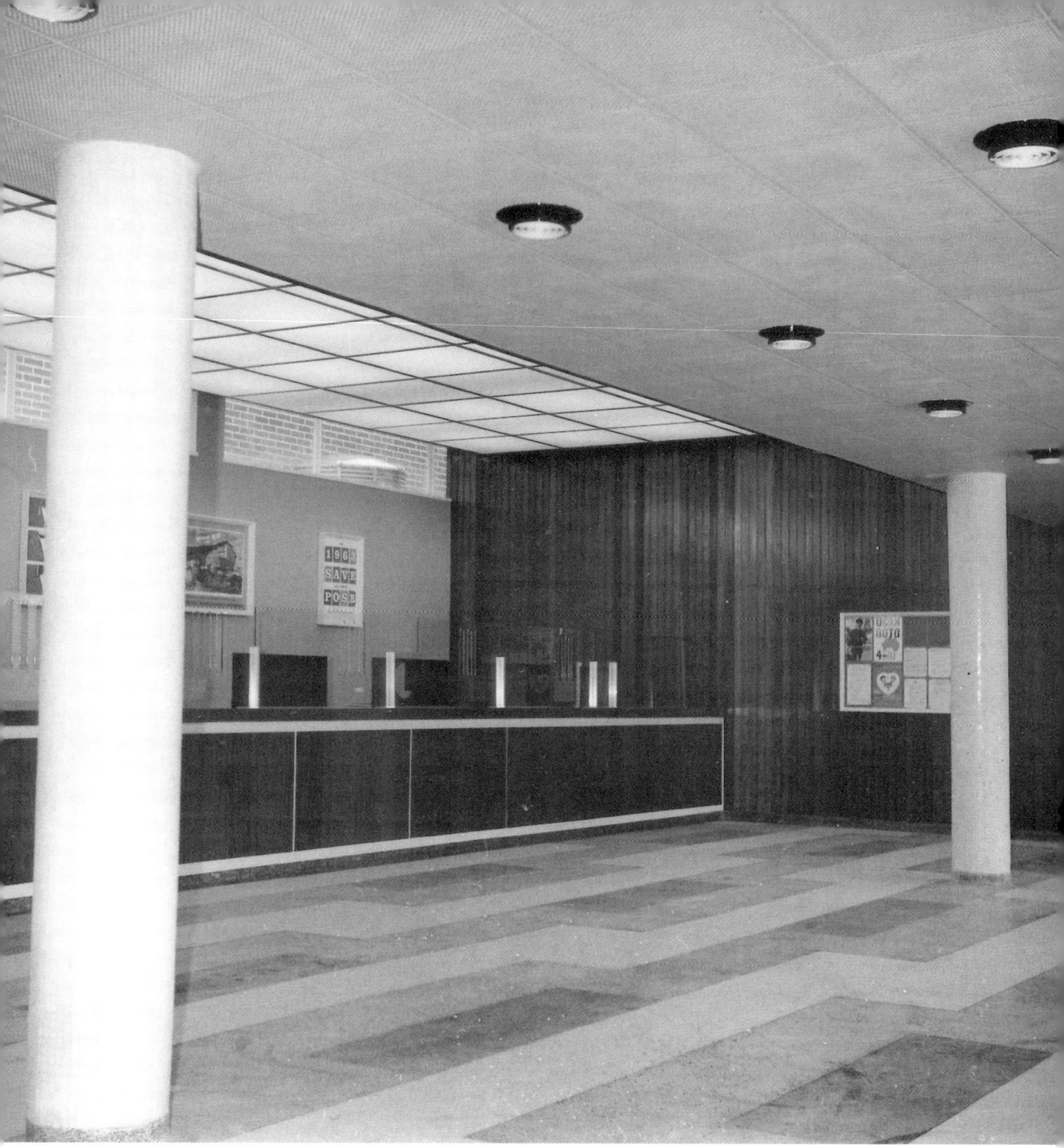

The interior of the new post office, opened in 1963. Closed down just a few years ago when post office counters were franchised, this view will stir many memories of past busy days when such emptiness was unknown.

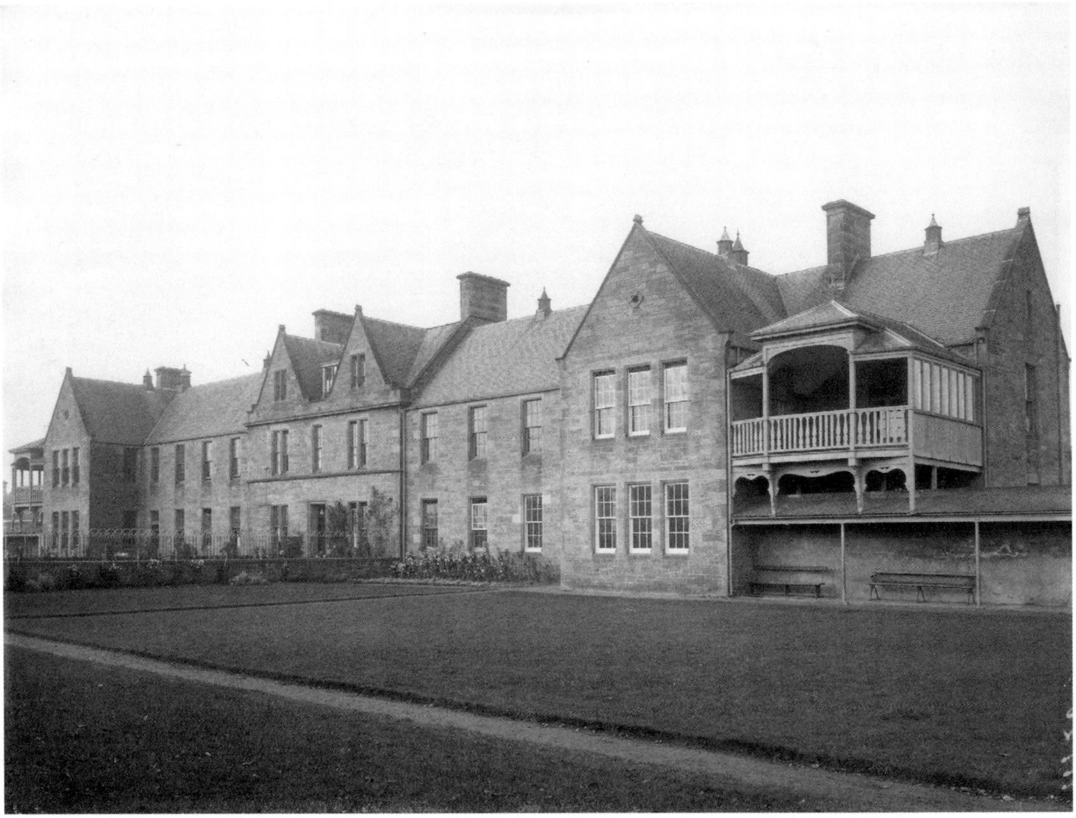

Craigmoray, the poor house. The stigma of being sent to the poor house still terrified old folk in the 1970s. In spite of proposals to retain the building and refurbish it for other uses, it was finally demolished and the nursing home that replaced it was renamed. It is on record that the poor house board gave the inmates a celebratory dinner, 'a most sumptuous feast with several courses . . . and an abundance of ale', in 1889 to celebrate the wedding of the Duke of Fife to Queen Victoria's granddaughter. These celebrations are recorded in the picture on page 10 (top).

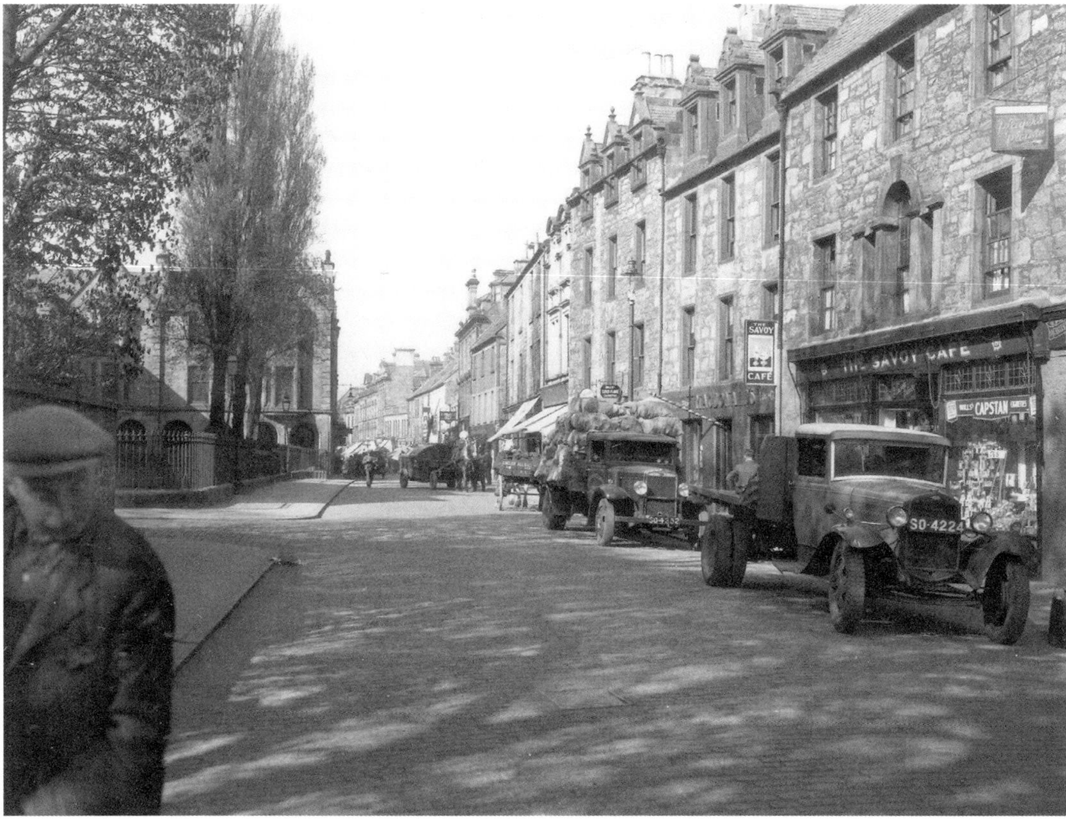

Nos 15-25 High Street looking west. Opposite the old County buildings, which were demolished in 1939, and just along from the Little Cross, these shops were the first buildings to be restored by the Elgin Fund and the character of the old piazzas restored.

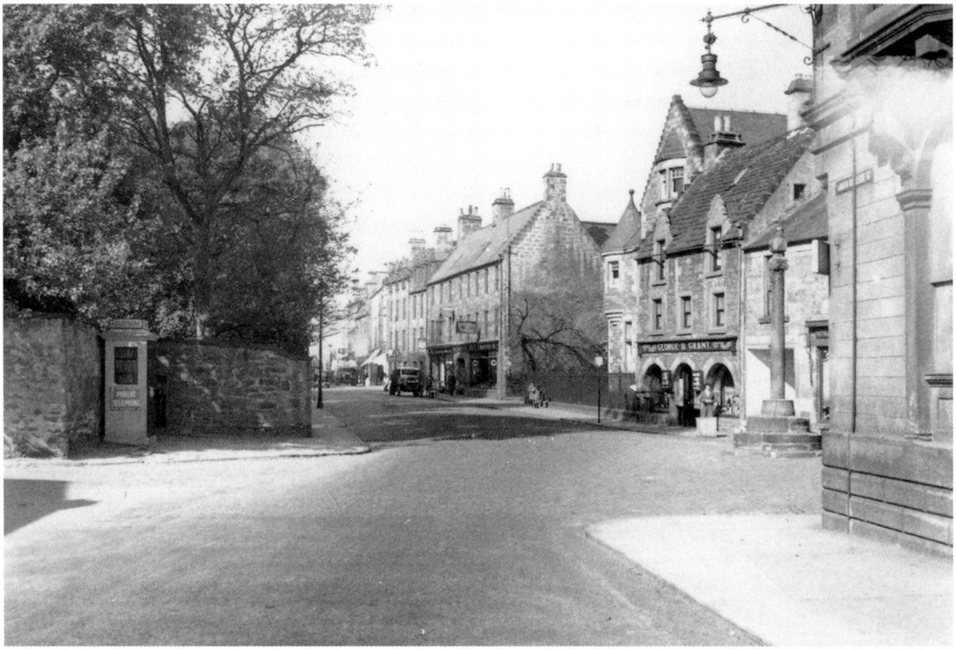

Facing the High Street, Little Cross House overlooked the site of the best well in Elgin. This early seventeenth-century well was still in operation at the beginning of the nineteenth century, until it was covered over during road re-surfacing in 1956. This picture appears to have been taken in about 1940.

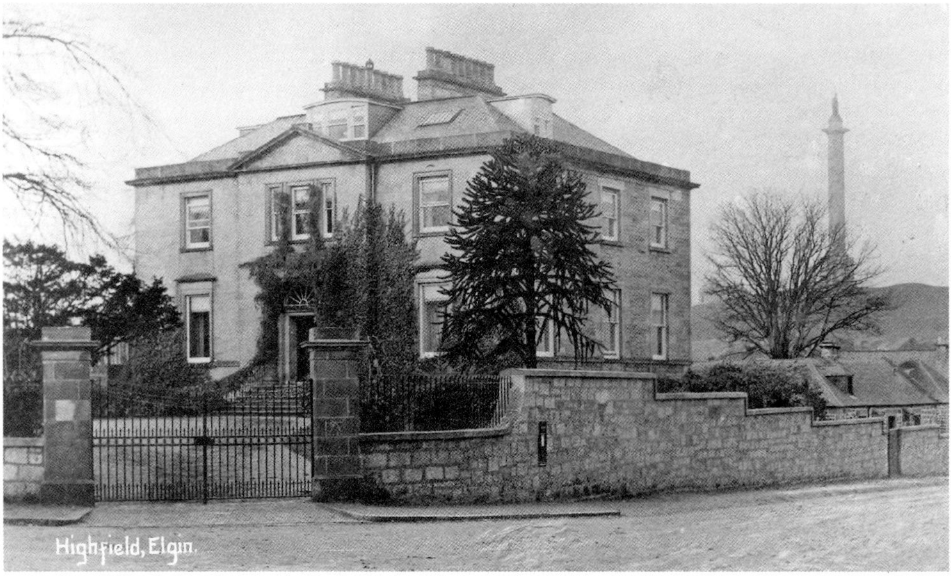

Highfield House was built in about 1820 as the town house for the Dunhars of Duffus and Highfield. In the fifteenth century the Dunbars were the Constables of the Castle of Elgin and the King's Regent in Moray. In the middle of the last century this was the home of the Lord Provost of Elgin, Alexander Cameron.

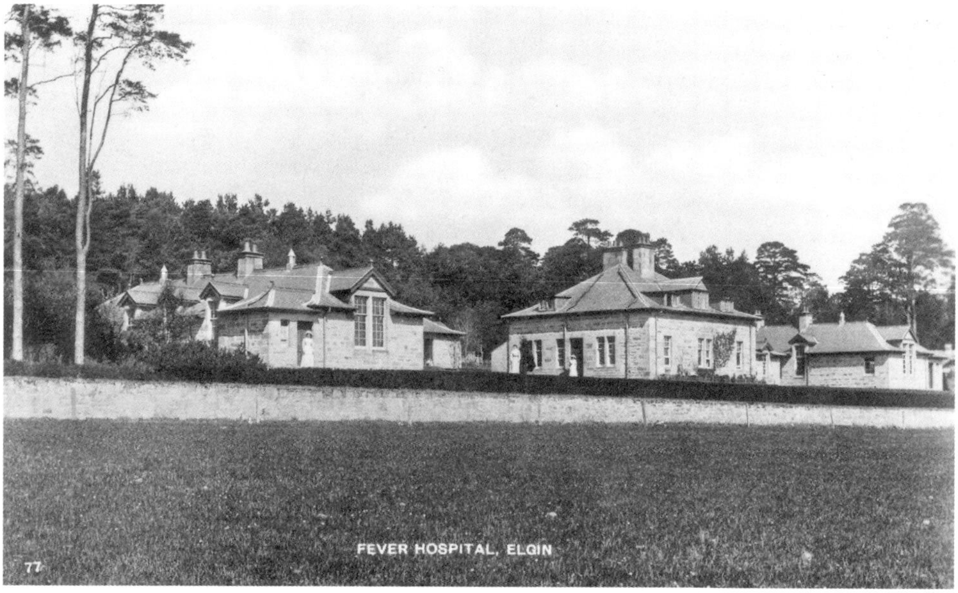

Spynie Hospital. This was once the isolation hospital where patients with tuberculosis were wheeled outside — still in their beds — and ranged in an orderly line to gain the full benefit of the fresh air. The long uniforms worn by the nurses in the doorways date this picture as beginning of the century.

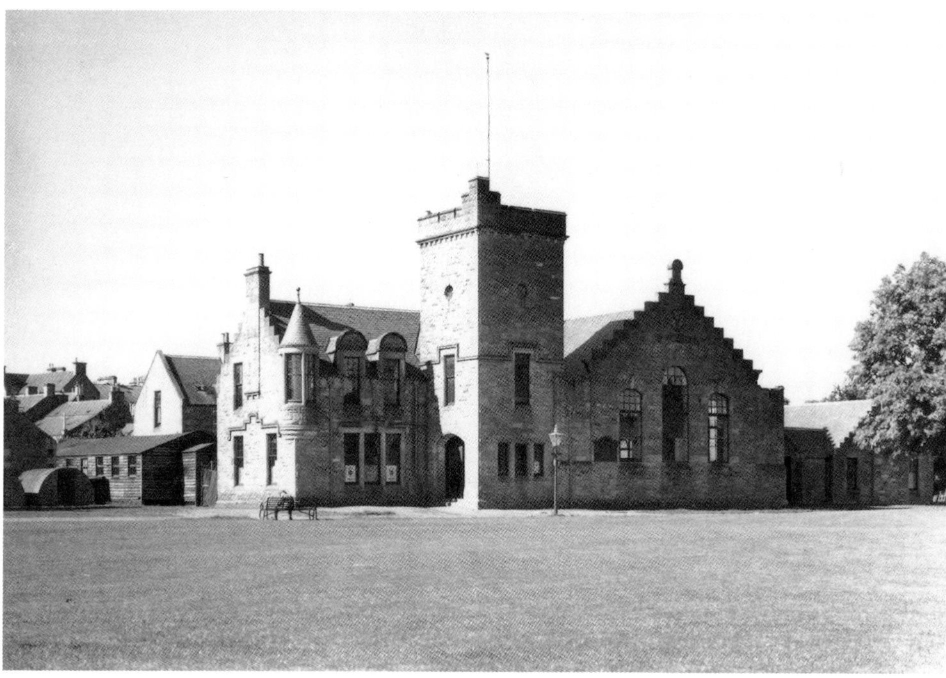

The Drill Hall on the site of Hervey's Haugh. It was the drill hall for the Seaforths, a volunteer force who distinguished themselves in the Boer War. This building was completed in 1906 and contained the first gymnasium in Elgin.

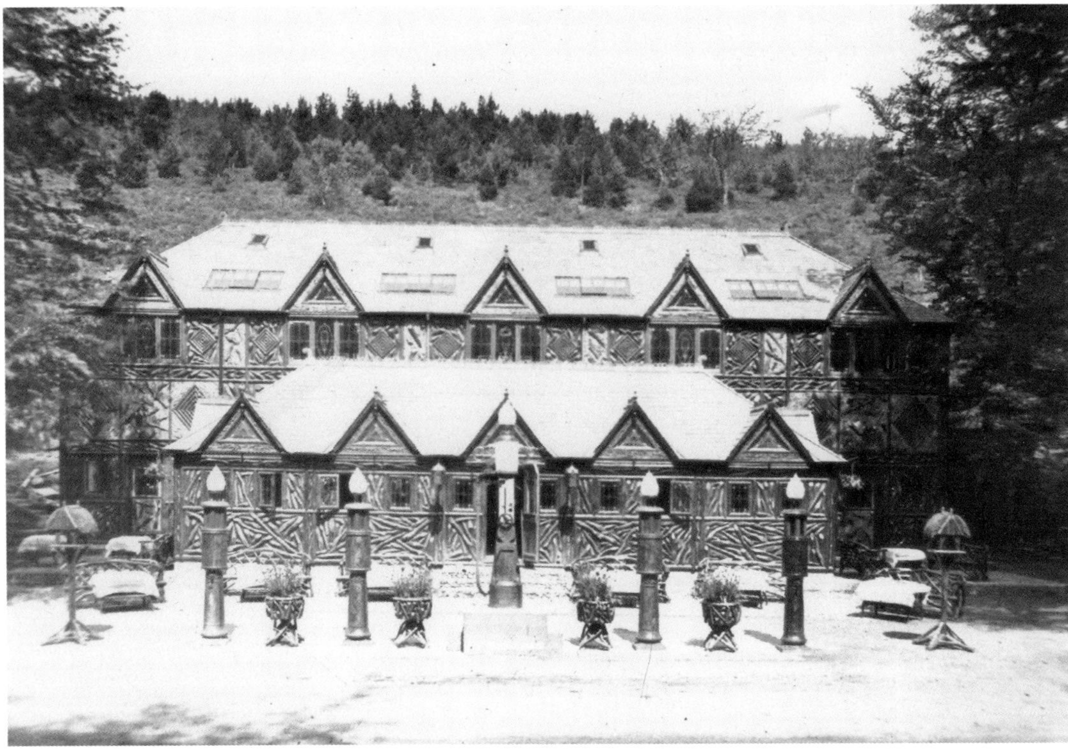

The Oakwood Motel. This is an early picture of the motel which was built in 1932 on the western outskirts of Elgin. After fifty years growth, the trees to the rear almost engulf the building now. The owner, Dougal Duncan, having made a trip to Canada, had the building constructed out of split and unsplit logs. For many years the motel was a popular venue for dances and social gatherings. People would walk through the oak woods to the motel in search of an ice-cream on a Sunday afternoon.

Section Five

Changed Places Around Town

Here are some familiar names but unfamiliar views showing how dramatically some things have changed over the past century. Looking back it is apparent just how much the petrol engine has changed the shape of the town and altered the pace of life. Daniel Defoe wrote of Elgin, ' . . . the country is rich and pleasant, so here are a great many rich inhabitants, and in the town of Elgin in particular . . . the gentlemen leave their Highland habitations in winter and come and live for the diversion of the place, and plenty of provisions; and there is, on this account, a great variety of gentlemen for society. This makes Elgin a very agreeable place to live in.'

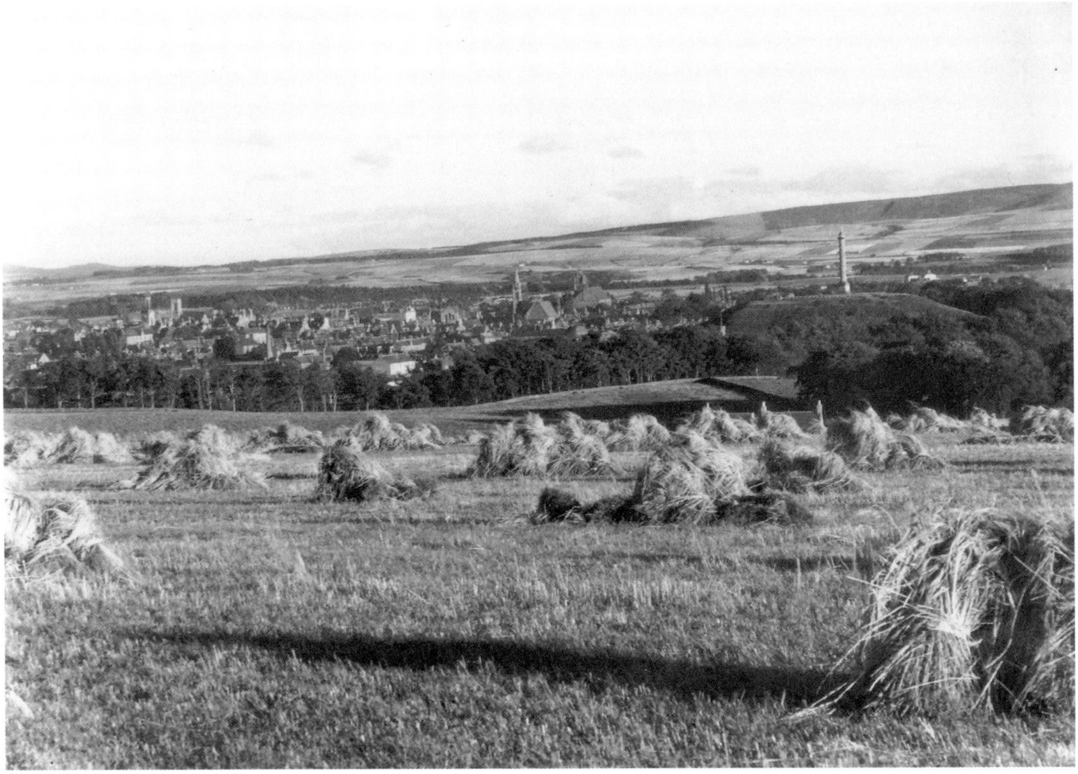

Town panorama from Morriston. After the Second World War there was great housing development in this area. Such stooks are a rare sight nowadays and these have been replaced by quality housing schemes.

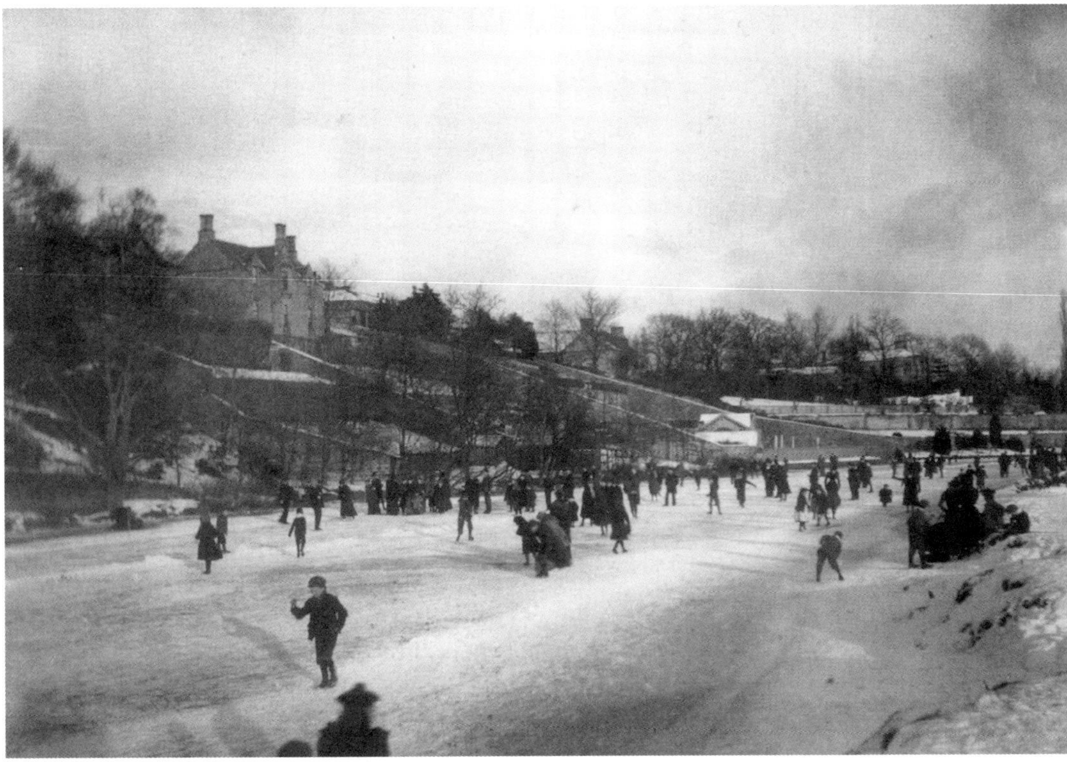

The frozen Lossie providing good entertainment at Bishopmill at the turn of the century. In ancient times the ridge of Bishopmill, overlooking the River Lossie, was called Frankoklaw. The first reference to a village of 'Bisaptung' is in 1363. A charter of 1566 calls the land 'Bischipis Mylne', referring to digging peat on the moor known as the 'Laverock Moss' or the 'Bischipis Moss'. A late Neolithic burial was found in the area, with one grave containing a bronze dagger and a man wrapped in what was probably ox-hide.

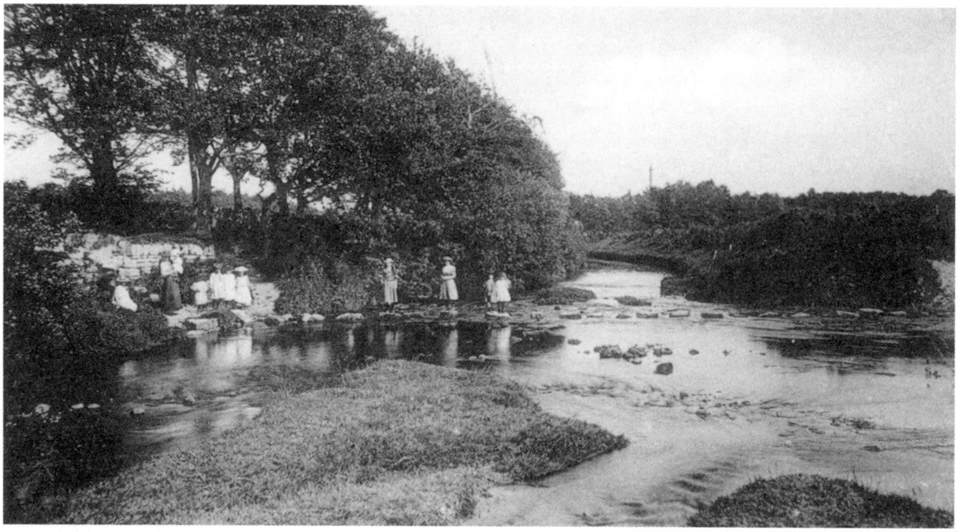

Looking east towards Morriston along the River Lossie. As the water from the town wells was very hard, and often brackish, clothes were washed in the river and maids would collect pails of water for the tea. This group of ladies at the turn of the century are simply enjoying a pleasant walk.

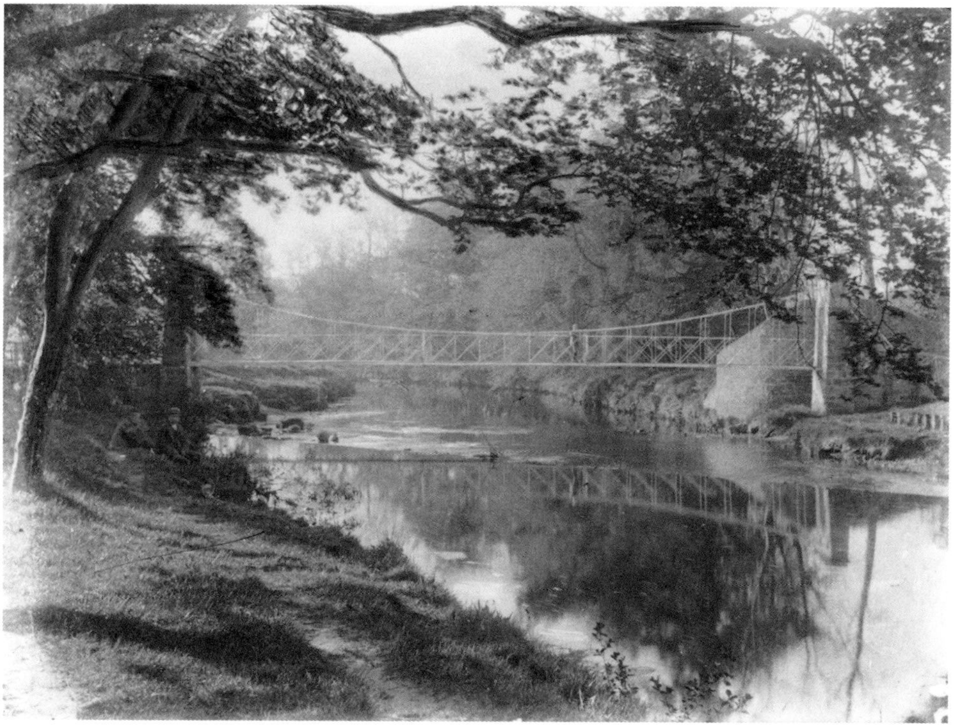

The Lossie at Marywell — Deanshaugh Bridge. It is said that the water of Marywell is colder in summer than in winter and has a higher specific gravity, according to local legend.

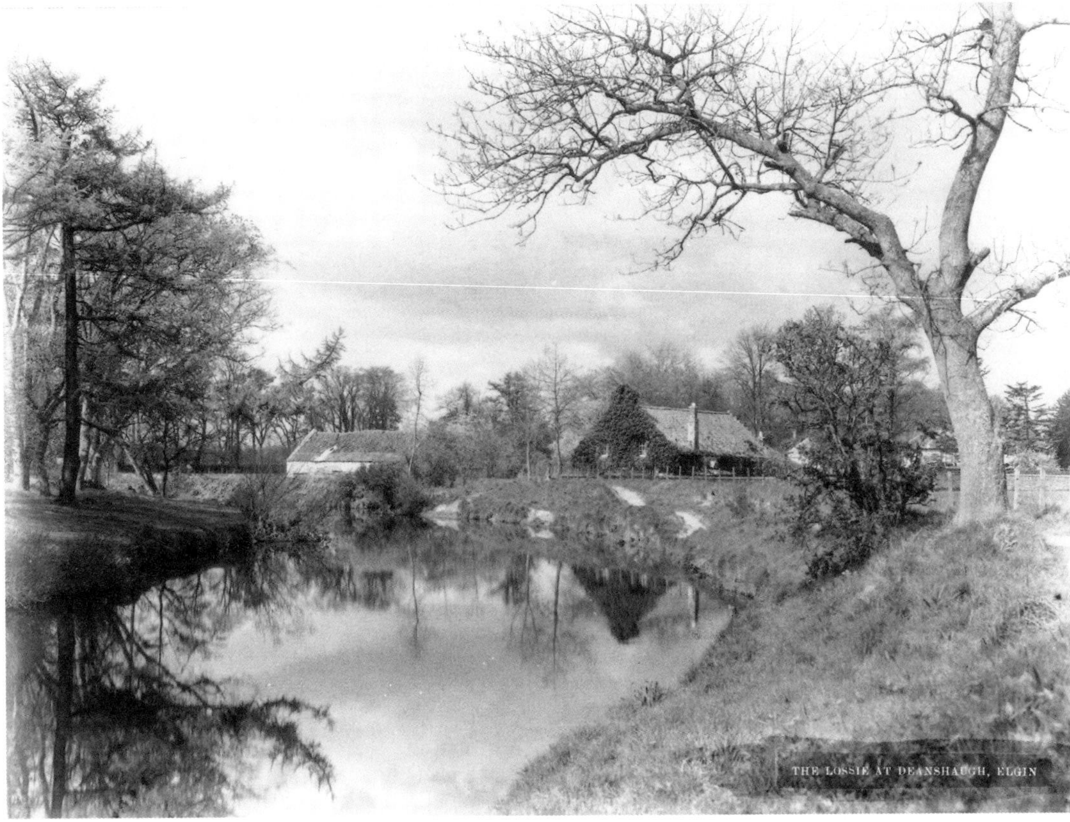

The Lossie at Deanshaugh. Passing between the Bishop's Castle at Spynic and the cathedral, the clergy crossed the Lossie by a bridge built in the early thirteenth century. The river changed course during medieval times and the old course is said to have run through the Haugh grounds close to the Episcopal church. It then passed near the Drill Hall, running round the east side of the pond in the Cooper Park and joined the main stream a little above Deanshaugh bridge. Towards the end of the eighteenth century a tobacco mill, a waulk (cloth fulling) mill, a flax mill and machinery for bleaching were all sited at Deanshaugh.

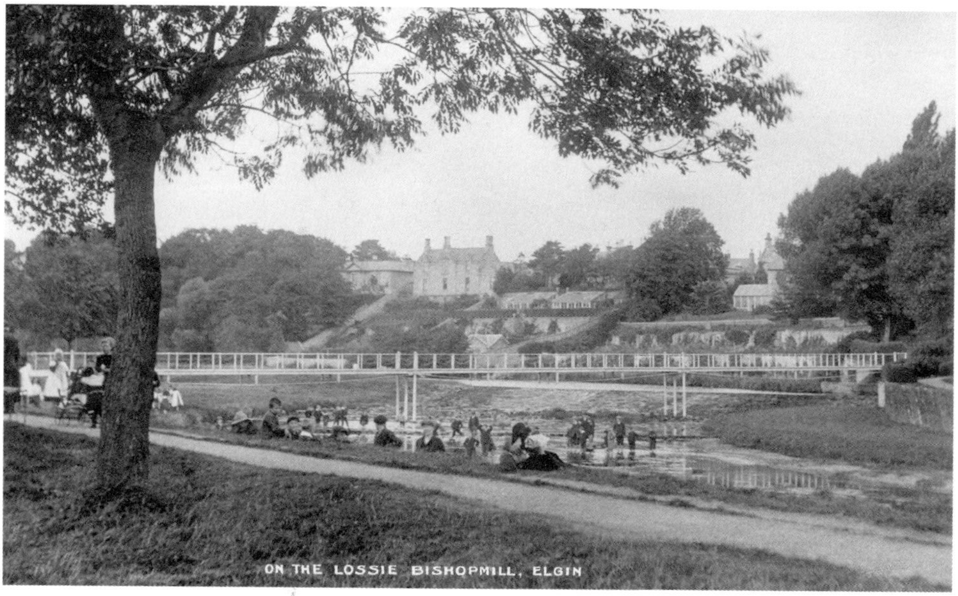

The Lossie at Bishopmill at the turn of the century. The Munro Bridge seen here was removed sometime before 1950. In 1566 the Bishop, Patrick Hepburn, granted a charter of land called 'the Bischipis Mylne', which included peat digging on the moor called the Laverock Moss alias the 'Bischcopis Moss'. The property passed into the hands of the Dunbars of Burgle, then to Robertson of Bishopmill. In 1798 the area was acquired by the Earl of Findlater, who did much to improve the village on the hill overlooking Elgin.

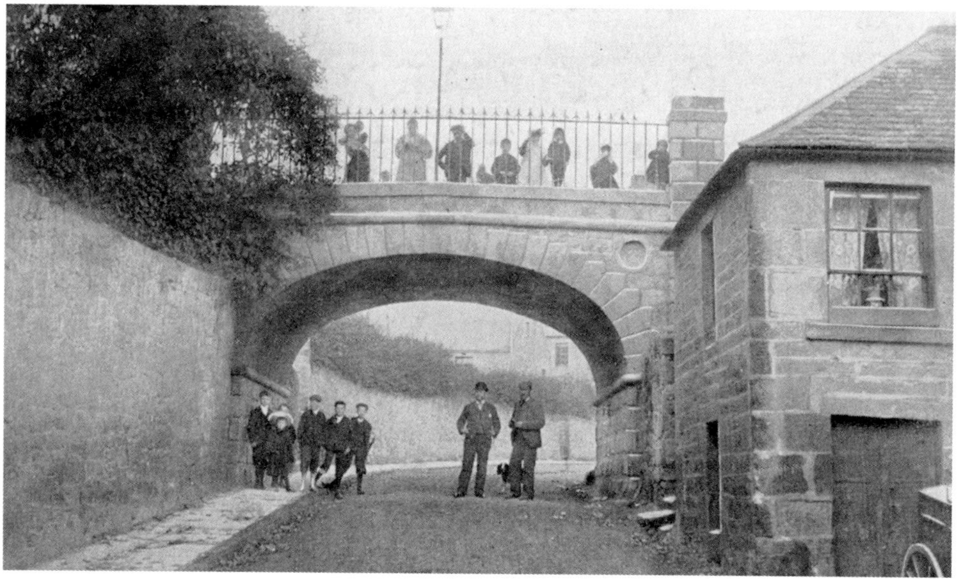

The Dry Brig, Bishopsmill. The Elgin to Lossiemouth road, constructed in 1820, passed via a deep cutting through Bishopsmill village and a bridge was built to reconnect the divided High Street. This Dry Brig was removed in 1898 and Bishopsmill High Street was again divided.

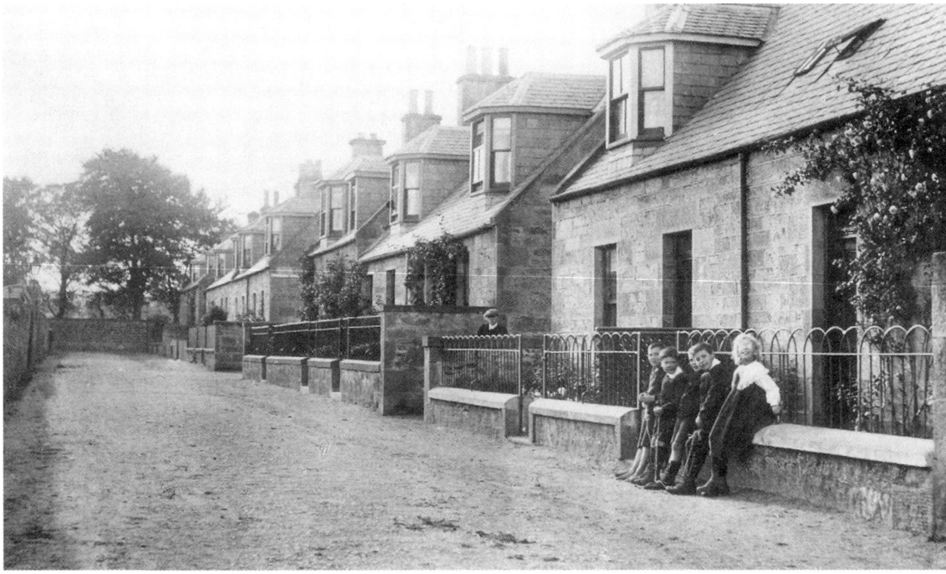

Blantyre Place, Bishopmill at the end of the last century. Bishopmill was laid out in an east-west grid in 1798 by the Earl of Findlater.

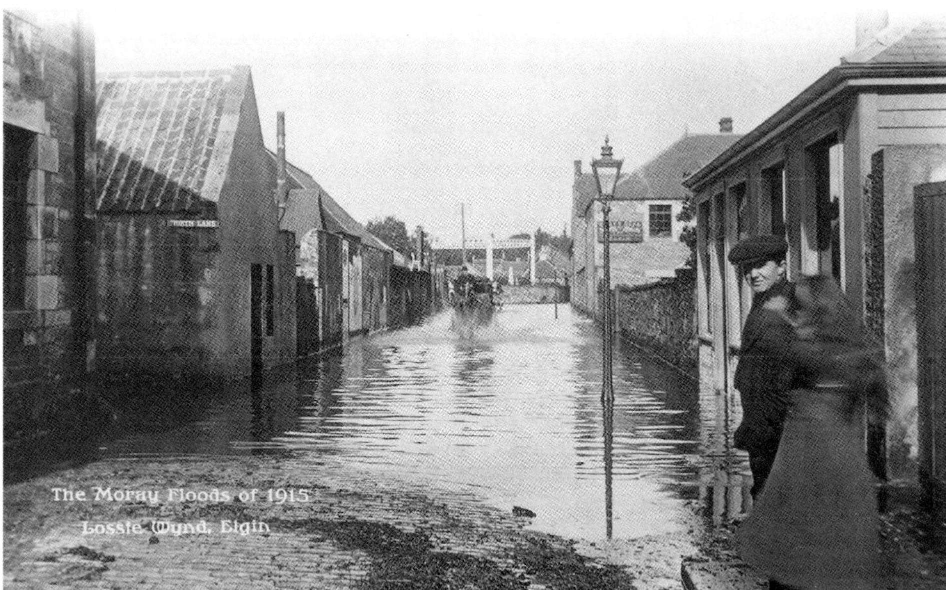

Floods in Lossie Wynd in 1915, when floodwaters cut off Bishopmill and Elgin. Lossie Wynd was once the main north entrance to the town and was once known as Carseman's Wynd, before becoming The Shambles Wynd, and finally being known as Lossie Wynd. North Port, where tolls were collected, stood halfway up this street until 1787.

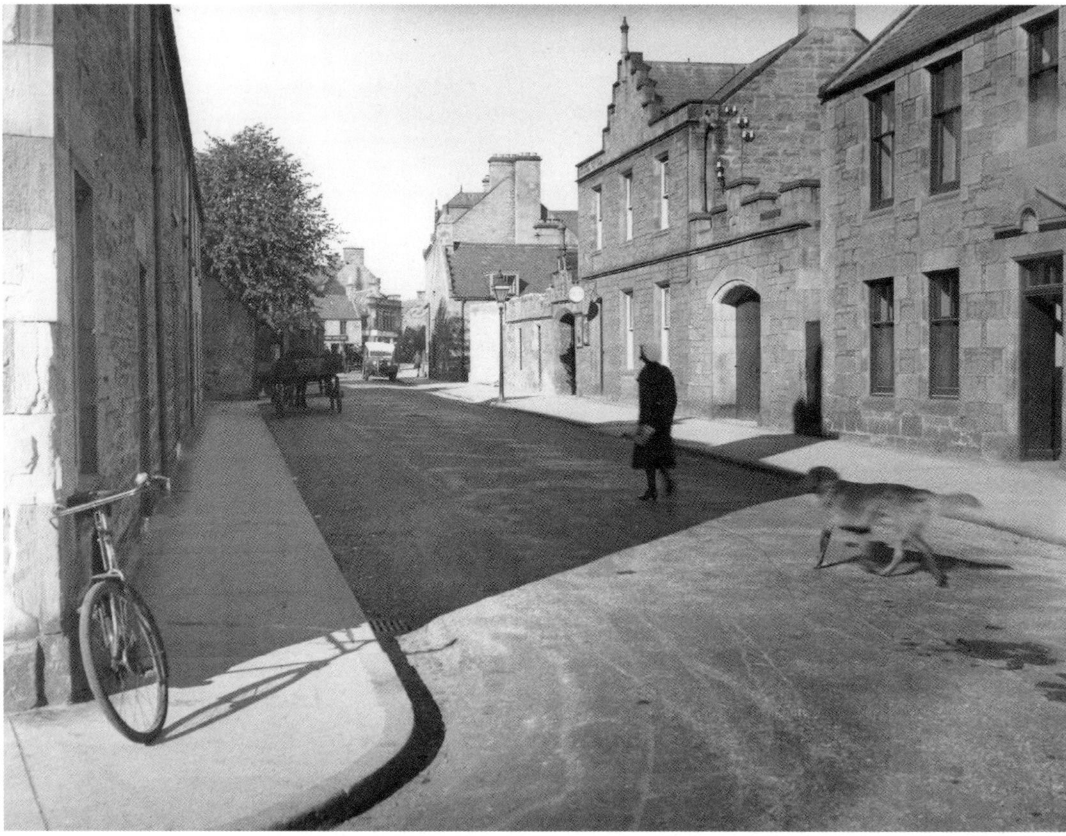

Greyfriars Street. The police station and prison were situated here from the middle of the nineteenth century until being demolished in 1965, replaced by a car park. The new police station, opened in 1963, was built on the site of the old town hall. The sign on the back of the lorry reads, 'coal 2/3d 1 cwt bag'.

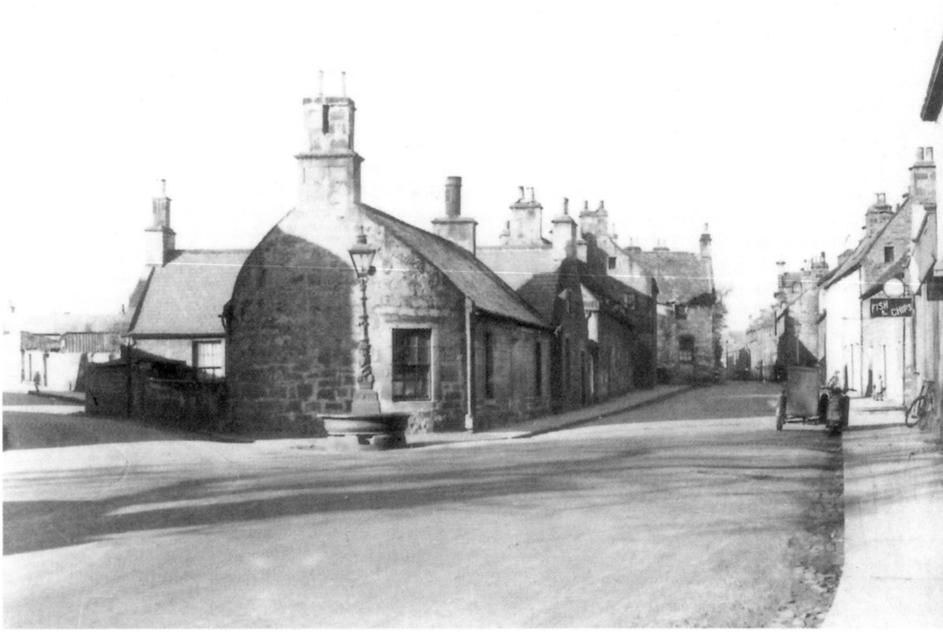

These old buildings were demolished in 1935 when the eastern approach to Elgin along South College Street was widened.

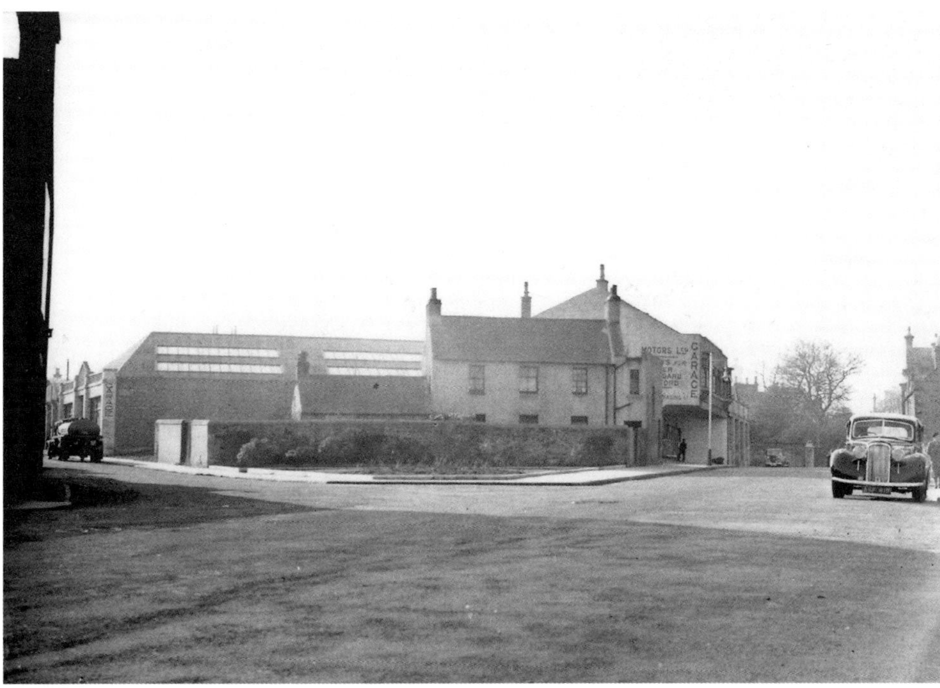

South College Street in 1948. The flat above the garage was in Art Deco style with Art Deco windows. The whole area is now totally changed following further road developments.

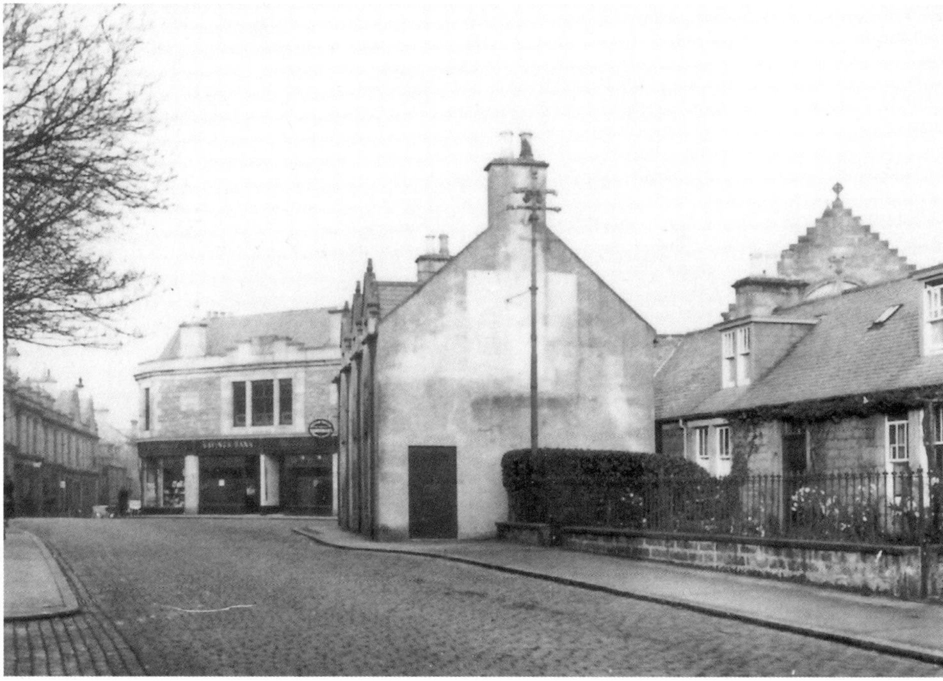

Moss Street. As can be seen by the tree on the left of both pictures, this view towards Commerce Street is taken from the same place and shows the gradual changes over the years, although the cobbles remained. The large building in the top picture was demolished in about 1936 when the road was widened. On the corner a step down led into Taylor's grocery shop.

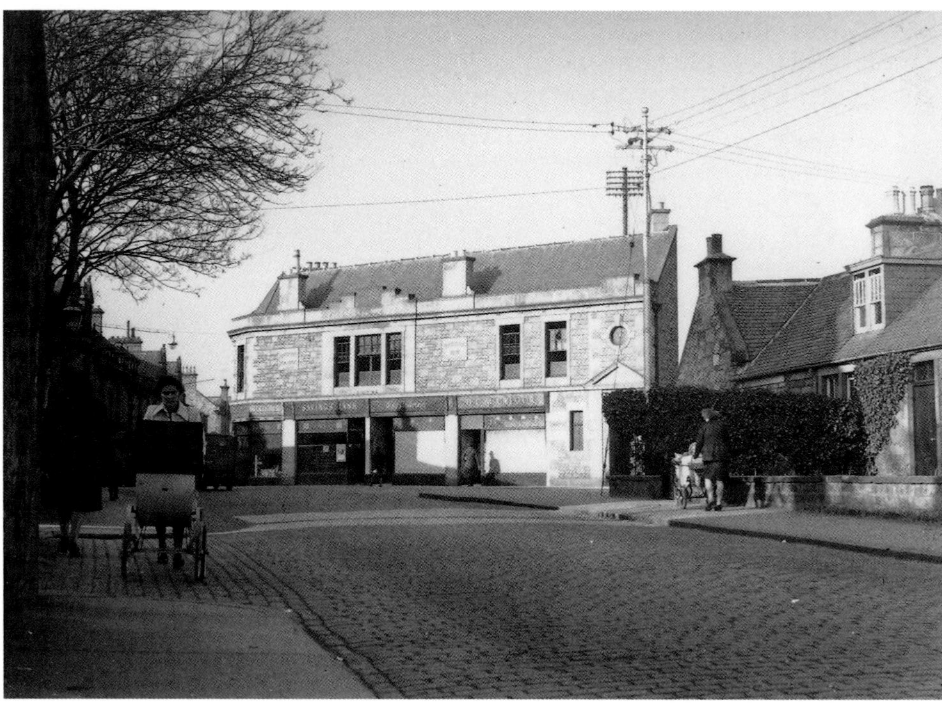

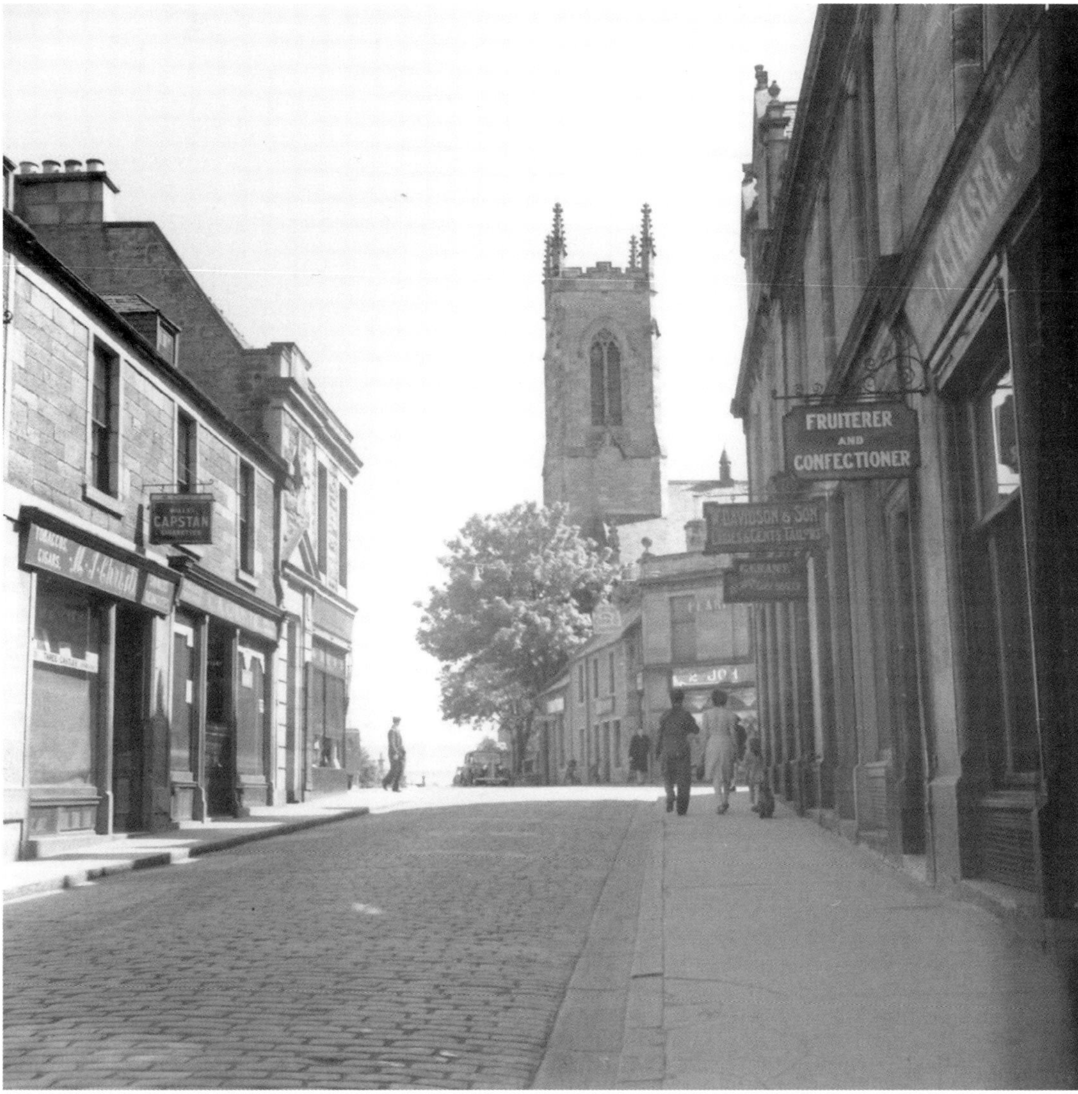

Commerce Street. Taken just after the Second World War, this is the view looking up to Moss Street. The same tree seen in the pictures on the previous page can be seen on the right, larger and in full leaf.

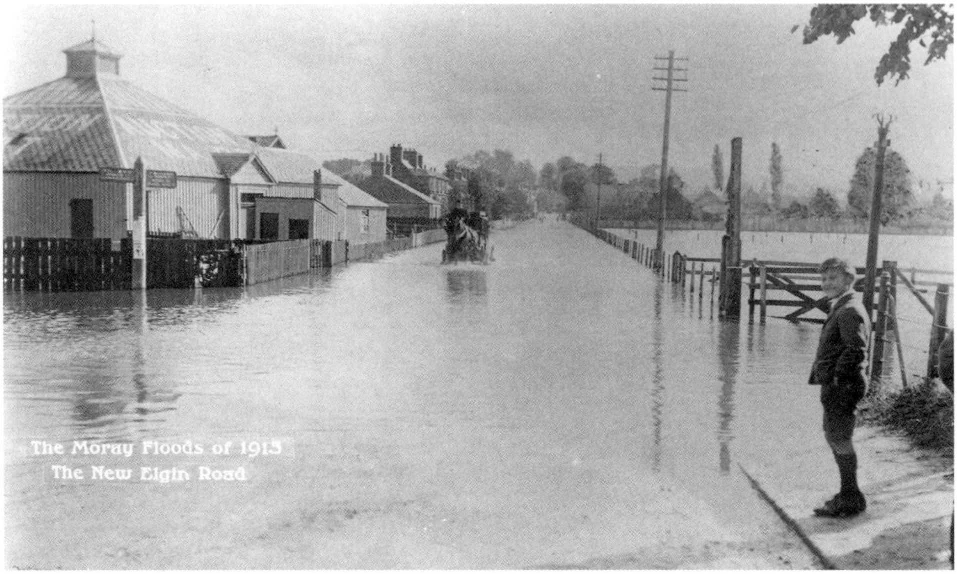

New Elgin floods. During the floods of 1915 New Elgin was cut off from the town. The village of New Elgin was built on the Muir of Elgin after the land had been acquired by the convenery of incorporated trades in 1760. This group of assembled trades went back to before 1234 when a royal charter was granted to allow free trade within the burgh of Elgin. The Moss of Strathcant, fed by the burn of Tyock, lay between Moss Street and the village, which explains why this area was so prone to flooding.

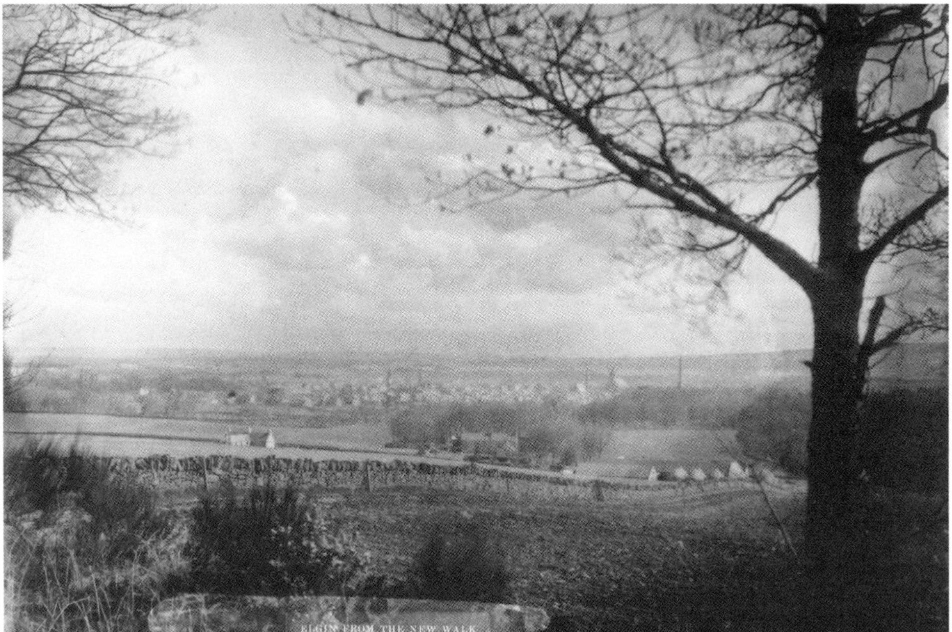

A view over Elgin taken from New Walk before additional houses and the High School were built.

Section Six

Closes, Homes & Castles

By the 1840s Elgin had become fashionable, with many neo-classical buildings and elegant villas springing up. While inequalities still exist today, most of us can take for granted the running water, good lighting and ready heat available. In the recent past the struggle for warmth and adequate accommodation was less equal. While some of the following dwellings are not actually within the town, their existence has made a vital contribution to the history and development of Elgin. The big houses provided employment as well as some security for loyal servants. Many folk would find the fierce discipline, long hours and lack of personal autonomy intolerable today — and too great a price to pay for tenure that could be terminated on a whim.

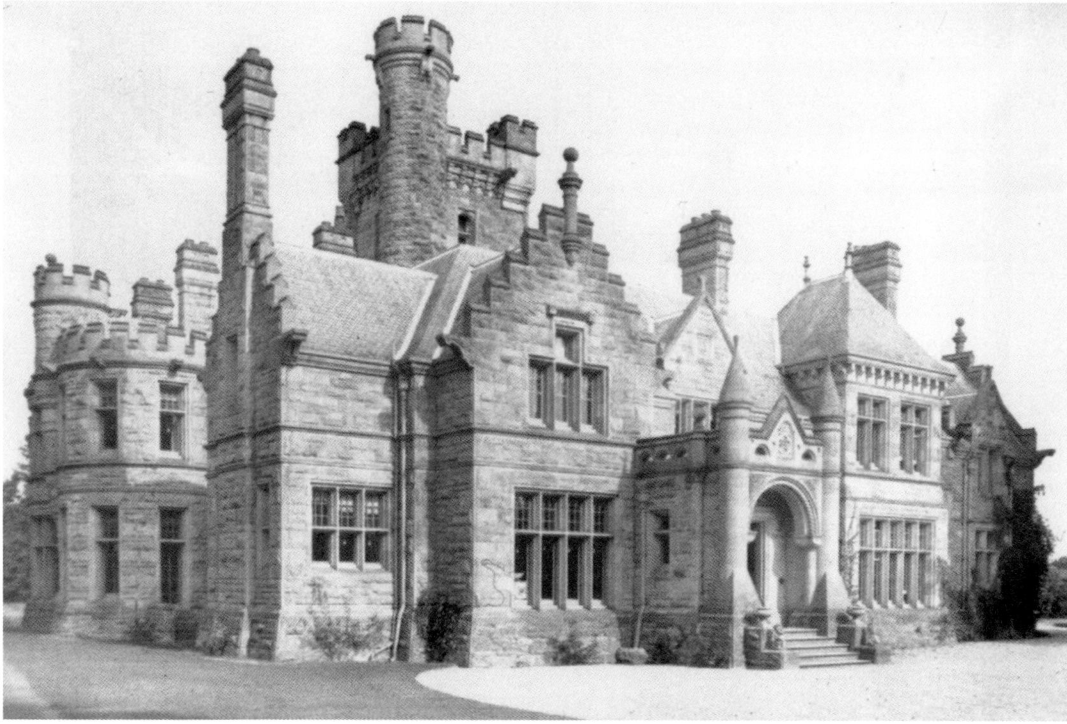

The Haugh, built on the west of the site of Blackfriars Haugh. It is on record that in 1750 the thirteenth century Blackfriars buildings and burying place were razed to the ground. Tradition persists that the people of Bishopmill used the gravestones to build their houses. As the old buildings were cleared, many silver coins, rings, seals and antique silver spoons were found — and sold in Edinburgh. The Haugh was completed in 1883 and was used in both world wars to accommodate service personnel. In 1946 the house was gifted to the town by Mrs H. C. Bibby and was used as a pre-nursing training centre and later as a music department for the Elgin Academy.

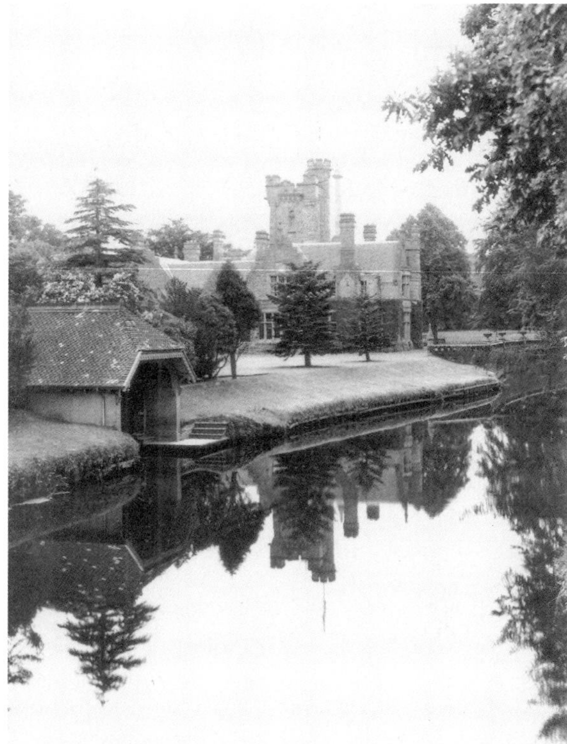

The Haugh. In 1882 the prominent lawyer A. G. Allan commissioned William Kidner to remodel the Haugh. Kidner had spent some time in Shanghai and this exotic influence can be seen in the design.

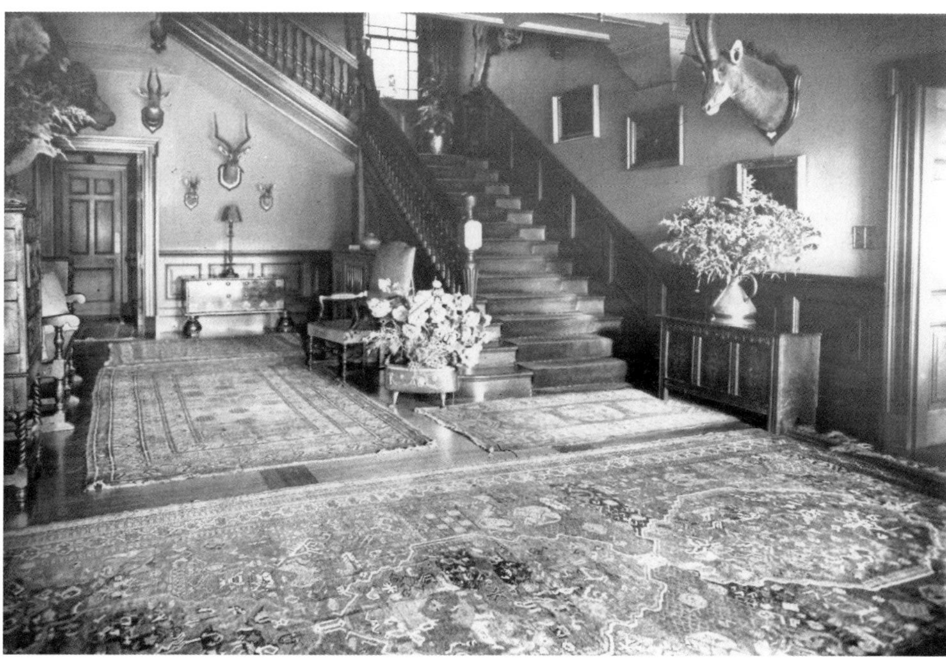

The entrance hall of The Haugh. This was how it looked before the onslaught of pre-nursing feet.

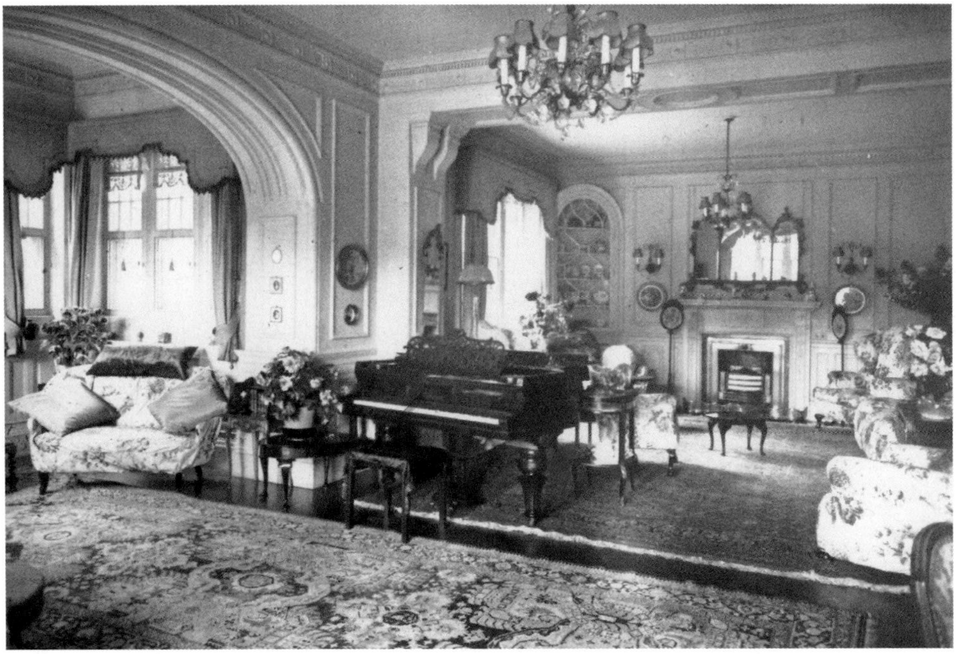

The Haugh drawing room. A fascinating glimpse into an elegant and comfortable room. Cut flowers and flowering pot plants are much in evidence. These photographs were probably taken around 1946, when The Haugh was gifted to the town.

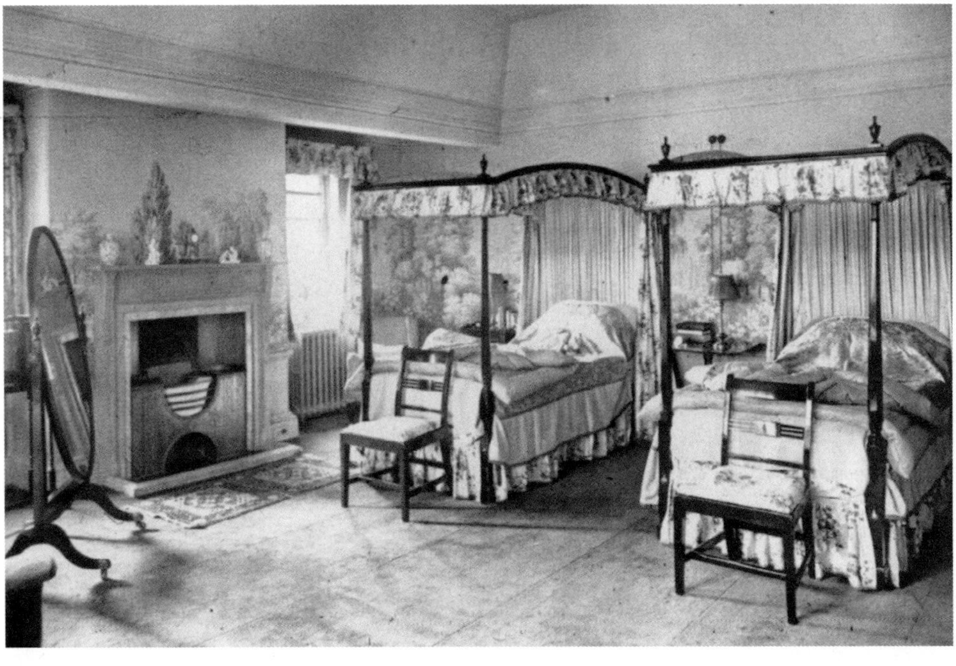

One of the bedrooms in The Haugh. It is interesting to see the landscape views which decorate the walls.

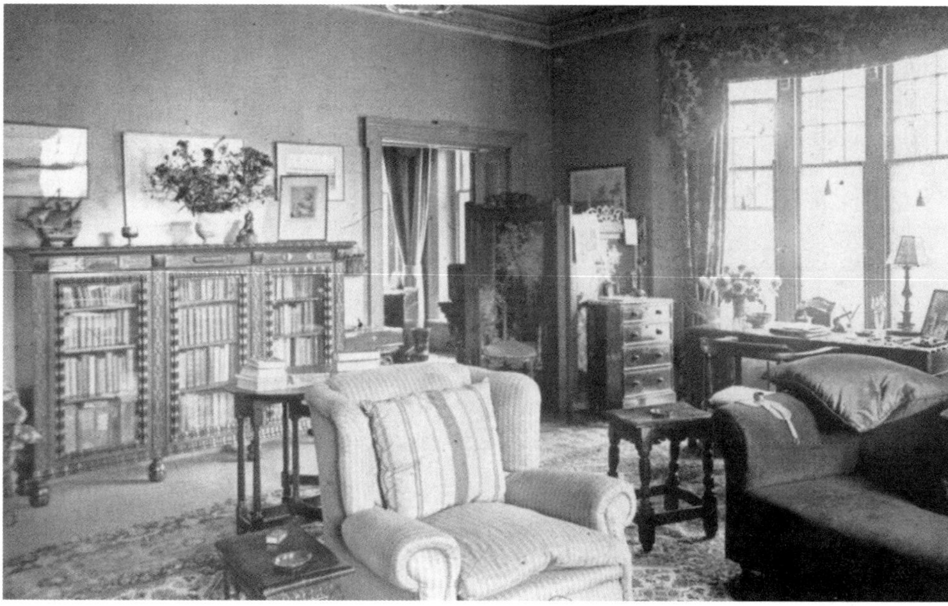

Another elegant and comfortable room in the Haugh, with more flower arrangements.

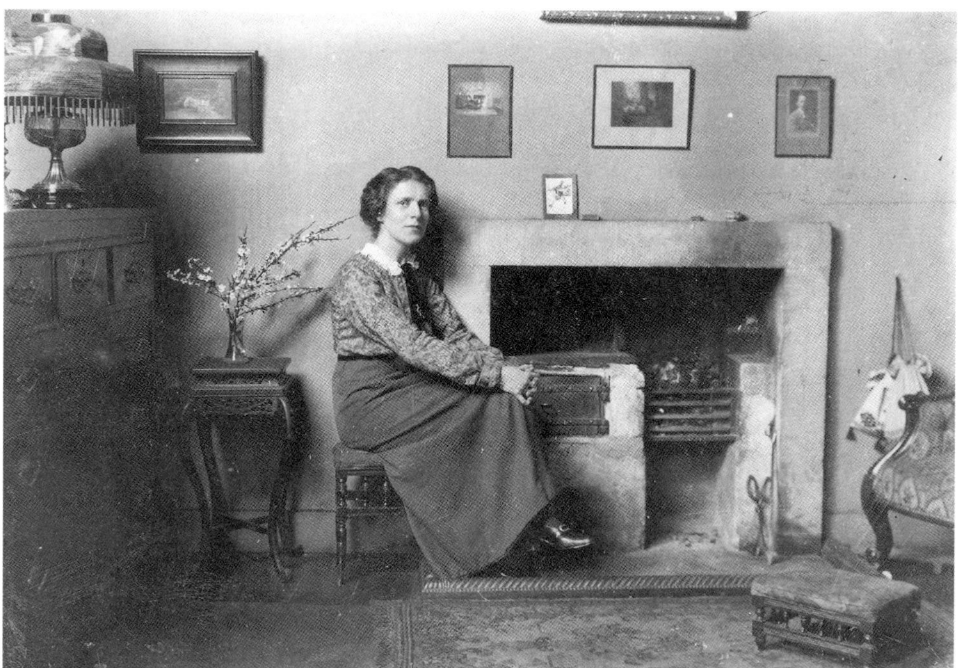

A more modest Elgin living room. Judging by the sprig of pussy-willow in the vase, it is spring time and doubtless the room has been well 'thoroughed' for the occasion. Evidence of past struggles with the fire can be seen in the smoky mark above the fireplace.

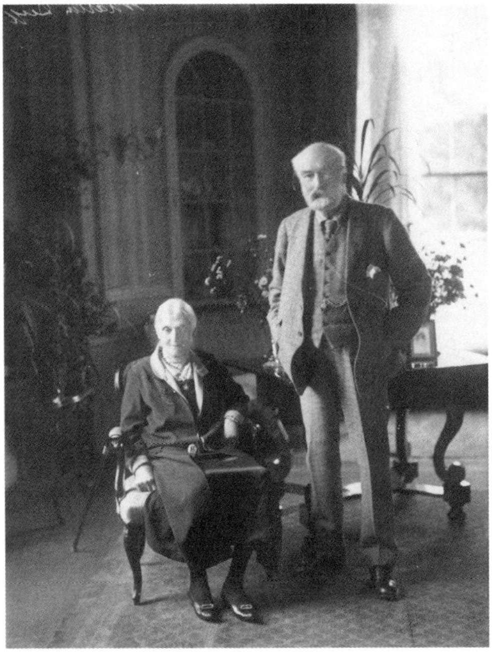

A pleasant portrait of the Warton-Duffs at home taken more than sixty years ago. These were the owners of Orton House.

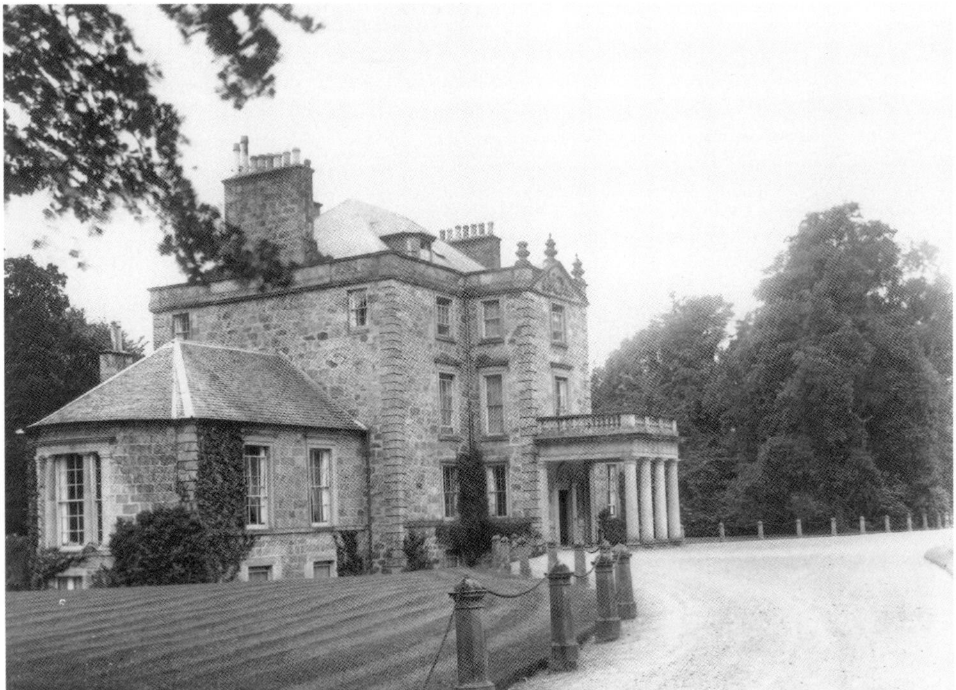

Orton House, *c.*1930. This tall classical house was built in 1786 with additions in 1826. The three main bedrooms were on the ground floor, the first floor being occupied by a magnificent suite of rooms. A library was situated on the second floor.

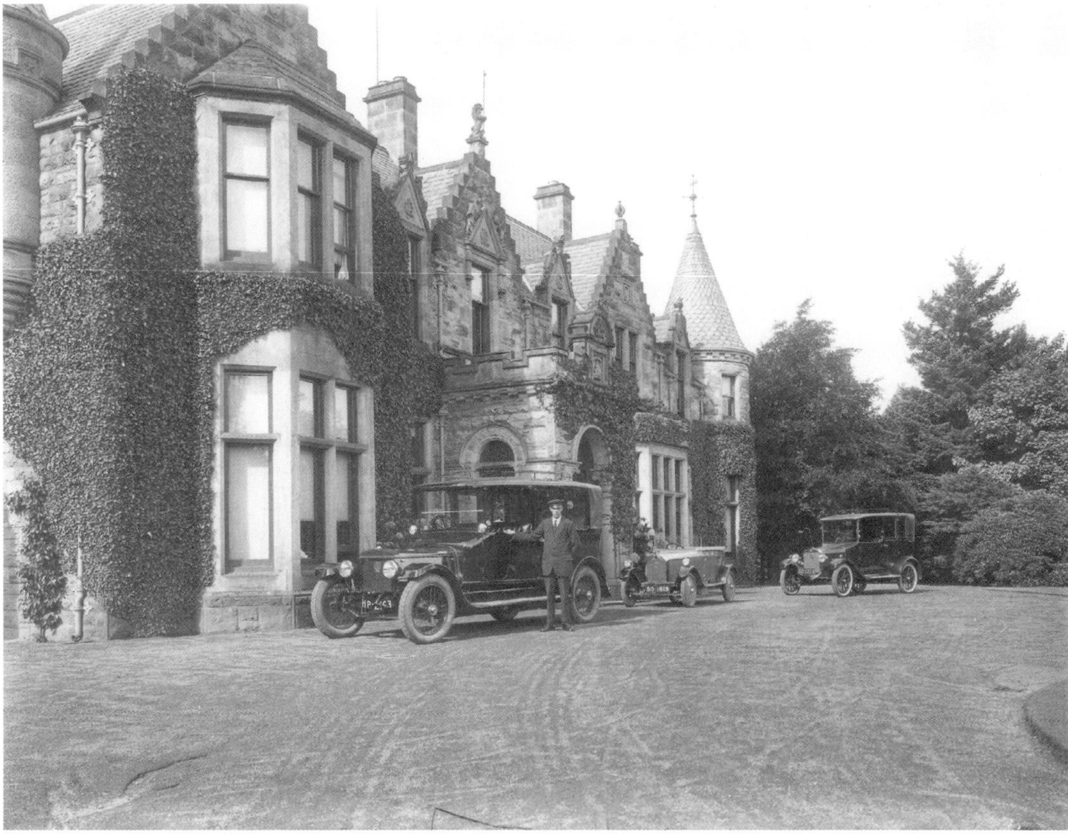

Glen Grant House, built in 1885. The Grants had distillery connections and much local influence. One of Major 'Glennie's' protégés was his batman, 'Byways', who was found as a native child by the roadside in Africa and brought back to Moray at the beginning of the century. 'Byways' became a popular figure, at one time playing football for Rothes. Believed to be over ninety when he died, his grave may be found in Rothes cemetery.

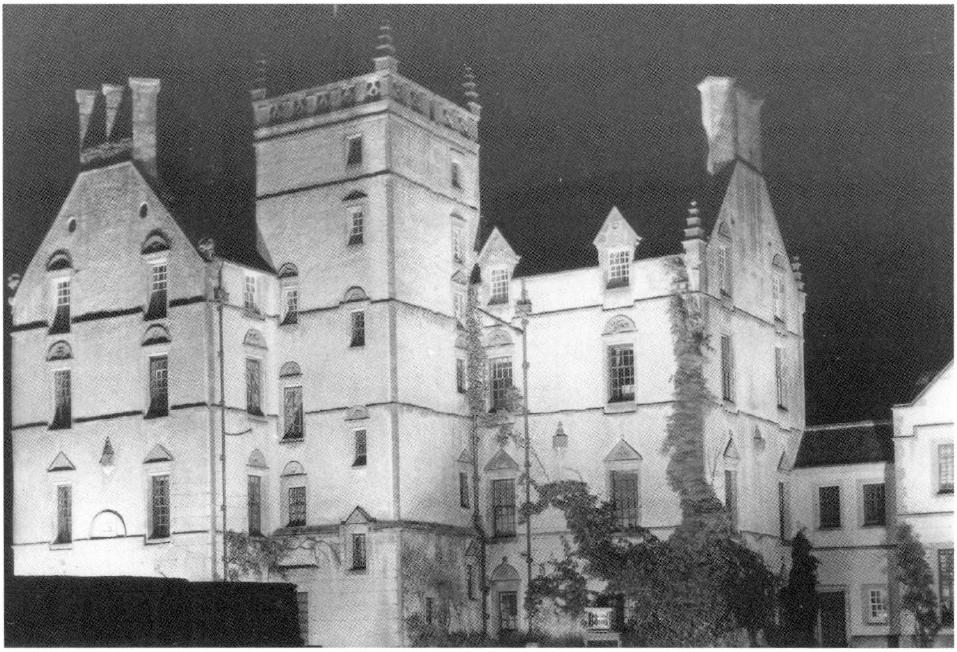

Innes House. The name Innes reflects the fact that the site was once an island. In 1157 Berowald from Flanders was given a charter for the land between the lochs of Cott and Spynie. Built in the mid-seventeenth century, it is an example of the transition from tower to house.

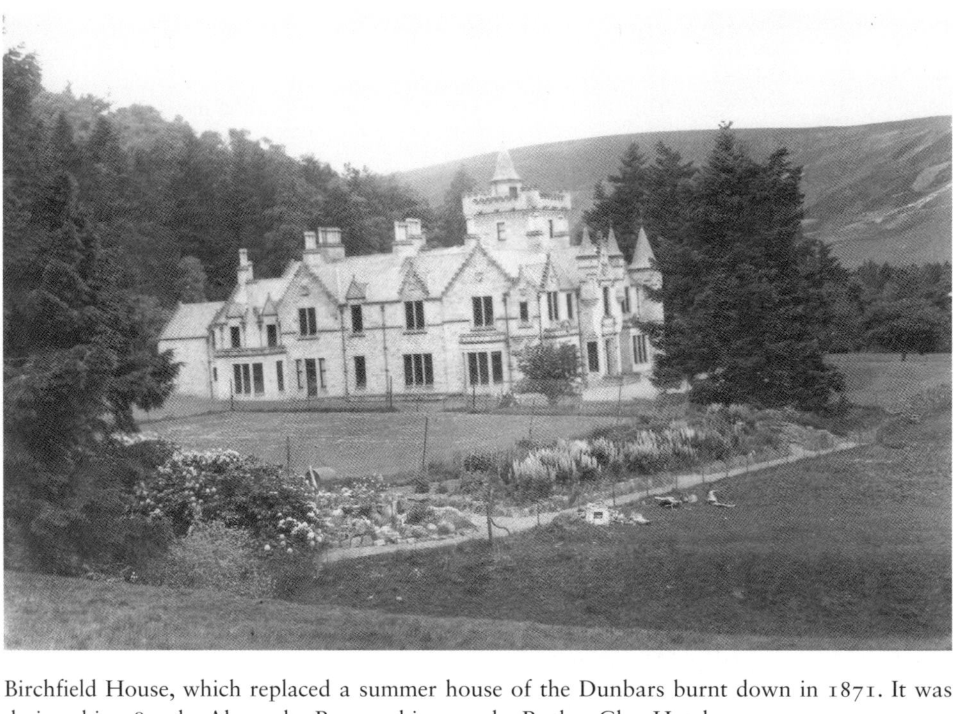

Birchfield House, which replaced a summer house of the Dunbars burnt down in 1871. It was designed in 1893 by Alexander Ross and is now the Rothes Glen Hotel.

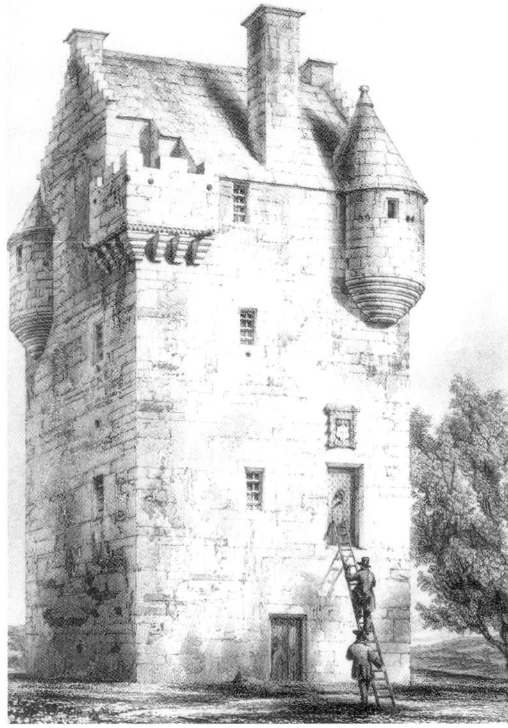

Coxton tower was built before 1644 for Sir Alexander Innes. It is in complete contrast to Innes House (built for another Innes) and was an anachronism in its day. Predators were discouraged by the two corbelled turrets and the first-floor entrance was originally reached by a ladder. The stairs were added in 1846. With thick walls, each of the four floors stone vaulted and a roof of stone slabs, it was made as fire-proof as possible.

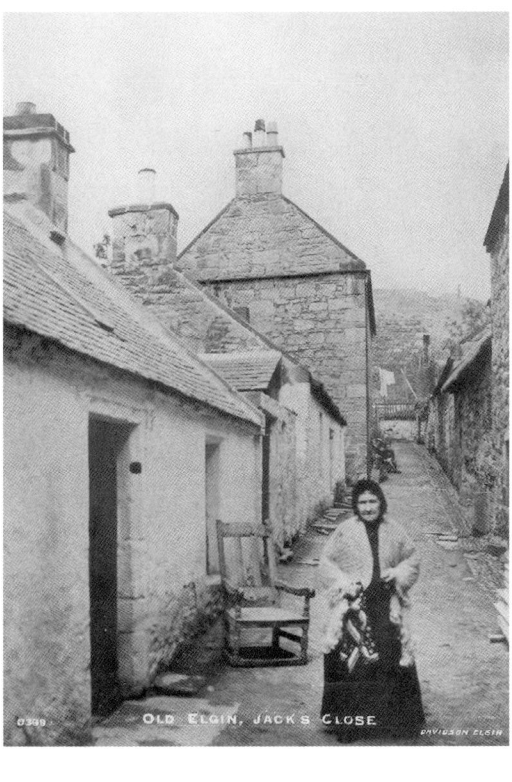

Jack's Close. A typical old Elgin close.

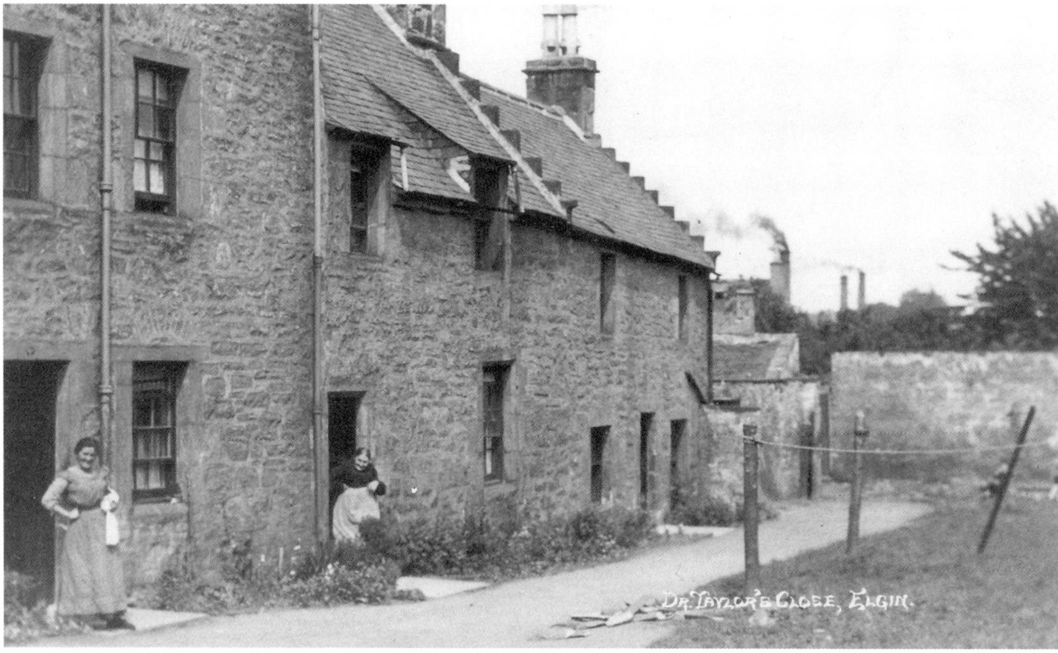

Taylor's Close. The surviving closes, wynds and alleys of Elgin are mostly eighteenth century but typical of seventeenth-century pends, running off the High Street. The windows and doors face east and the buildings are generally lower and more rustic than those facing the High Street.

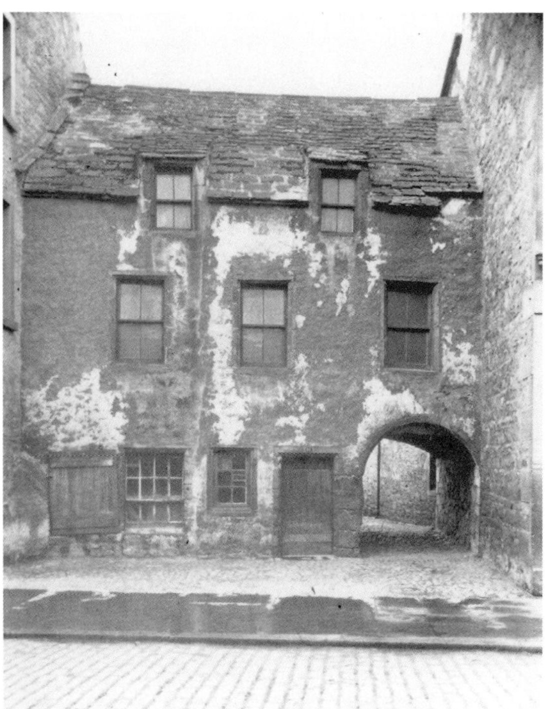

Another old Elgin close, taken at the turn of the century when cobblestones were common. This one is opposite the court house.

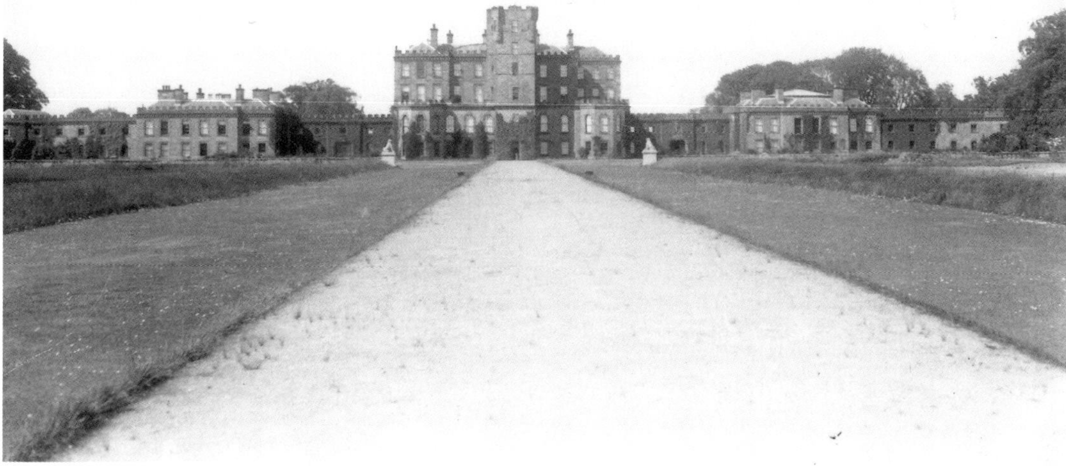

Gordon Castle, once described as the most magnificent edifice north of the Forth. It was begun in 1479, then extended and rebuilt in 1769, resulting in a castellated building 538 ft long. Having been sold to the government in lieu of death duties in 1938, and having suffered army occupation, it was bought back in 1953 and, except for the central tower, the central block was demolished.

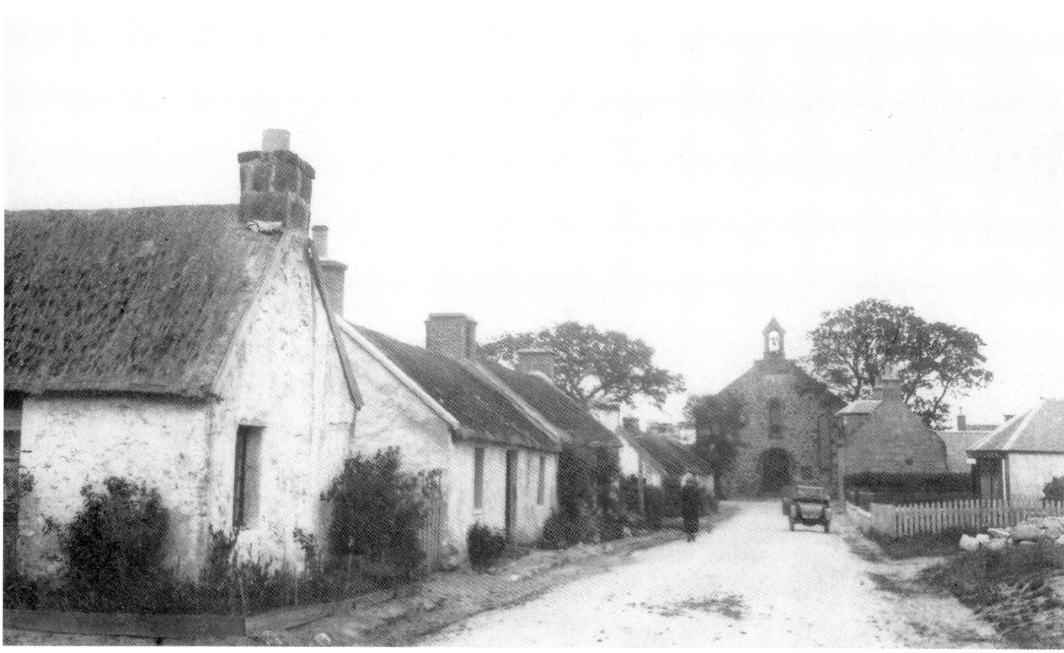

Urquhart village at the beginning of the century — in complete contrast to the picture above. A priory was founded at Urquhart in 1125.

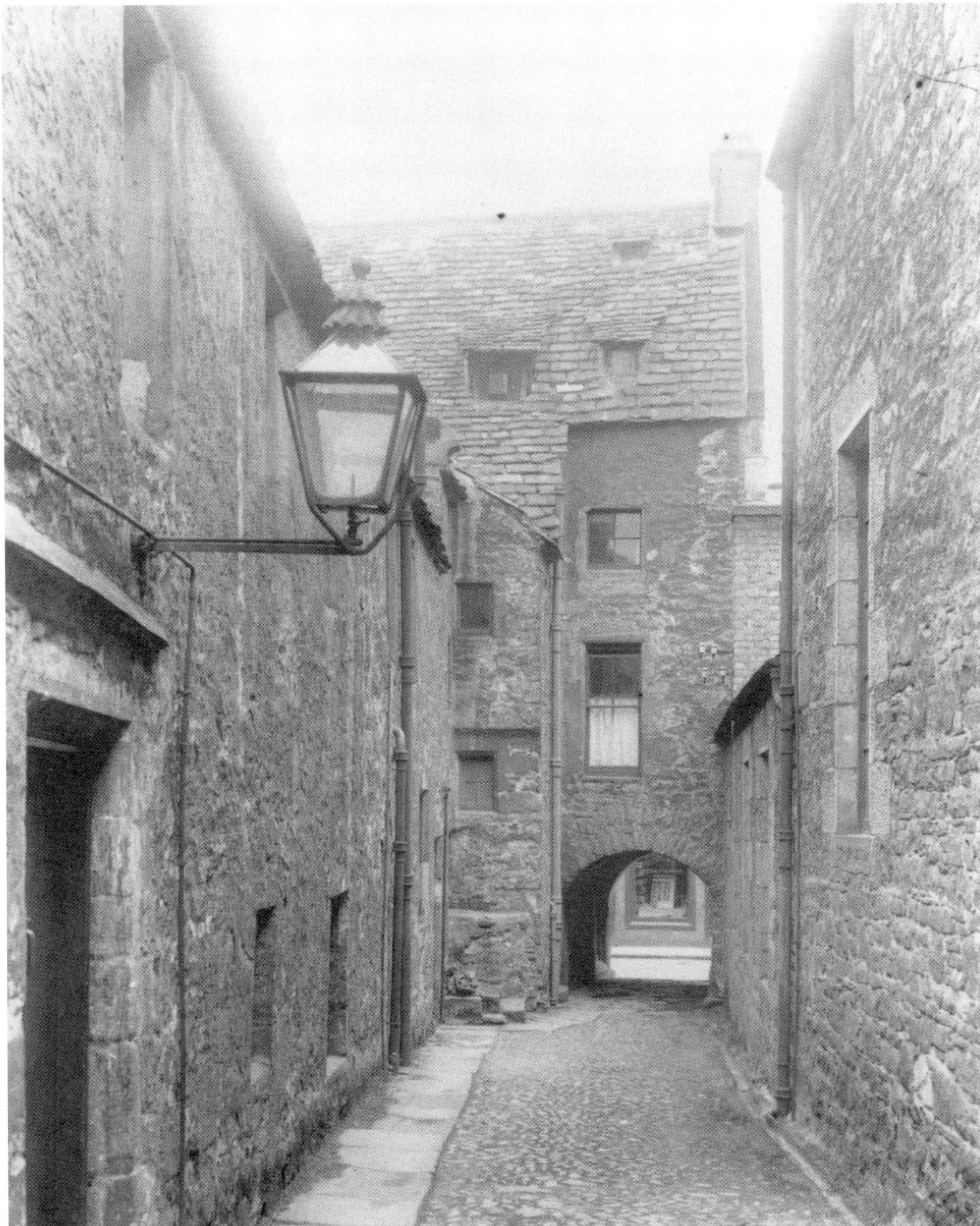

The Red Lion Close, 44 and 46 High Street, is dated 1688. The ten pace length of the buildings on either side of the entrance to Red Lion Close show the original width of medieval tofts. Stage coaches were accommodated at the Red Lion Inn, and it was there that Dr Johnson stayed. He was mistaken by a busy waiter for a well-known regular drinker and was served an inferior meal, which gave him cause to 'complain for the first time of a Scottish table' .

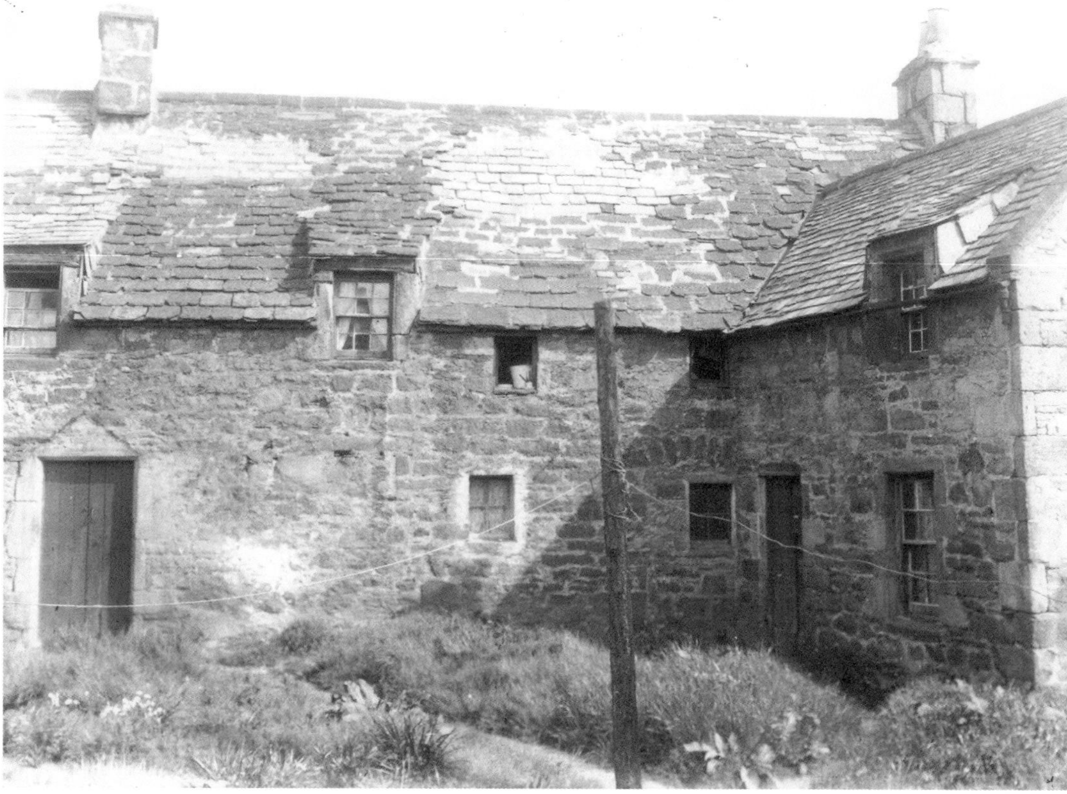

This old Elgin building provided the subject for a technically excellent and atmospheric photograph at the beginning of this century. The small sash windows cannot have allowed much light into the back rooms and the building would appear to have differing floor levels, probably due to additions and alterations over the years. Signs of a relieving arch, to the right of the pole, can be seen, probably above an earlier door or entrance-way. It is interesting to speculate just how many individuals and families inhabited these buildings at any one time and shared the backyard and drying green.

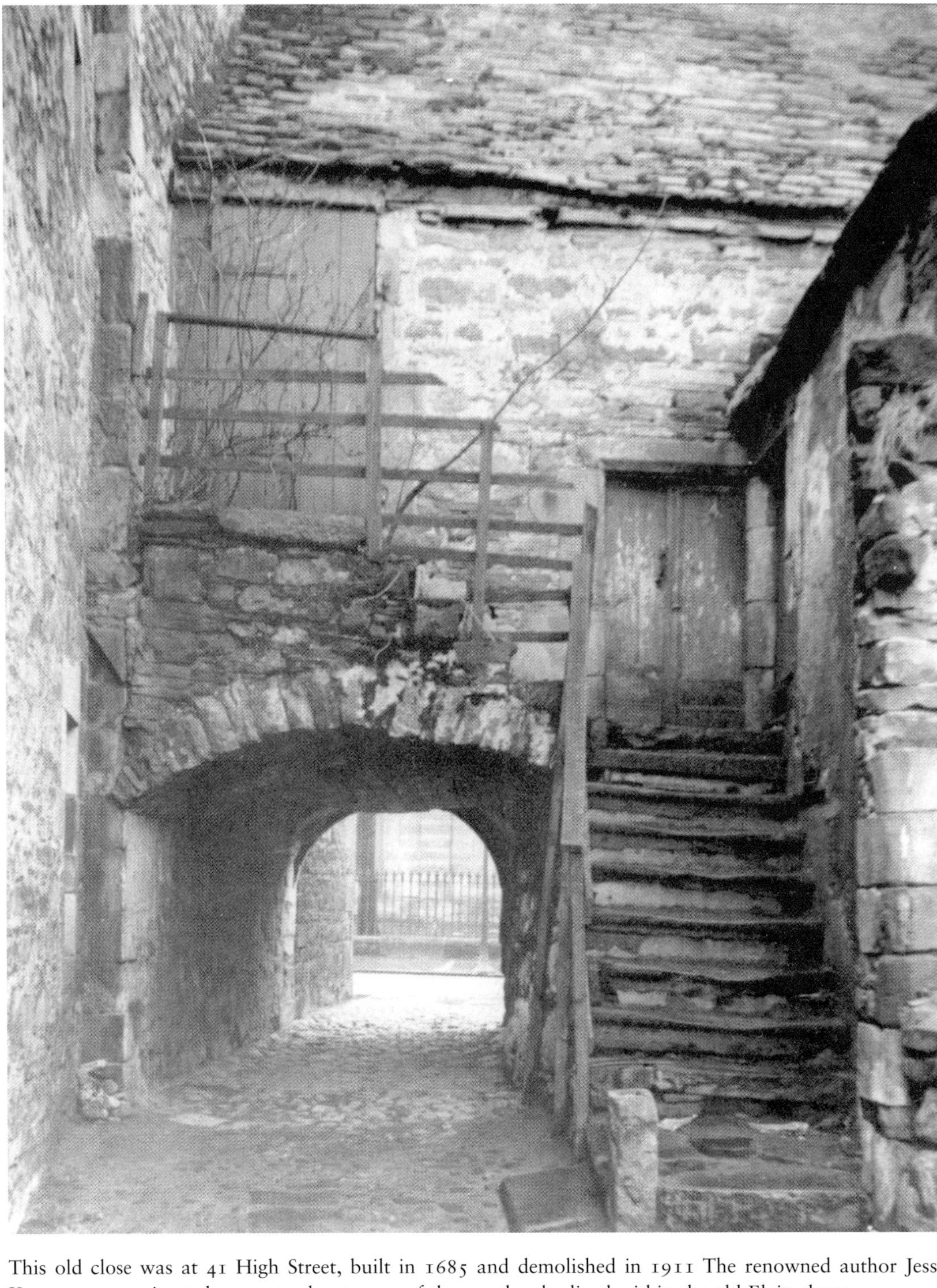

This old close was at 41 High Street, built in 1685 and demolished in 1911 The renowned author Jessie Kesson wrote animated accounts about some of the people who lived within the old Elgin closes.

Section Seven

An Education

For centuries Elgin has always understood the value of providing a good education and its schools have enjoyed a good reputation. Countless photographs exist of classes of children grinning or scowling at the camera throughout the years. However, for a change, following the first three photographs of traditional schools are a series of pictures of Aberlour Episcopalian Orphanage. This represents education with a difference. Many Elgin children spent their early years in this orphanage under its strict but kind auspices. Without such a refuge their prospects in a world before welfare benefits would have been grim indeed. Many people were ashamed to admit to spending their formative years in an orphanage and there are not many illustrations of life within these institutions. The Aberlour children were lucky ones who could be justifiably proud of their schooldays.

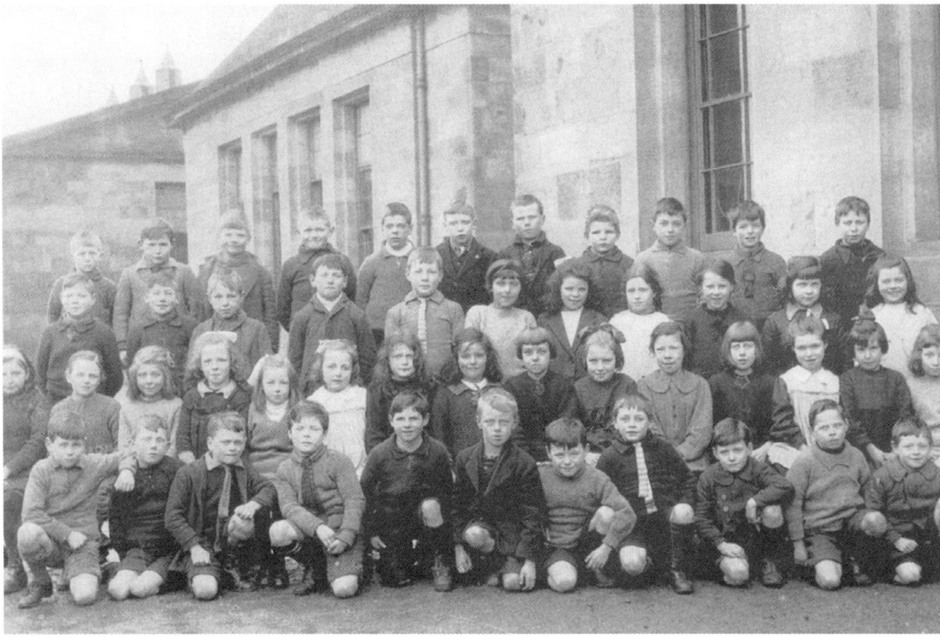

East End School. Back row 3rd from right is C. Wilken and J. Falconer is 2nd from right in front row. The Free School, as it was first known, was part of Anderson's Institution. After transferring to the Burgh School Board it became known as the East End school. Founded in 1831 after an endowment from Major General Anderson, the institution was created as the 'Elgin Institution for the support of old age and the education of youth'.

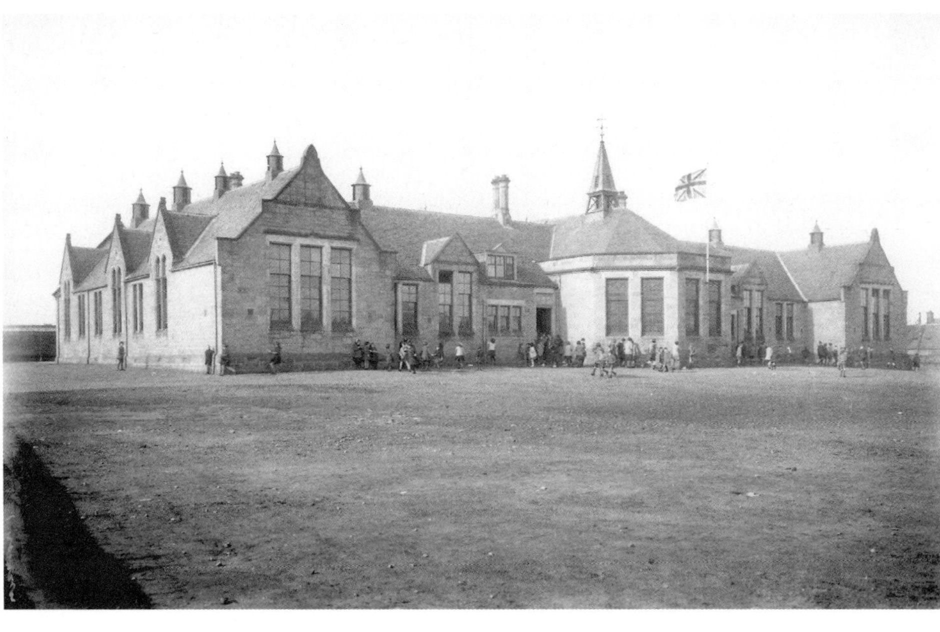

The West End school was erected around 1875 following the formation of the Burgh School Board.

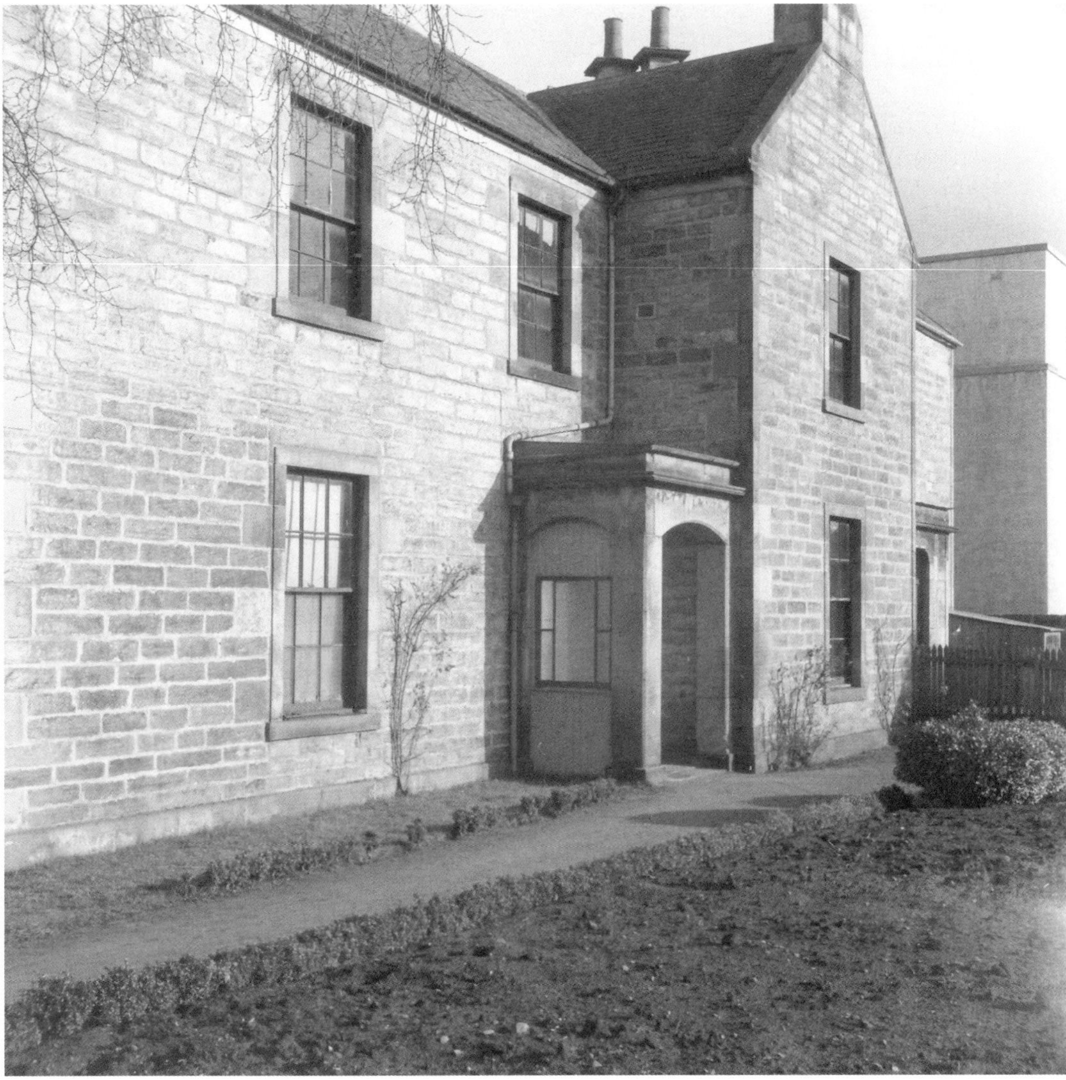

Weston House Academy was set up in 1859 opposite Highfield House. Alexander Graham Bell, inventor of the telephone, was a pupil and teacher here. After its demolition, stones from the building were used in a long garden wall beside the Doocot Park in New Elgin.

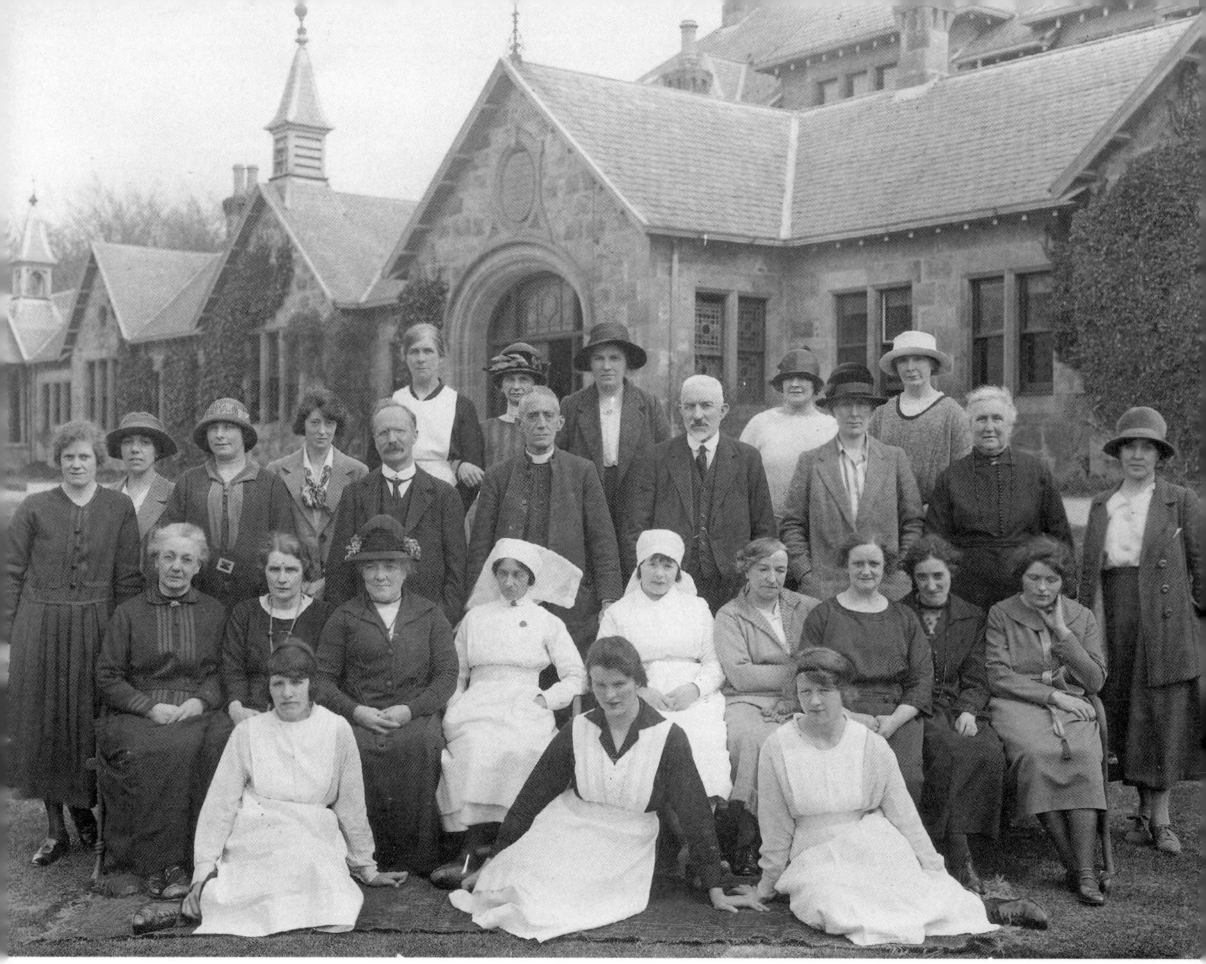

Some of the staff at the Abelour orphanage. Standing, fifth from the left, is John White. Next to him is Canon Jenks the headmaster. While the regime may have been severe, many of the children were given a good basic training and discipline to enable them to survive in a society without welfare benefits. The boys at the orphanage helped tend the large gardens at the Home Farm, which provided the orphanage with fresh milk, fruit and vegetables. The girls were trained in cooking and domestic work.

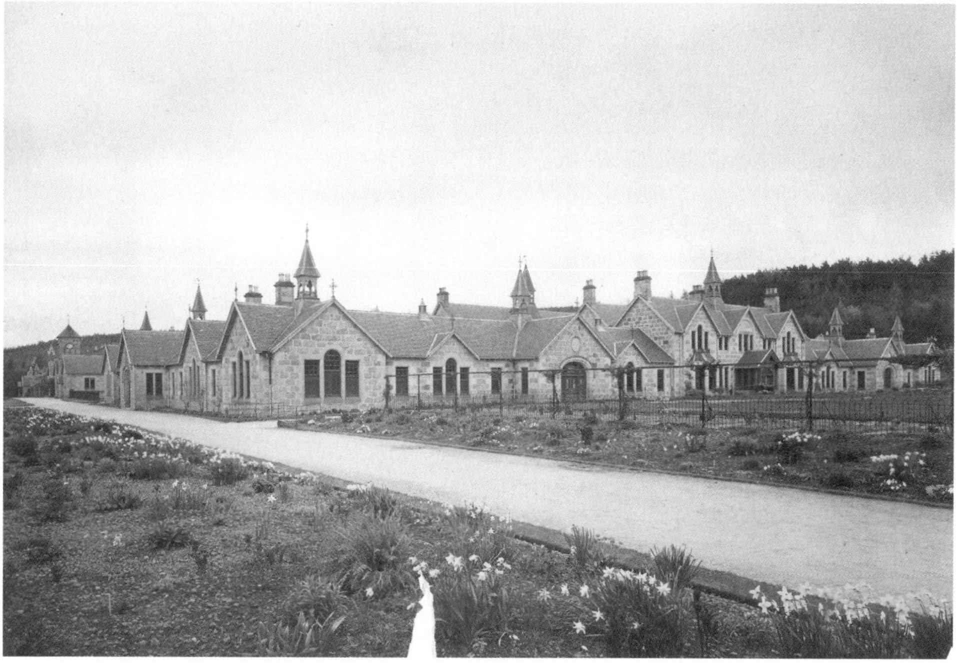

Abelor Episcopalian Orphanage was a large, purpose-built building. It was founded in 1875 by Canon Jupp, a native of Sussex. In its heyday it catered for some 500 children and included a school, a church, a swimming pond and an isolation hospital. The orphanage was finally closed in the 1960s, and all that survives is the clock tower, erected in 1889.

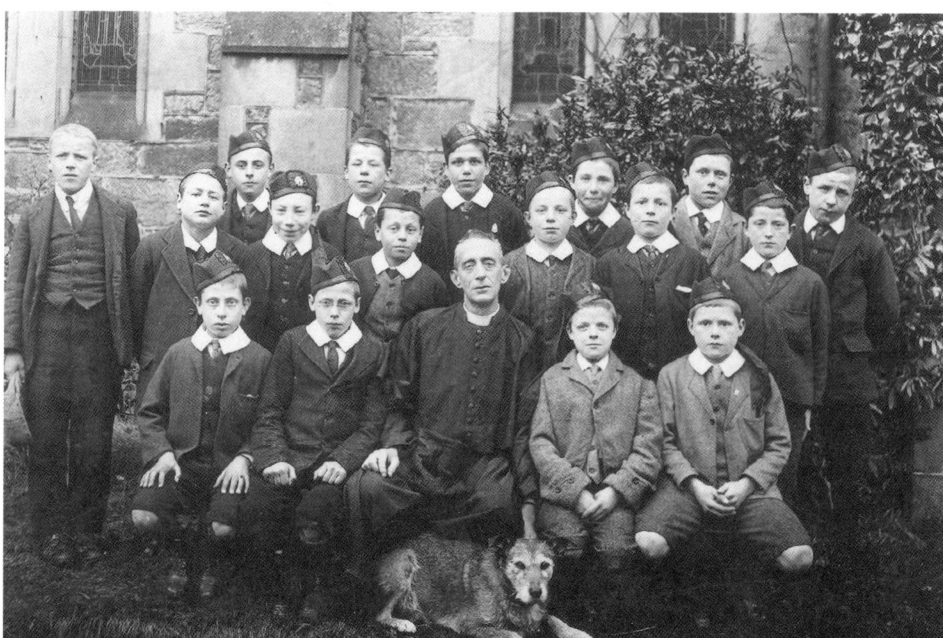

Some boys from the Aberlour orphanage with Canon Jenks and his dog 'Lintie' in the 1920s.

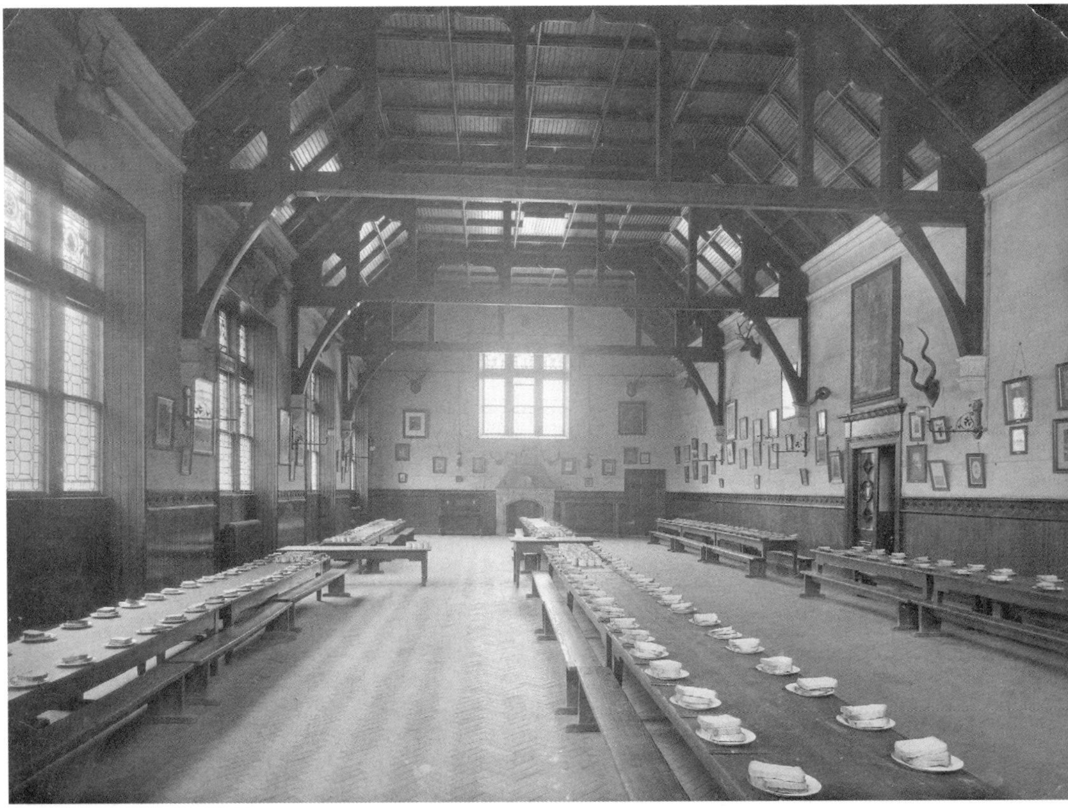

Aberlor Orphanage dining hall. With so many children to discipline it is not surprising that things were well ordered, even regimented. The children would march into the dining hall and stand in ranks according to their age groups at their respective tables. Once there was absolute silence, grace would be said before they were allowed to begin the meal.

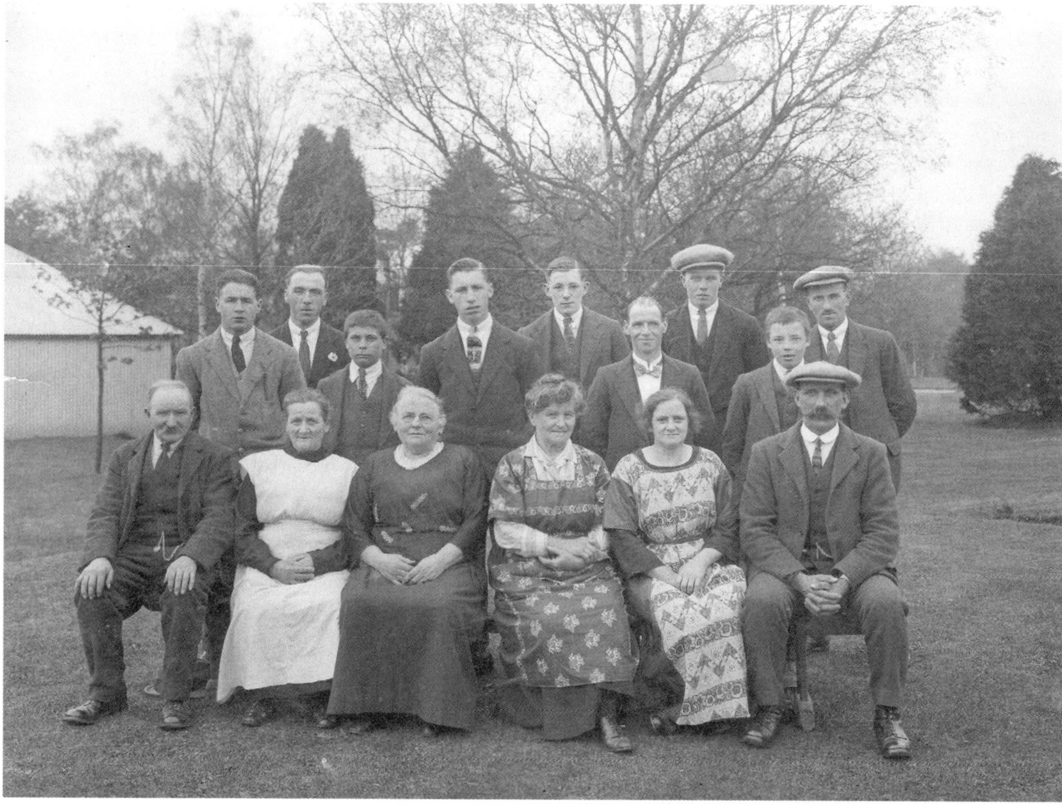

The staff of the Aberlour Orphanage. Seated on the left is the head gardener, Lachlan Macdonald, known affectionately as 'Old Lachie'. His daughter married one of the orphanage boys whom he had trained. Many children were placed in the orphanage because their surviving parent could not look after them properly, and more than 4,000 children passed through its doors.

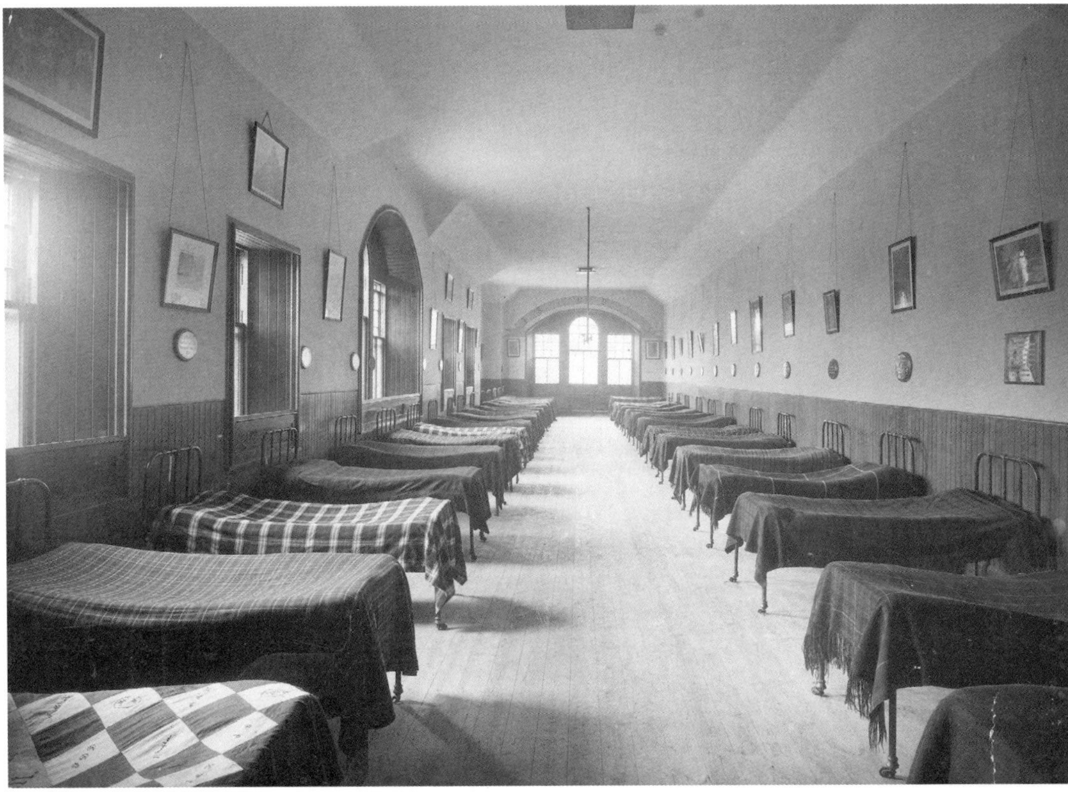

This is a typical children's dormitory at Aberlour Orphanage. There are no cupboards, personal lockers, carpets, pictures, slippers or personal effects of any sort — and no toys or books. During the influenza epidemic of 1920-1, six of the chIldren died in spite of all the attention they received from the caring staff.

Section Eight

Weel Kent Faces

The local newspaper archives are full of the faces of famous or notorious Elgin folk. It would be impossible to do justice to the variety of characters and the many hard working individuals from all walks of life who have made so many and various contributions to the life of Elgin. This is a small selection of those found among the collection from Studio Tyrell and many family likenesses can be recognized by those familiar with Elgin folk. All have names 'weel kent' once although perhaps forgotten nowadays, but they have made an impact on the life of the area.

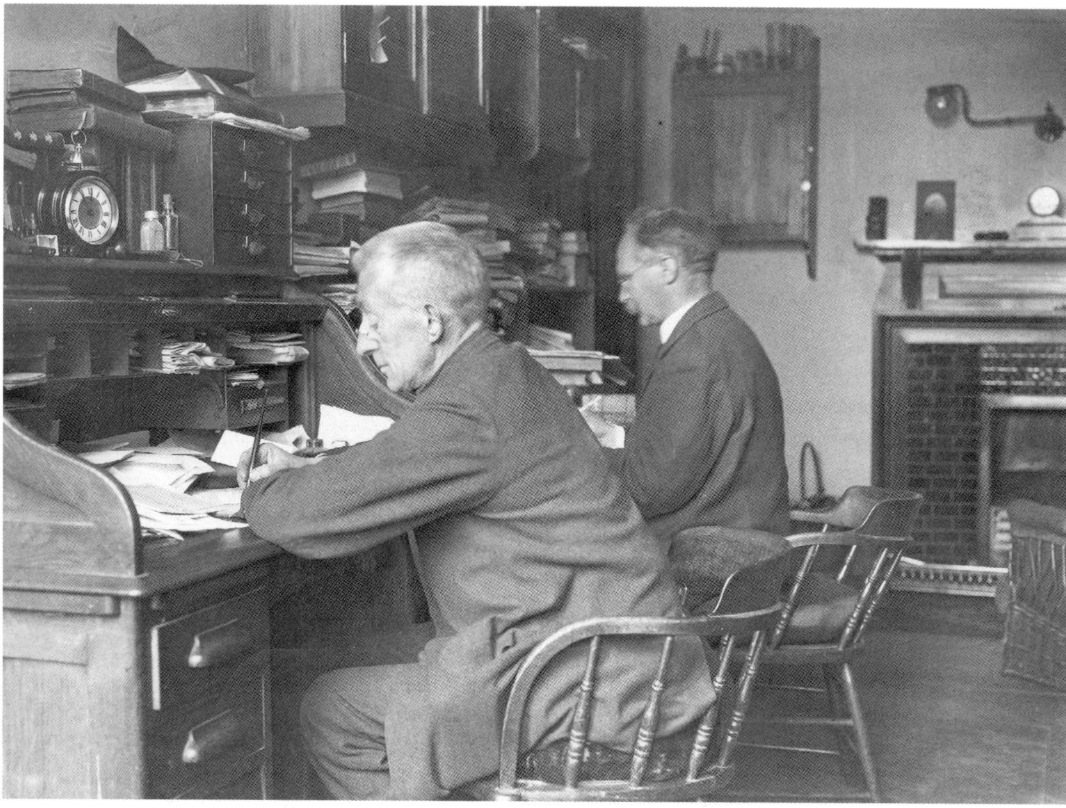

Canon Jenks, headmaster of Aberlour Orphanage, in his study with John White seated behind him. 'Whitey' was Assistant Secretary and Treasurer from 1876 to 1936. He instilled a great love of plants and wildlife into his charges. He was an outstanding botanist and gardener, with a special interest in begonias. His enthusiasm for cricket, photography and astronomy inspired many of the 4,000 children who were at the orphanage during the sixty years he was there.

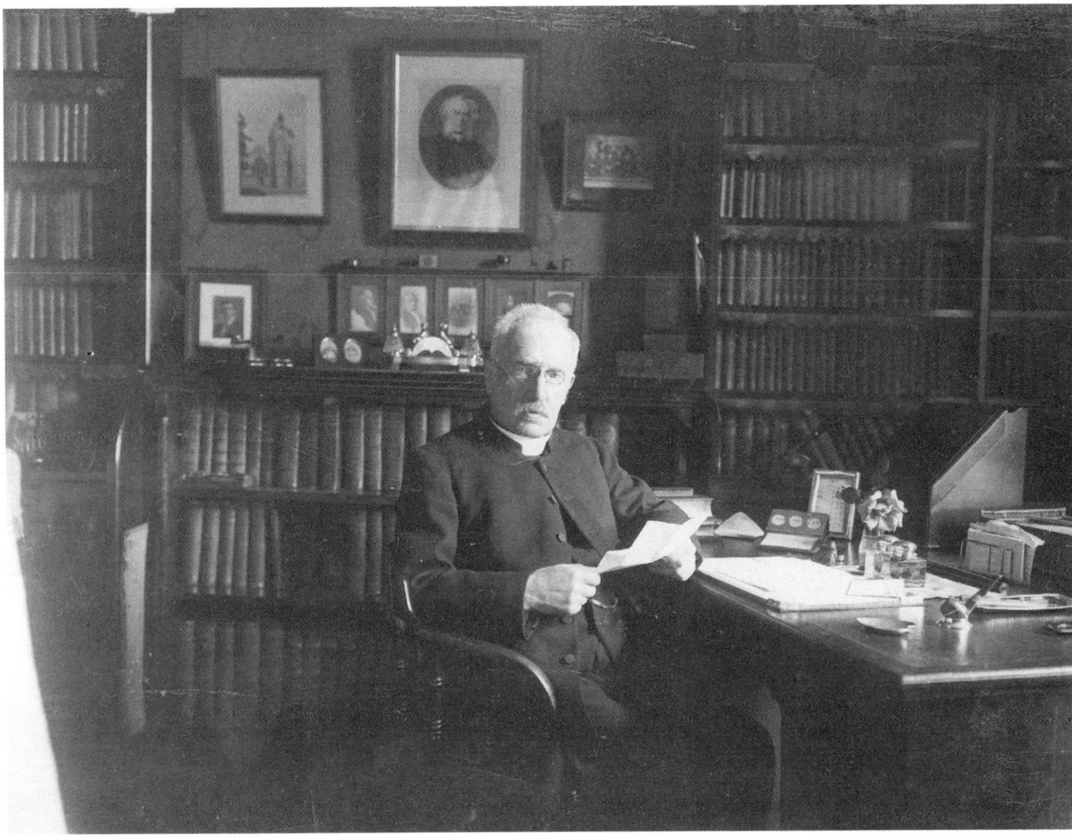

The Revd R. MacPherson, DD, son of the minister of Forres, was the Church of Scotland minister in Elgin from 1881. During his illustrious career he was on the examining board of the General Assembly of the Church of Scotland, chairman of the Governers of Anderson's Institution, member of the Burgh School Board and Chaplain-Colonel of the 6th Seaforth Highlanders. He served with the Volunteers in the Boer War.

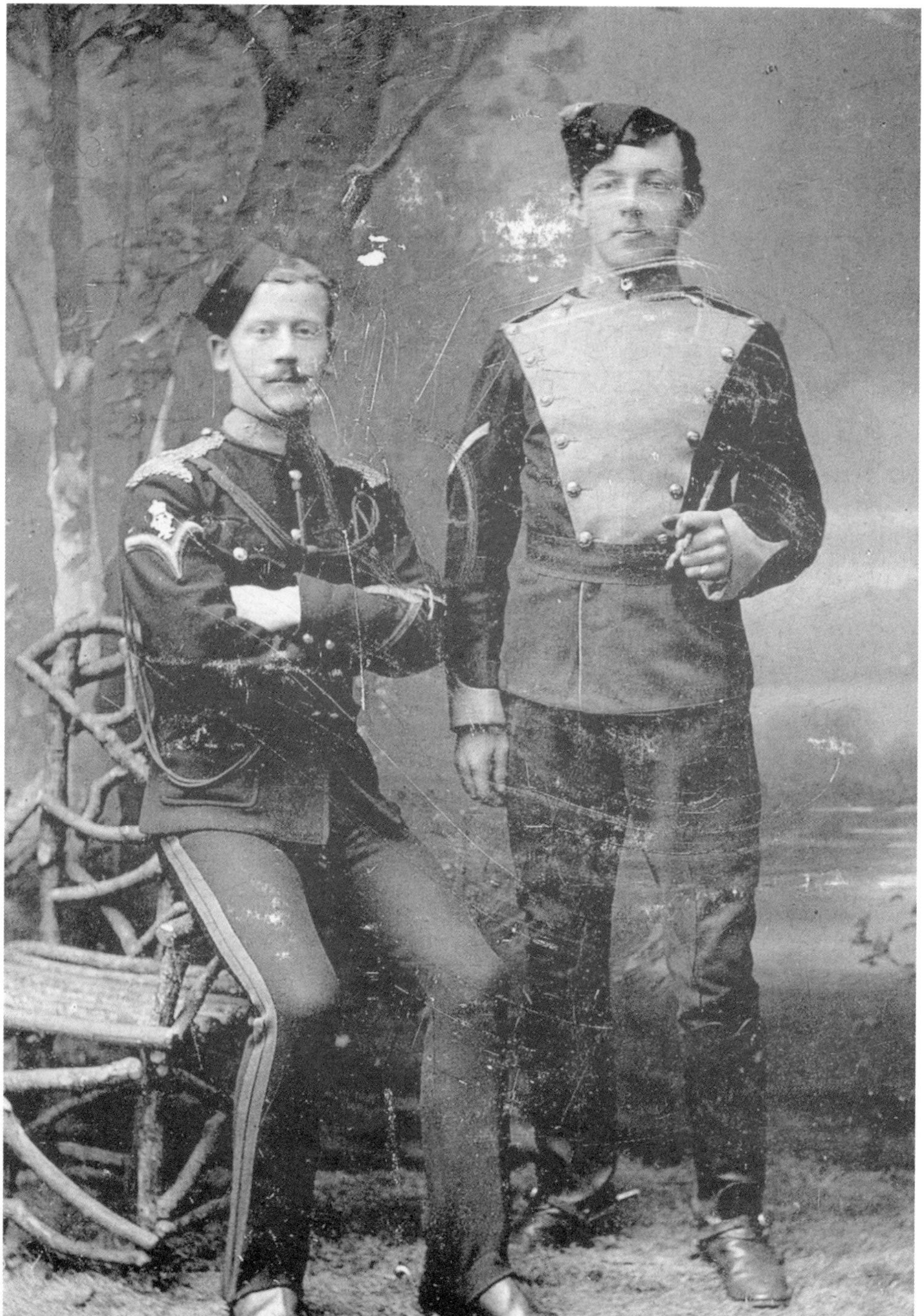

Two good friends. Standing is William Christie who died of drowning in Australia in 1910. His friend is a McGillivray whose mother had a paper shop. The picture was taken in the 1890s.

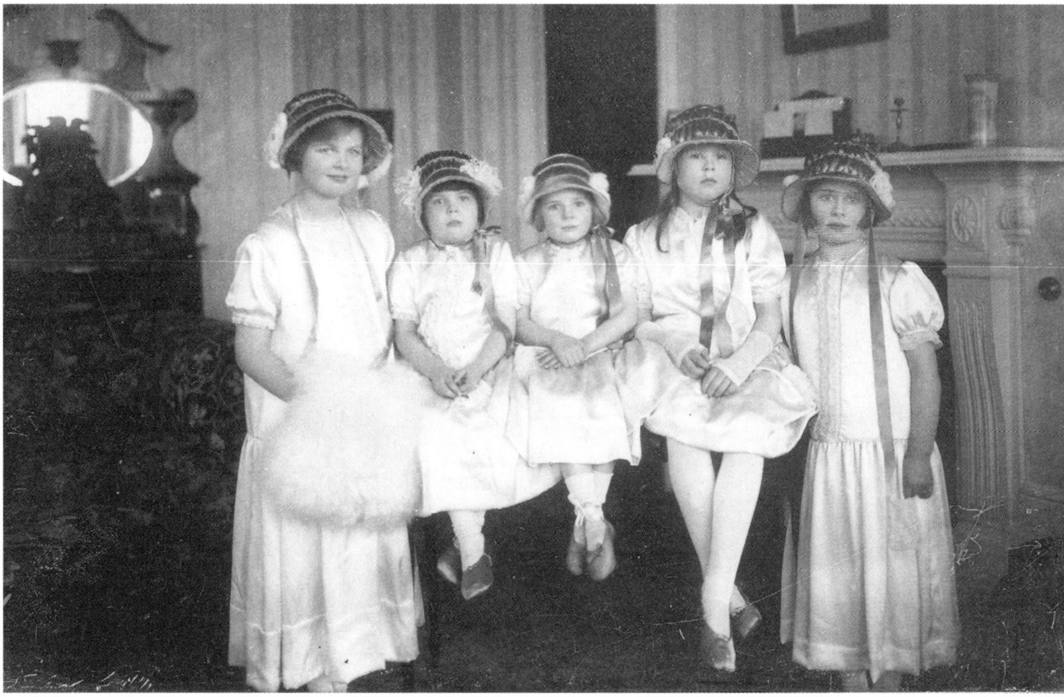

Flower girls. This picture is thought to have been taken in the 1920s, or '30s. Nothing is recorded about them, but the picture is enjoyable if only for the details of dress and house interior, as well as the delightful characters portrayed.

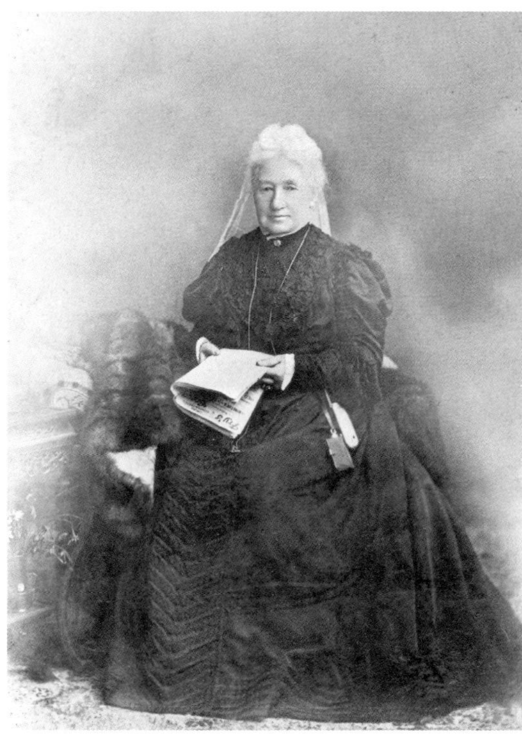

This lady is wearing a 'chatelaine', household keys and implements such as scissors attached to a chain from her belt. The advertisement on the back of the magazine is for Fry's chocolate. She is believed to be a Mrs Collier.

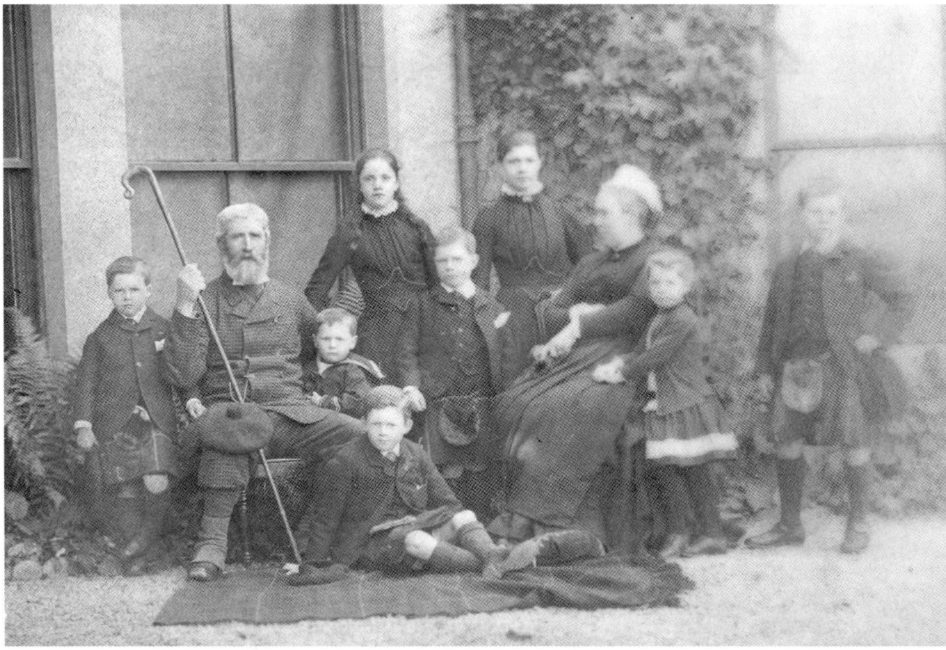

A typical Victorian family portrait.

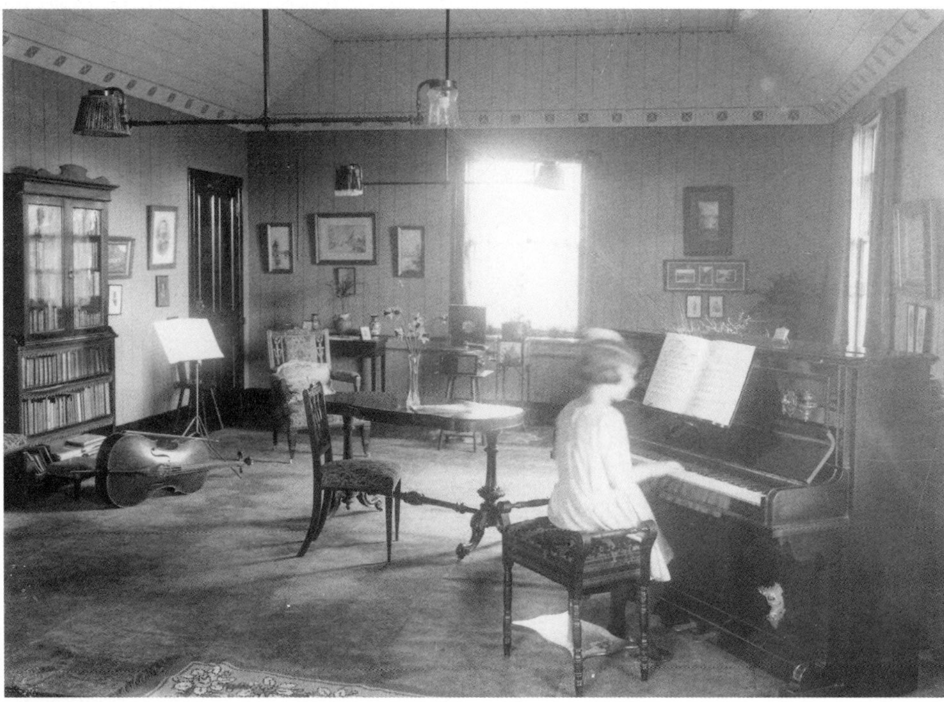

A 1920s music room. The light fittings are interesting, and on close inspection it can be seen that the piano is fitted with reliable candle holders.

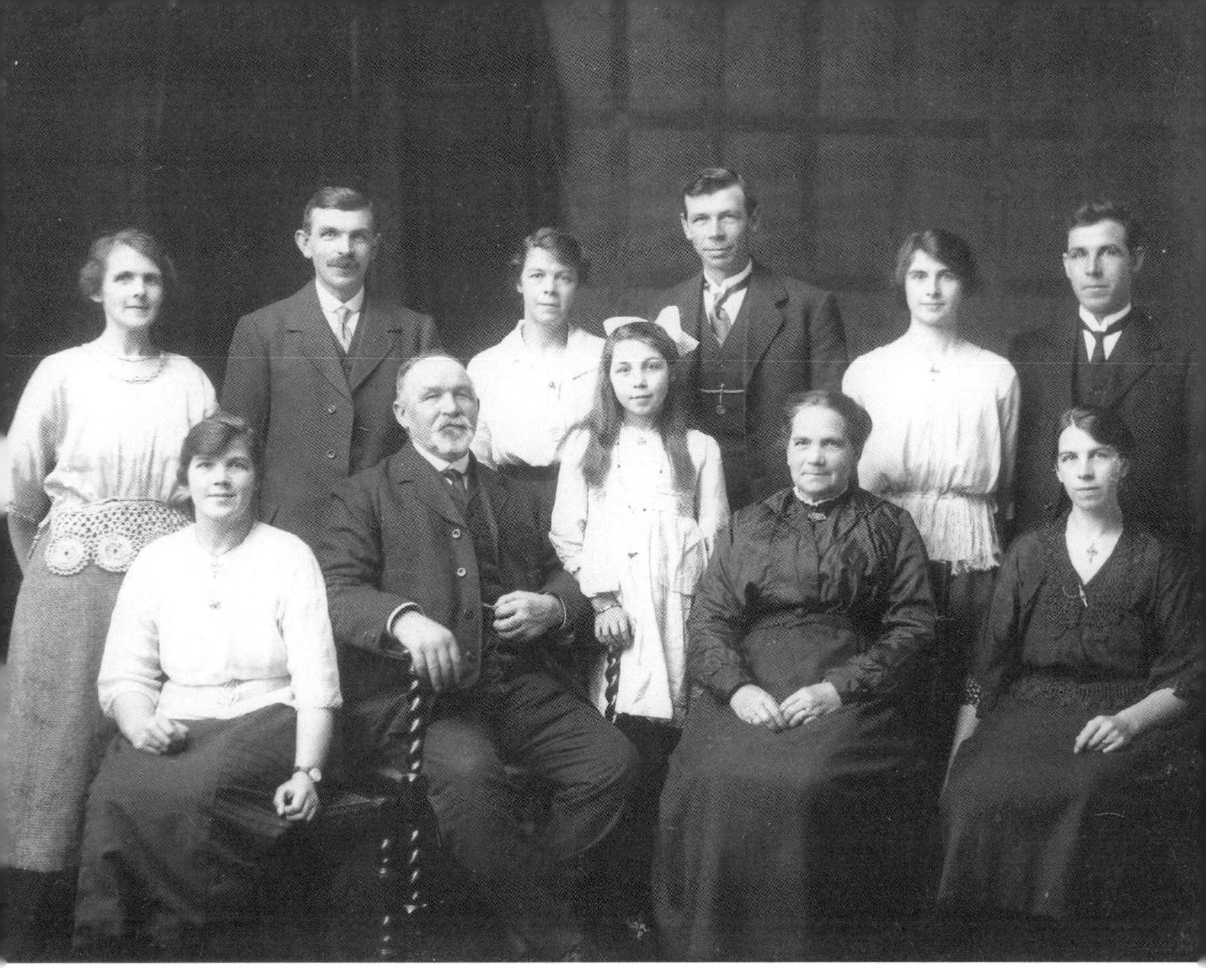

A gathering of a McPherson family taken in Studio Tyrell. The fashions of the 1920s are well displayed in this picture.

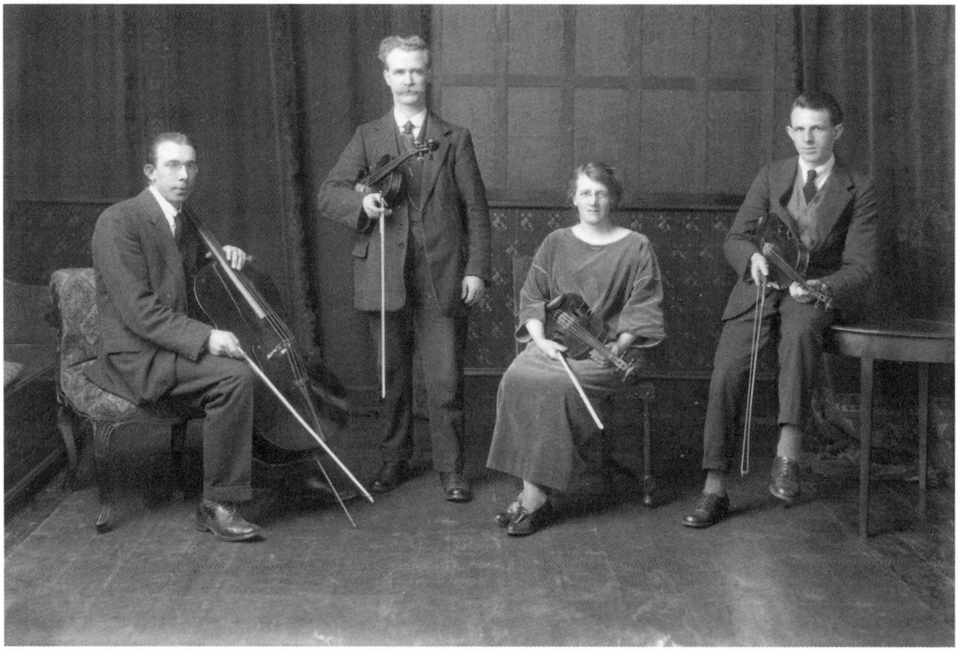

A string quartet. It is known that one of the members of this string quartet was Willie McPherson, a renowned violinist — thought to be sitting on the table.

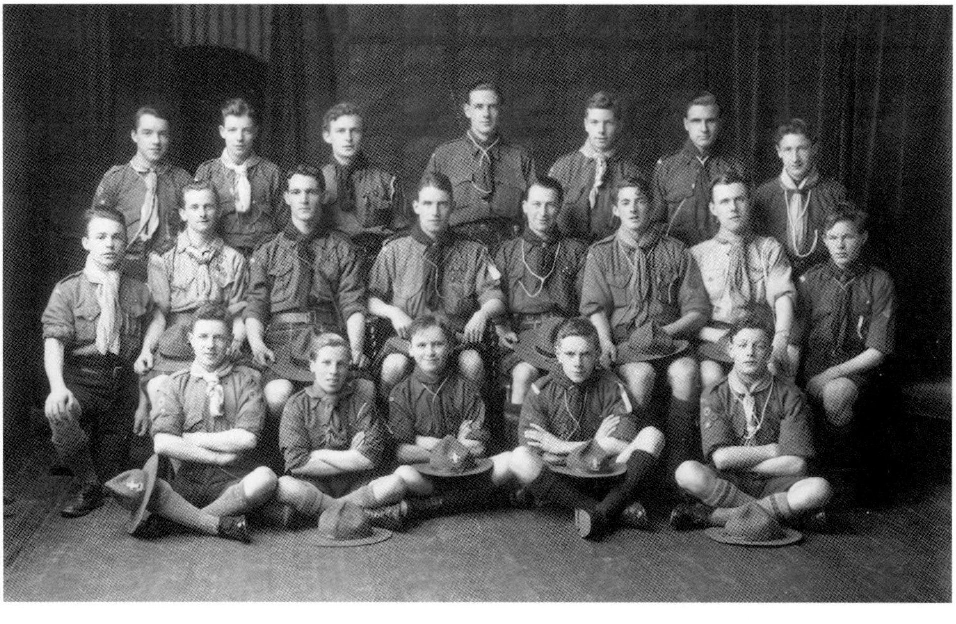

Scouts, 1926, two years after World Scout Jamboree. Top row from left;- Sidney George, Arthur Johnston, A. Murphy, Jim Stalker, W. Munro, A. Smith, S. Wood. Second row from left;- S. Murphy, Willie Robb, Horatio Smith, Willie Wittet, A. Patterson, Ian Fraser, Willie Penny, A. Rothnie. Bottom from left;- -?, I. Cumming, A. McKechnie, A. Donald, A. Robertson.

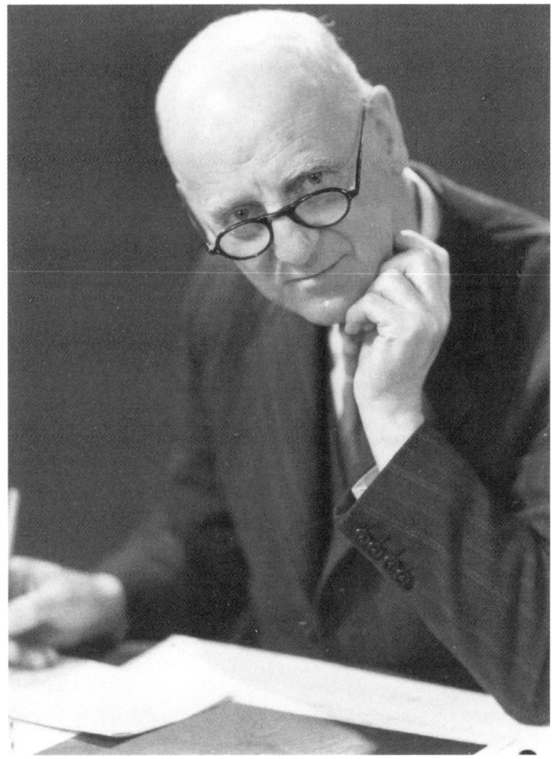

George Tyrell, of Studio Tyrell. After his death the business was taken over by Harry A. Waltuch. The studio had originally been founded by George Tyrell's sister who left George with the Elgin studio and went on to found another business in Inverness. Following his death in 1955 his widow continued with the studio, employing a succession of photographers.

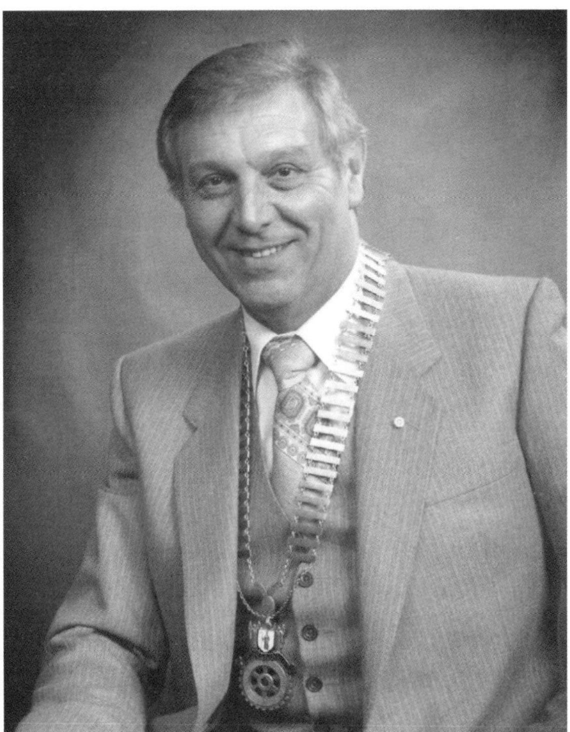

Tony Spring LBIPP, LMPA, owner of Studio Tyrell 1971-95. Arriving at RNS Lossiemouth aged eighteen, he studied photography and became head of the photographic section. He left the Navy after twenty-two years and bought Studio Tyrell in 1971. There he discovered boxes of smashed glass photographic plates dated between 1884-1920 which had been considered useless. Thankfully he managed to salvage some, and these he generously donated to the Elgin Museum when he retired in 1995.

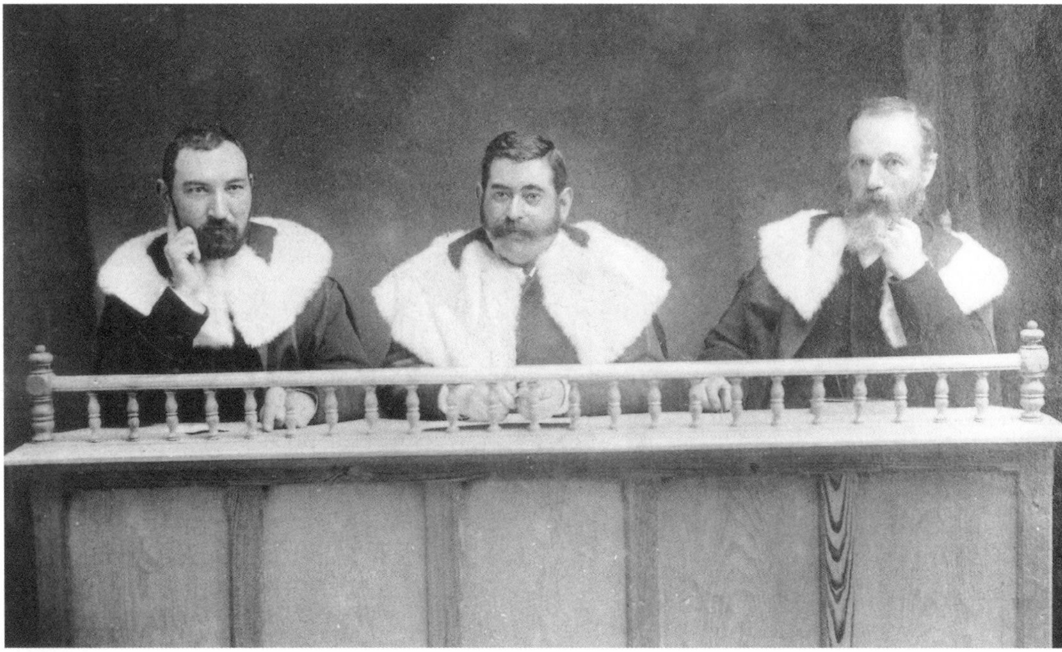

These early magistrates of Elgin, labelled 'The First Appointed Magistrates of Elgin', are unidentified. The earliest recorded chief magistrate was Thomas Wysman, Provost in 1261.

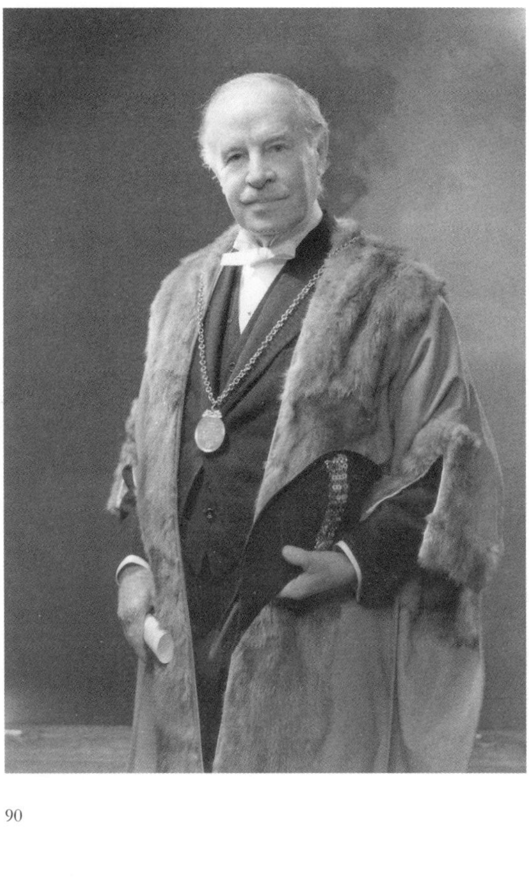

Lord Provost E. S. Harrison, owner of Johnston's woollen mill, also known as 'Ballie of the Beild,' who was given the freedom of the city of Elgin in 1964. The 'Beild', a word from his local Border country, was the name of his large rubble house, to the west of the town, designed in 1930 in the Scottish Arts and Crafts style. Harrison Terrace, Bishopmill, is named in his honour.

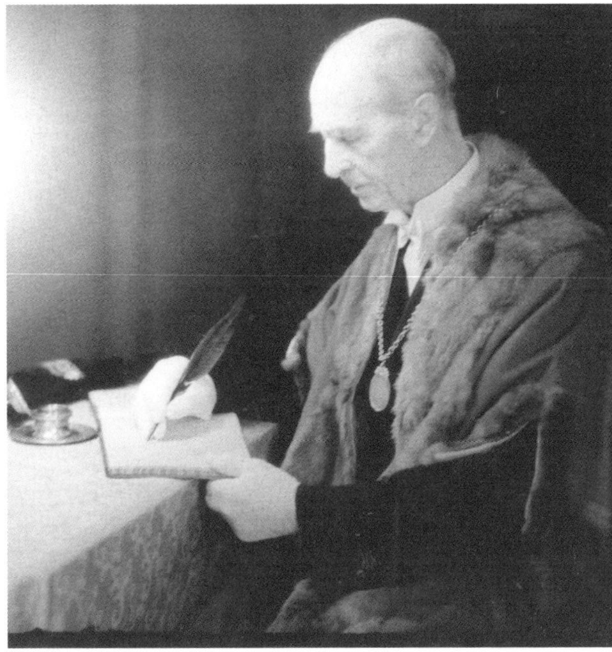

Provost John Brodie, 1879-1973. The earliest Provost Brodie was Alexander Brodie of Windyhills in 1755. John Brodie was Lord Provost from 1949-52, succeeding E. S. Harrison. He was a master plasterer, elder of the High Church and Commissioner to the General Assembly of the Church of Scotland. A Freemason for nearly sixty-five years, he was also an honorary member of the Moray Society.

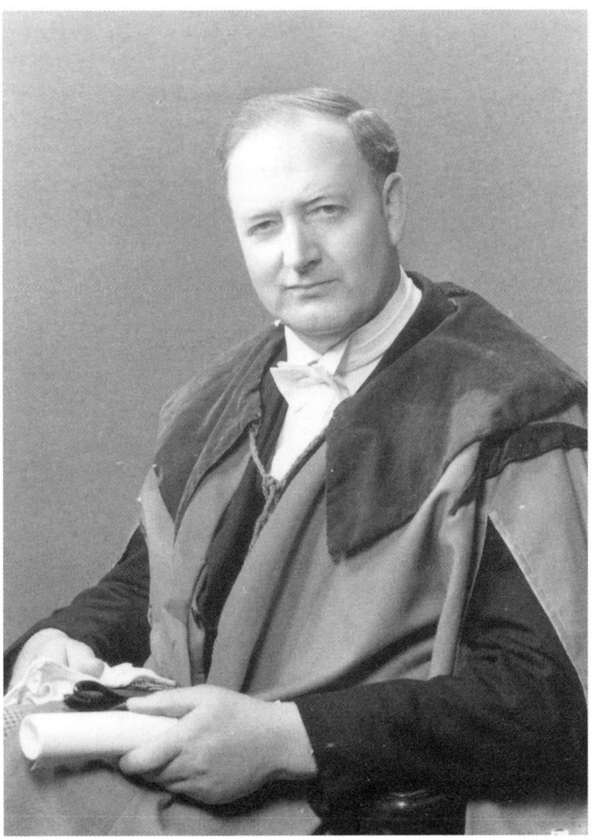

David Emslie. Formerly a policeman, he was a well-known, enthusiastic bee-keeper and became a partner in a local sports shop.

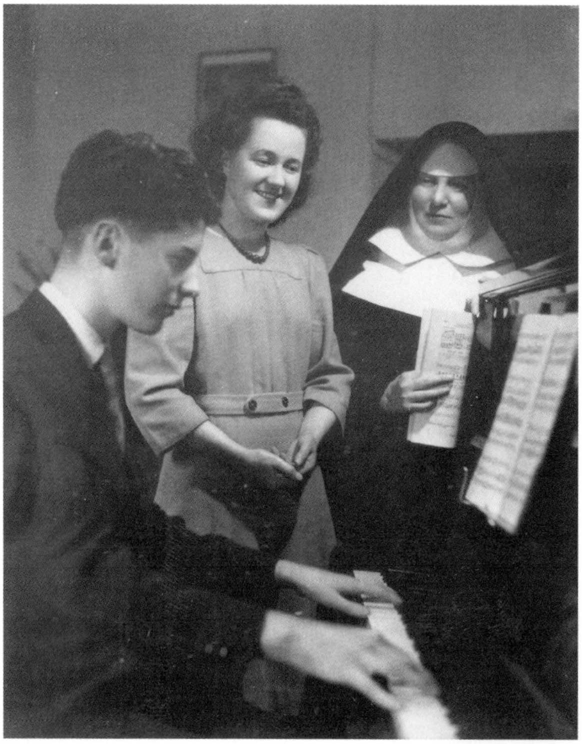

Sister Mary Winifred with pupil James Noble and vocalist Sheila Davidson. Sister Mary Winifred shared her musical talents with large numbers of Elgin youngsters.

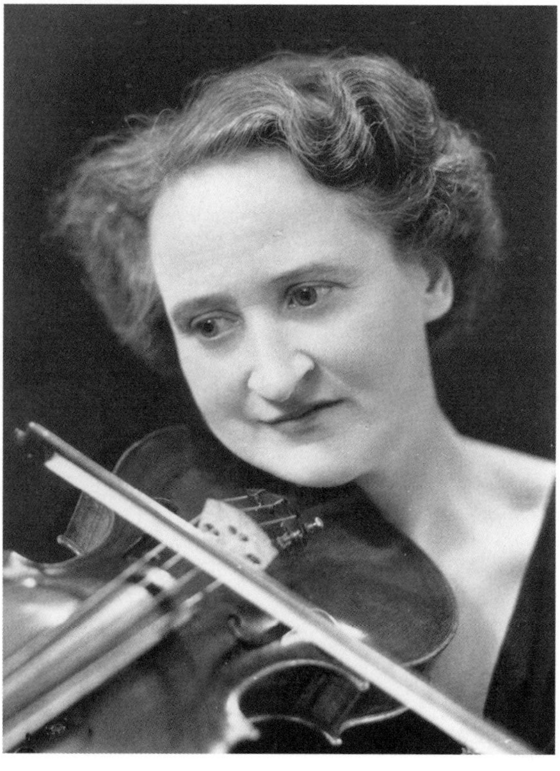

Kim Murray. Taught piano by her mother, Kim Murray graduated with a diploma from the London Royal Academy of Music in 1924 and began a prolific musical career. She passed on her skills to many successful pupils and was leader of an orchestra, gave recitals, adjudicated at festivals all over Scotland, and served on the advisory council of BBC Scotland. She was awarded an MBE in 1971 for her contribution to music. Never married, she devoted her life to sharing her love of music and died aged eighty-three, in 1985.

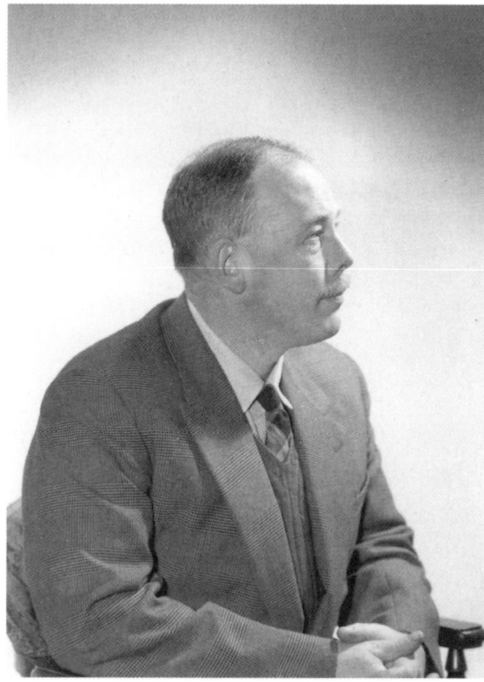

'Boy' Wood. James Wood was a well-known local character and author; some of his short stories were featured on BBC radio. He had an extensive knowledge of country life, was an excellent fisherman and a pistol shot. It is rumoured he possessed an intimate understanding of a variety of poaching methods and consequent expertise in cooking country fare.

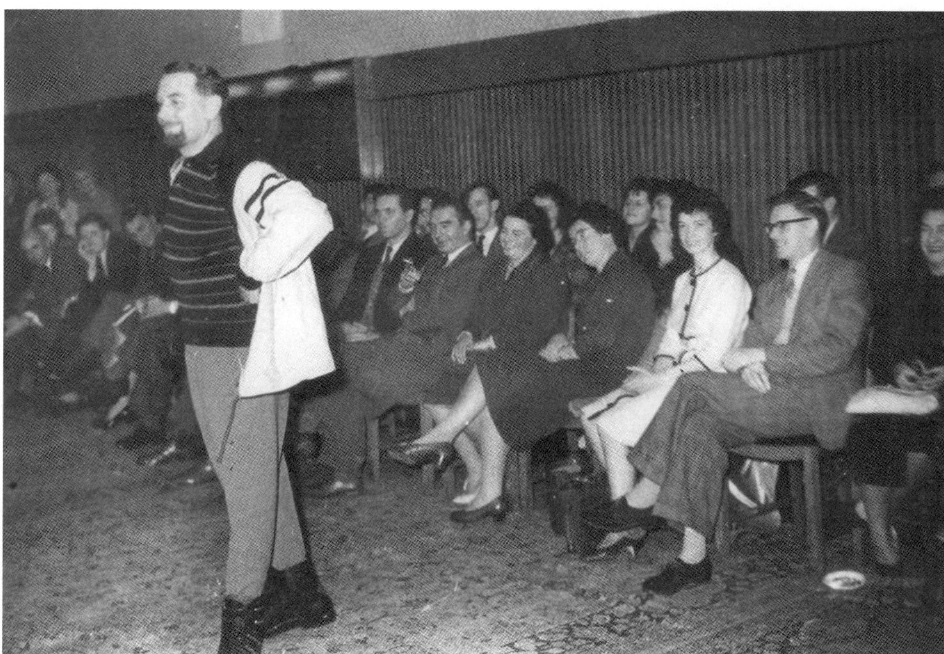

Sandy McDonald and Barry Gilhoulie are in the audience. Fortunately for the sake of Elgin architecture, after this brief foray into modelling sports clothing, Ashley Bartlam decided to stick to his day job! A well-known architect, he founded the Ashley Bartlam Partnership in Elgin which is still going strong, although he has now retired.

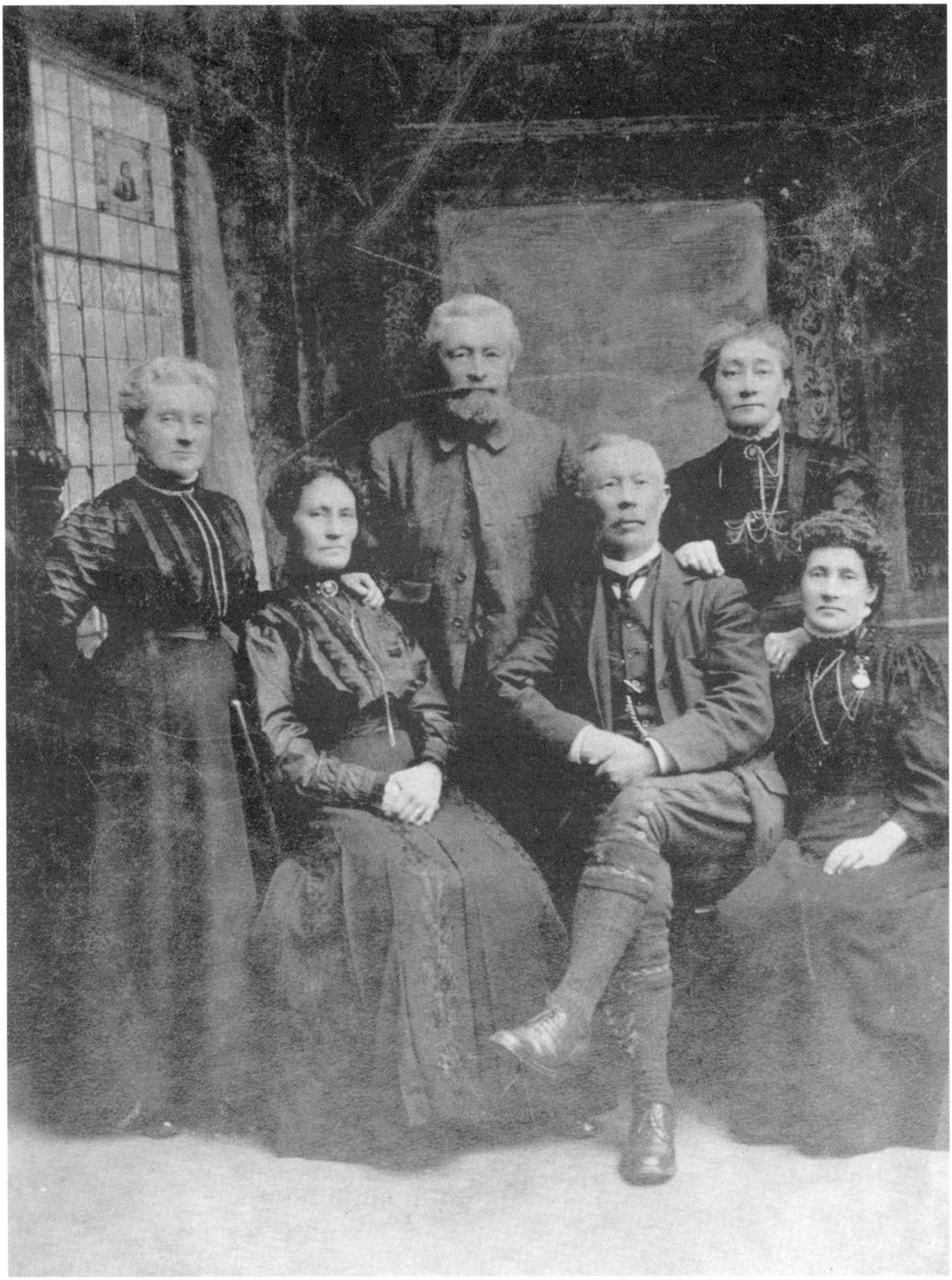

The Christie family. Taken before the two Christie sisters emigrated to Australia, this is a picture of the well-known family of hoteliers. Standing is George Christie, of the Tilt Hotel, Blair Atholl. Sitting is William Christie, of the Stotfield Hotel, Lossiemouth, who was Provost of Lossiemouth. Next to George is Isa (née Henderson), of the Aberlour Hotel. Standing on the left is Jane Christie (née Innes) of Milnefield Farm, New Elgin. Maggie and her sister, who both emigrated to Victoria, are on the right.

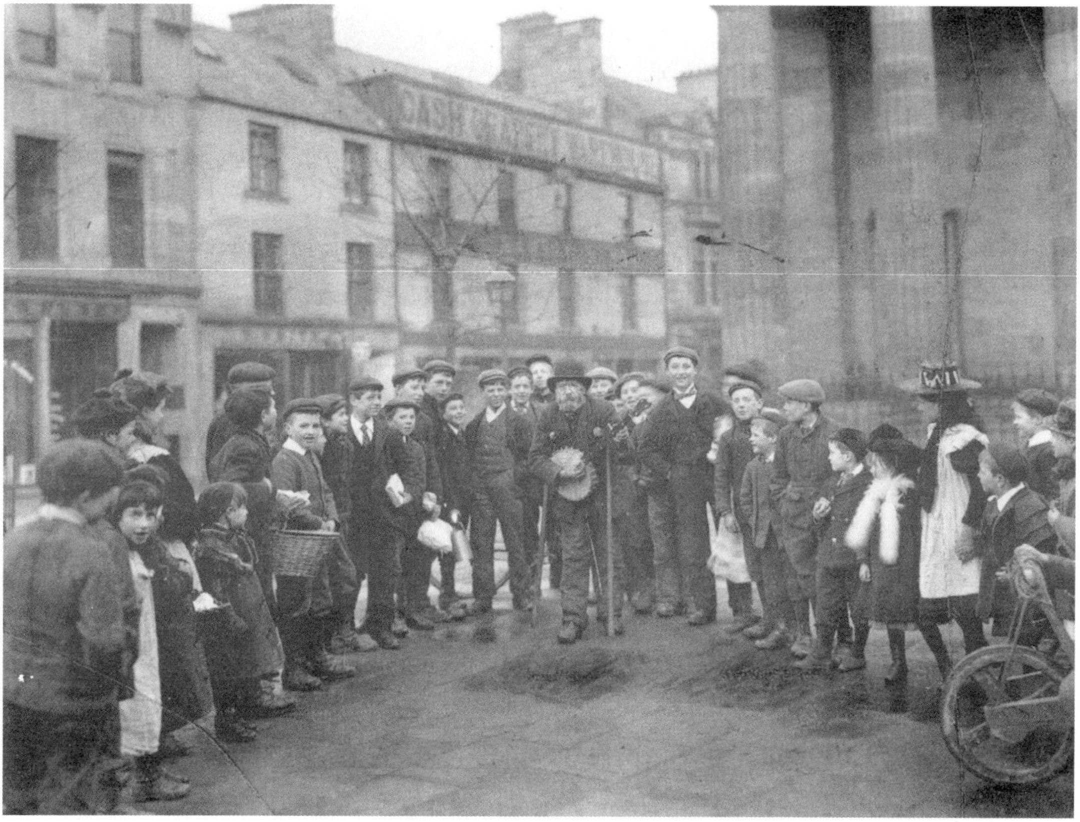

This must have been taken earlier than 1904, before the grand Ramseys building was erected. Elgin was home to a number of 'worthies' , many of whom entertained the town with their eccentricities, repartee and poaching exploits. They were tolerated within a community which knew the meaning of true poverty.

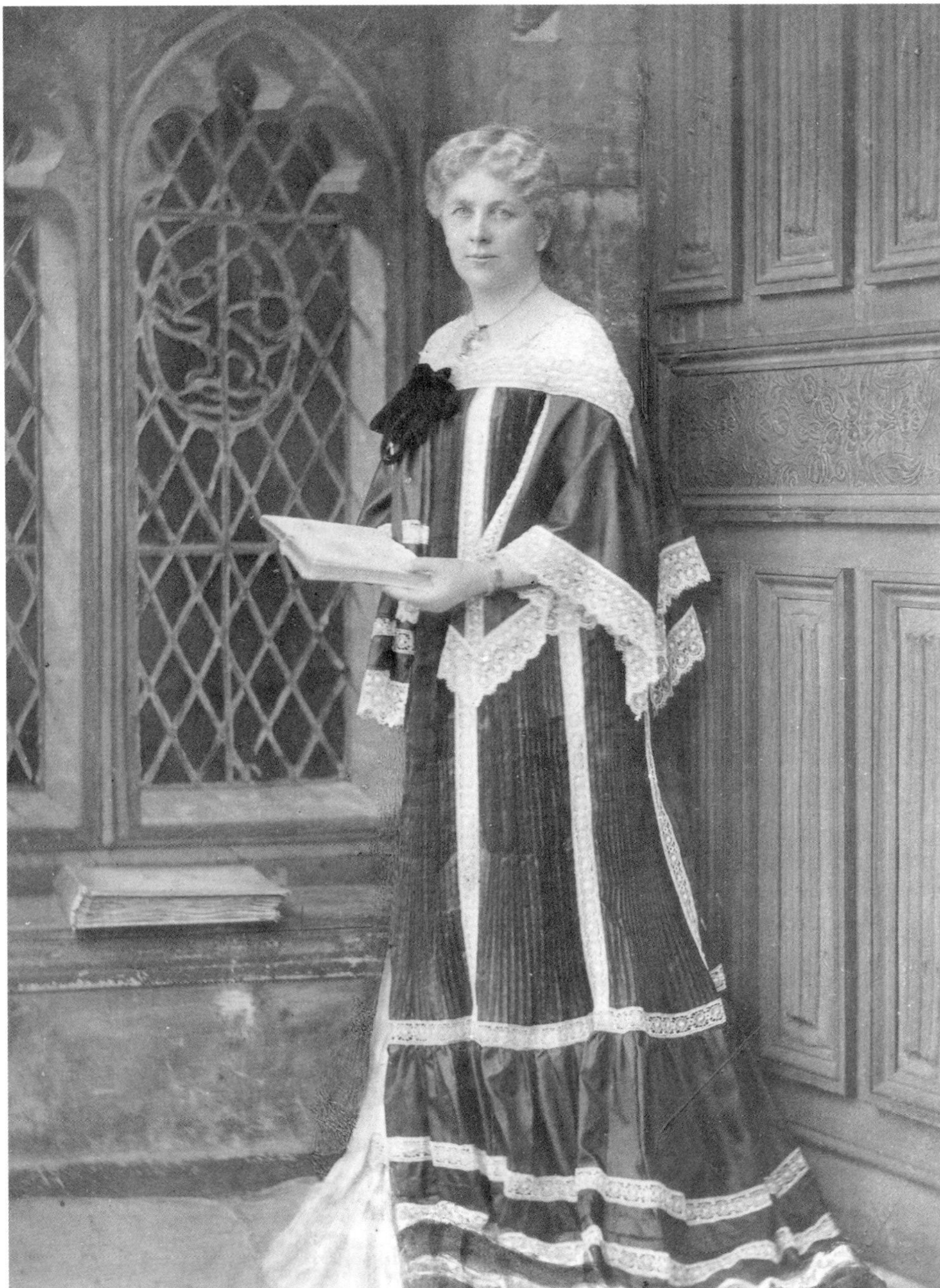

Another mystery picture from the hoard of glass negatives donated to the Elgin Museum. There is no name or indication of the subject but this obviously old picture is worth including for its sheer elegance! The hairstyle dates from the turn of the century or earlier, and the panelling and stonework appear to be that of one of the larger Elgin buildings, perhaps no longer in existence. Maybe a reader will be able to help with identification.

SECTION NINE

INUSTRIOUS ELGIN

In the early days not many photographs were taken of folk actually working. Lengthy interruptions to pose subjects would not have been welcomed, and work was not considered artistic enough to preserve for posterity. The following photographs give some insight into the various types of work, industrial, agricultural, administrative and clerical, which kept Elgin folk busy for long hours. Time off was precious and rare. Within living memory employees were expected to work on Christmas Day — usually harder than ever. The present long winter holiday breaks were unimaginable once.

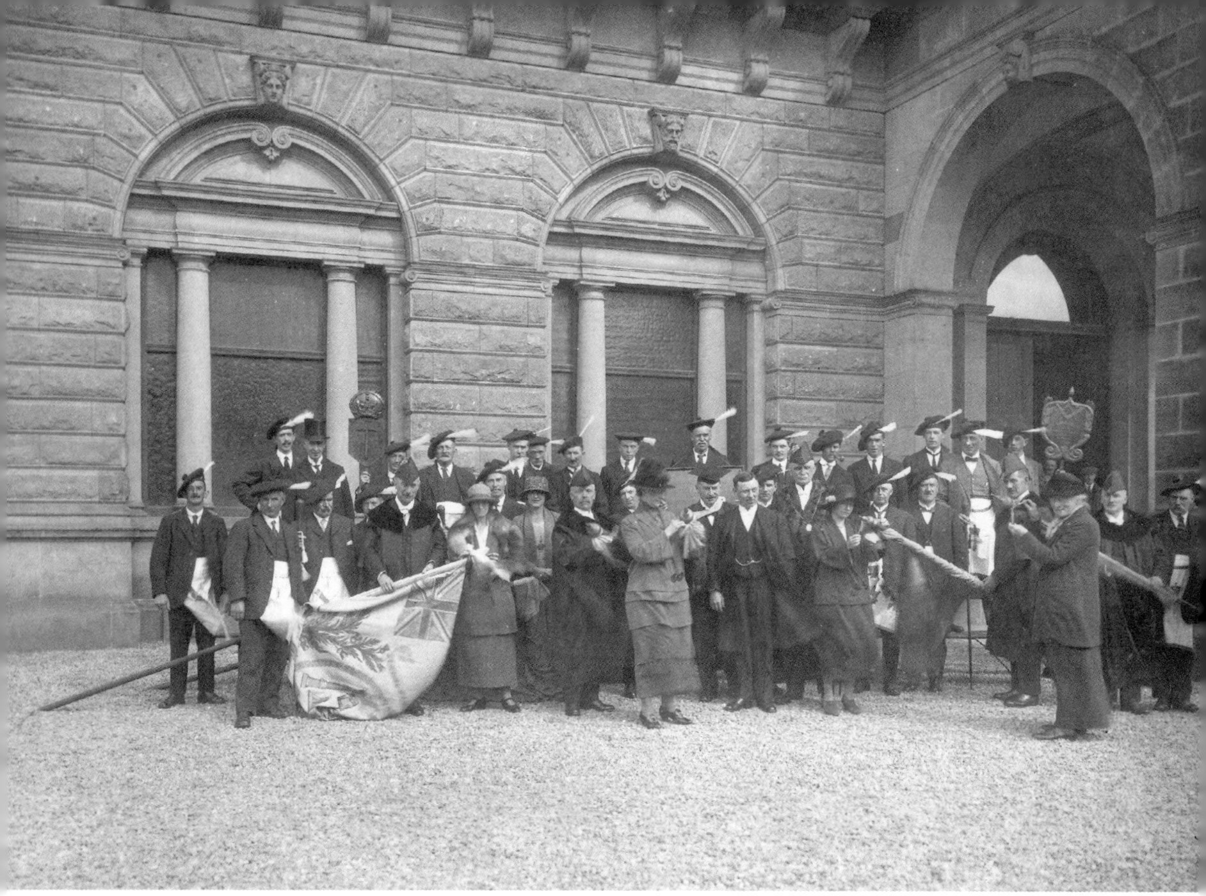

A group of the incorporated trades outside the old town hall. The craft guilds played a vital role in the development of the town. Scottish craft guilds were created by royal licence or by resolutions of town councils. In 1284 Alexander II granted a charter to the burgesses of Elgin conferring on them the right of a merchant guild. This is the oldest charter the town possesses. Under the charter the trades were entitled to form co-operatives. The policy of self-protection had, by the beginning of the nineteenth century, crippled local industry. Eventually all of this was removed by the Reform Act of 1832 and the political power of the trades diminished.

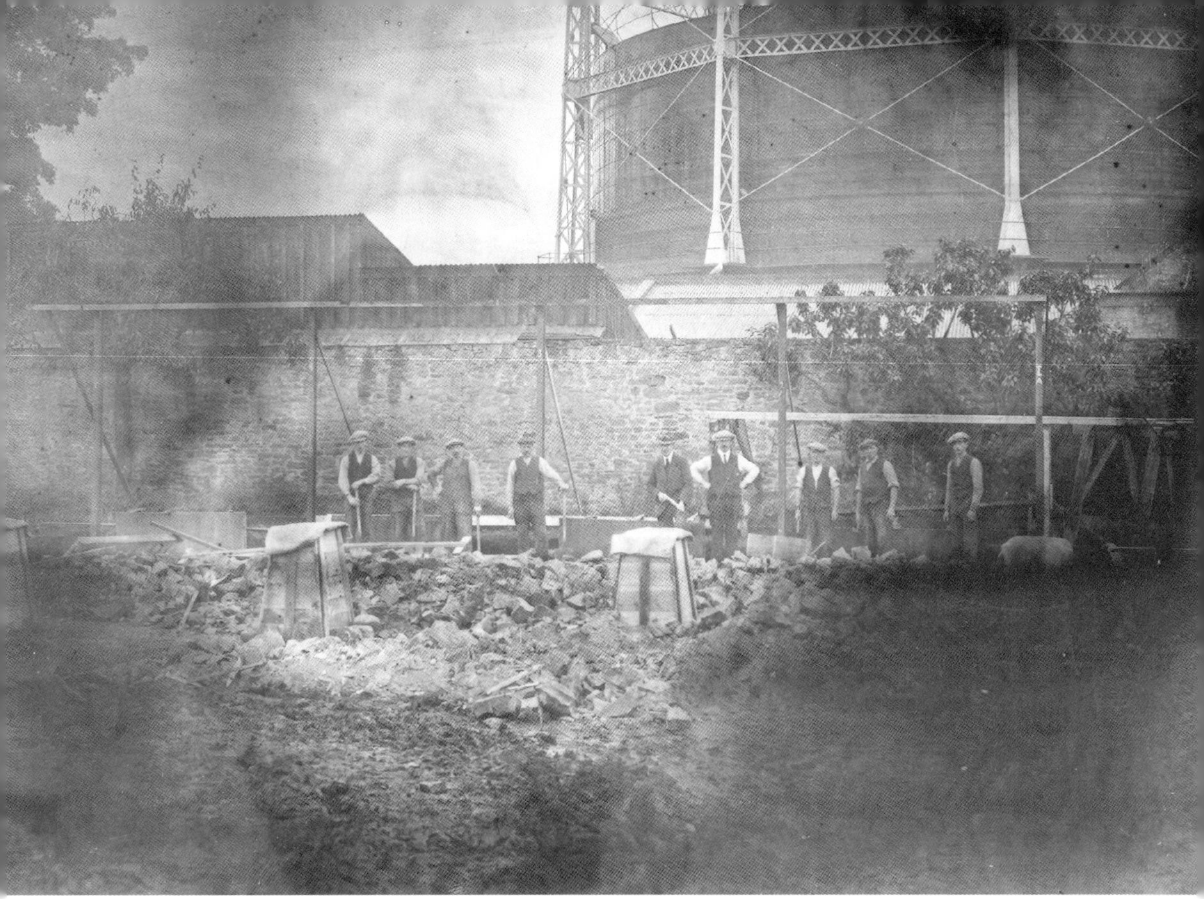

The gasworks. Gas was introduced to Elgin in 1831 and the gasworks were originally sited between Lossie Green and the Cooper Park. The man on the second left in this picture has been identified as John Christie by one of his descendants, who dated this picture as turn of the century. The old gasworks were demolished in 1933 after the new works had been constructed at Pinefield in 1931. The old gasholder was removed in 1949. Before the advent of gas, candles were used. Cheap, quick-burning tallow candles with cotton were used by the poor, while the longer-lasting, but more expensive, wax candles were used by the wealthier citizens. Jack's candle factory was at the Red Lion yard.

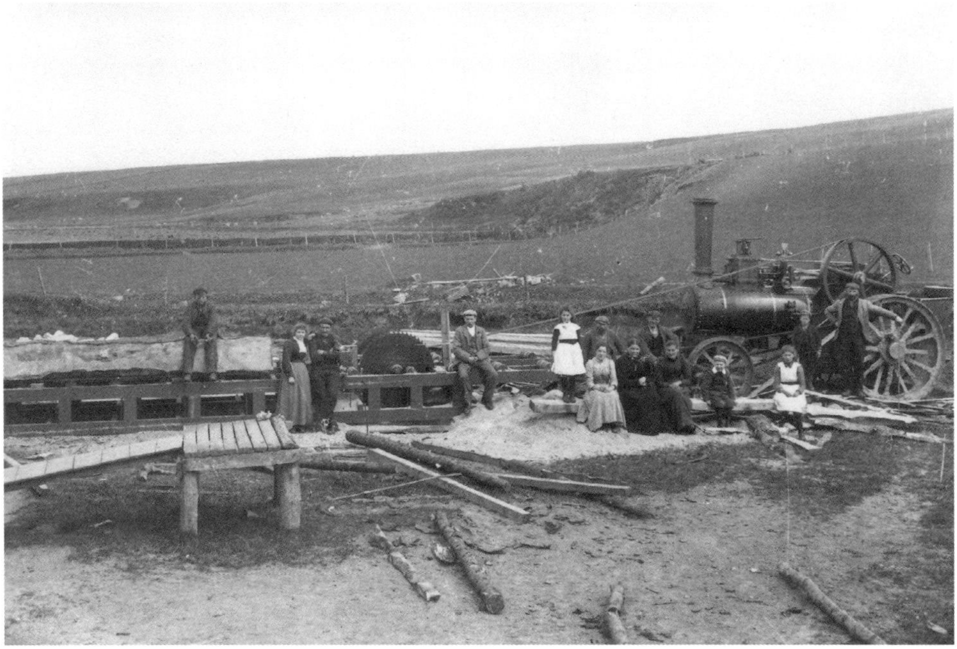

The three-wheeled steam tractor constructed for the haulage of guns in 1770 was the forerunner of the self-propelled steam threshing machine of 1842. The steam traction engines seen in these photographs were developed to be driven to the farms and used for jobs such as ploughing, threshing and sawing wood. It took roughly an hour and a half to raise steam before work could commence, and it is not surprising that by the 1930s the steam engine was replaced by the more efficient diesel engine.

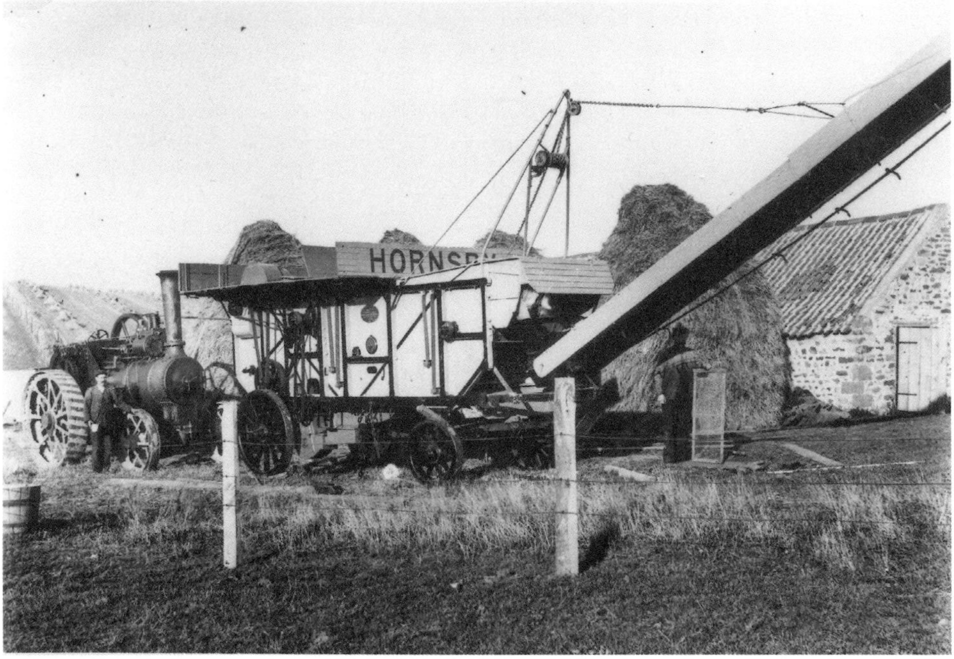

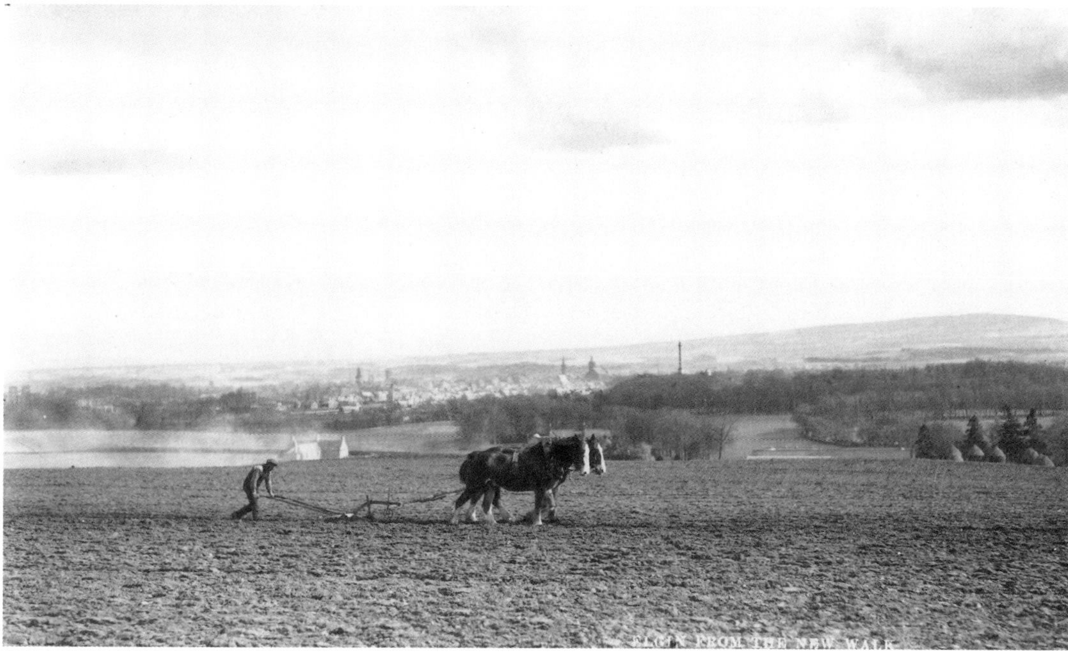

Looking over the town from New Walk. Horses were quickly made redundant once the less demanding tractor was introduced.

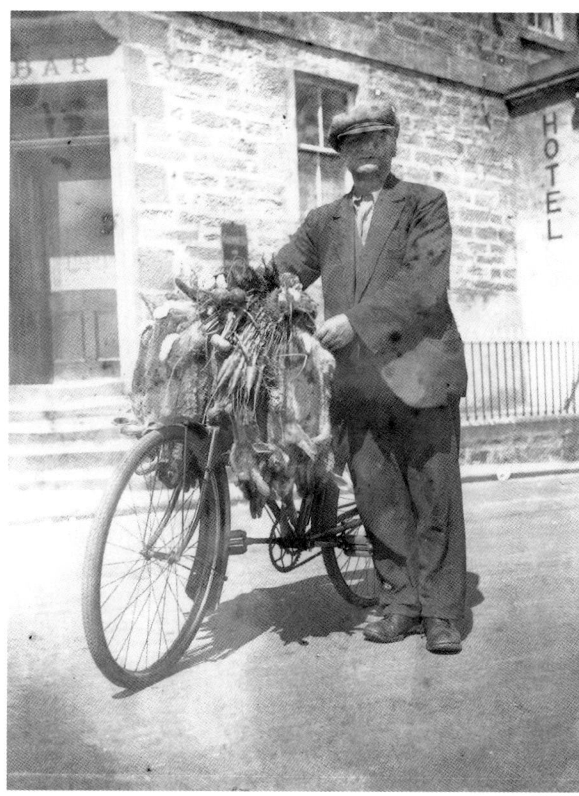

Rabbit-catcher, outside the Harbour Inn, Lossiemouth. This would appear to be an enterprising door-to-door salesman, carrying not only rabbits but vegetables as well. Rabbit-catching is still practised by some folk in Elgin who have their own select and appreciative landowners and customers!

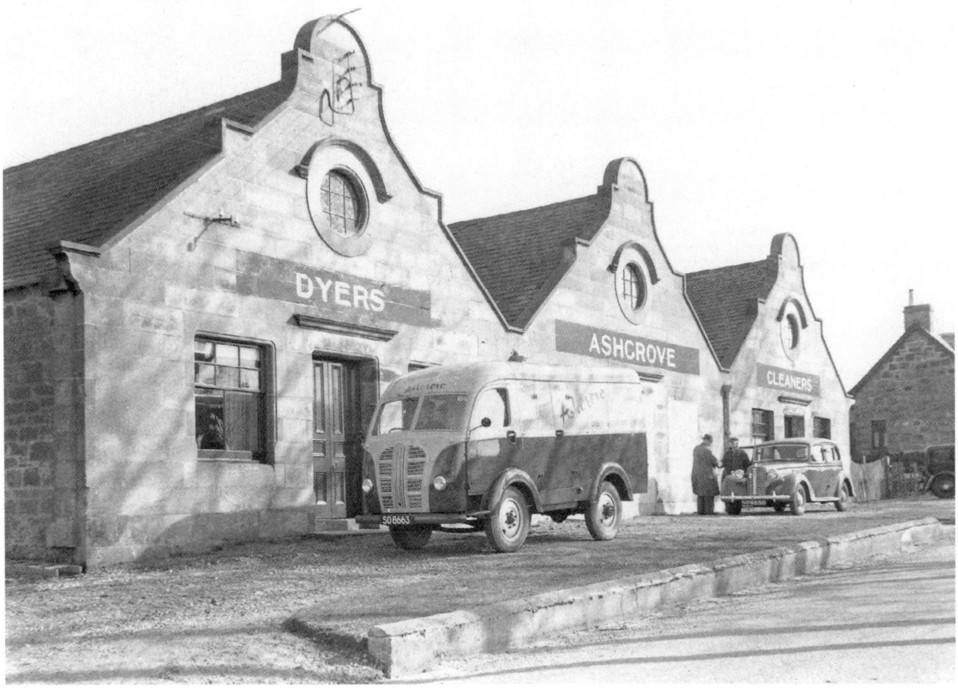

The Ashgrove Cleaners was a flourishing business in New Elgin. When removed from its site at Milnefield it was replaced firstly by a bacon factory, then a bond house for Campbell, Hope and King.

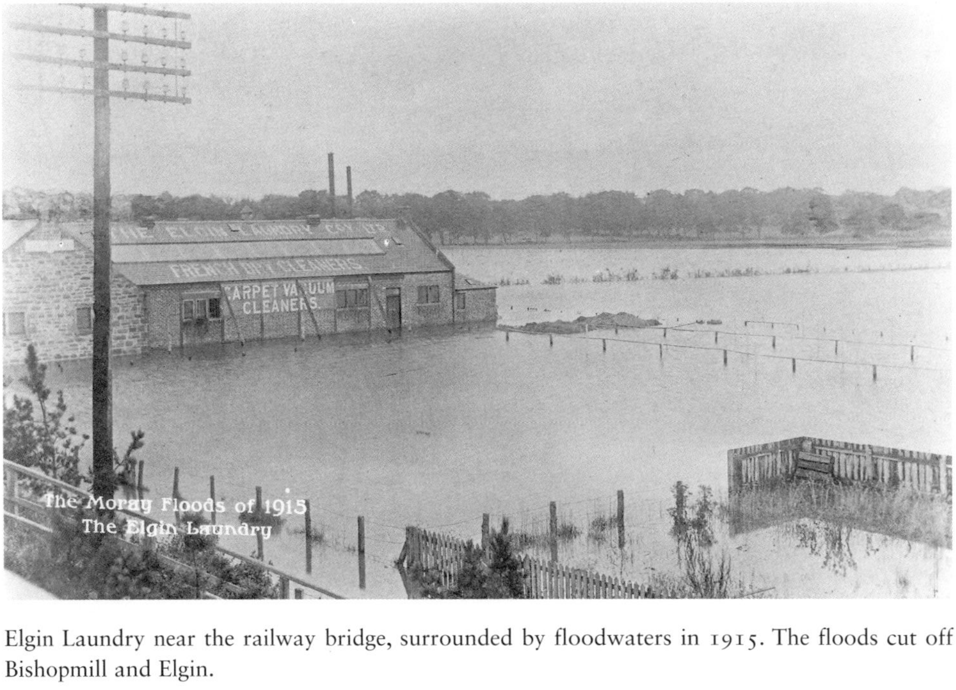

Elgin Laundry near the railway bridge, surrounded by floodwaters in 1915. The floods cut off Bishopmill and Elgin.

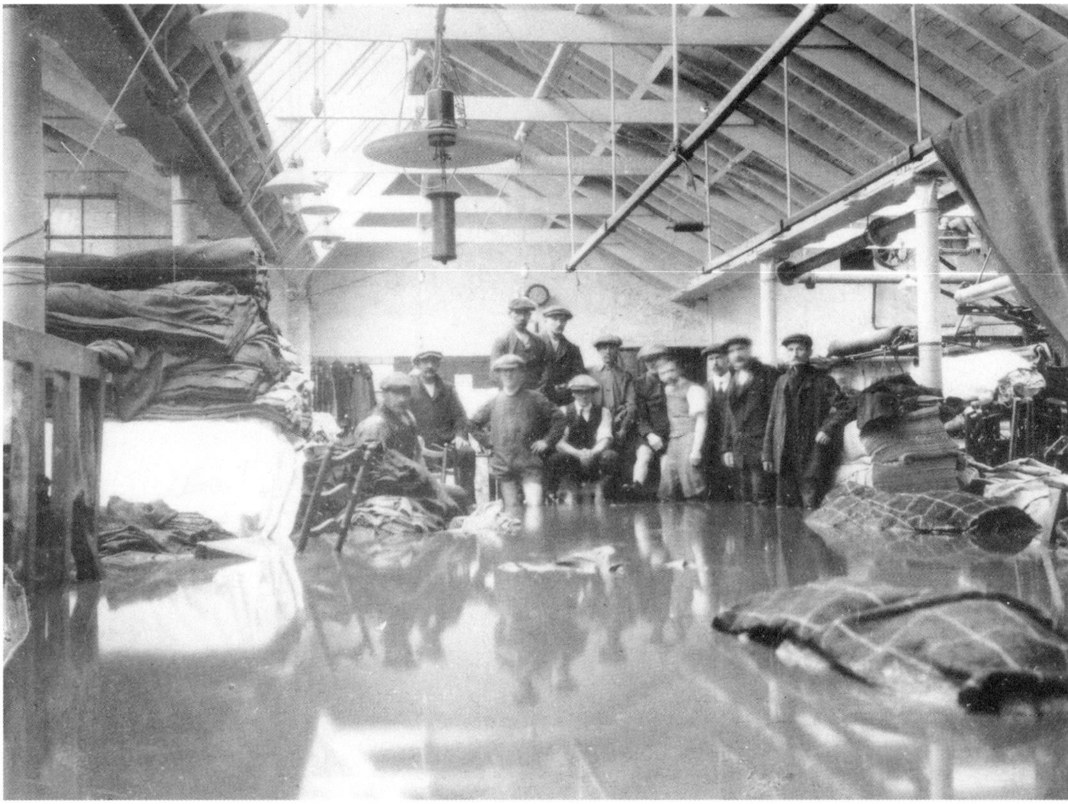

In September 1915 rain fell for nearly forty-eight hours. The River Lossie burst its bank in several places and the area from Elgin to Mosstowie was turned into a vast lake. At the railway stations the water reached the platforms. The Johnstons, Newmills mill was flooded out, and the workers are seen here surveying the damage.

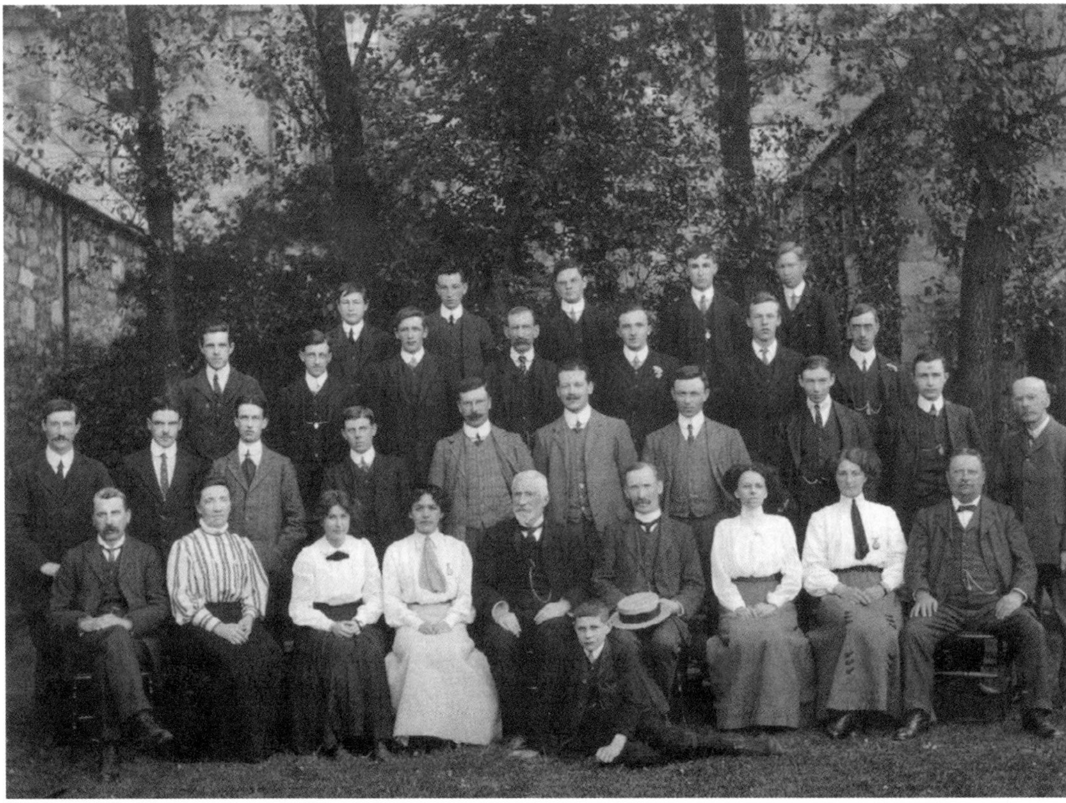

The combined staff of the Royal Bank and the law firm Stewart & McIsaac. This was taken either in 1910 or 1914. Front row, seated, left to right: Mr Alex Russell, joint Bank Agent with Mr McIsaac; Mrs Spence, caretaker; Oohna Stewart (Mrs Gordon); -?-; Mr Hugh Stewart; Mr James McIsaac; -?-; Bell Grant (Mrs Cockburn); Mr Howie; standing behind Mr Howie, I.W. Mackie, cashier. Second row: Bob Cruickshank, who worked for Stewart & McIsaac for 65 years; fifth from left, Henry Savage; sixth from left, J. A. Clark. Third row: J. Spence, caretaker, fourth from left; I. Calder, far right. Middle of back row: S. Morrison. Many of the young men seen here never returned from the Somme.

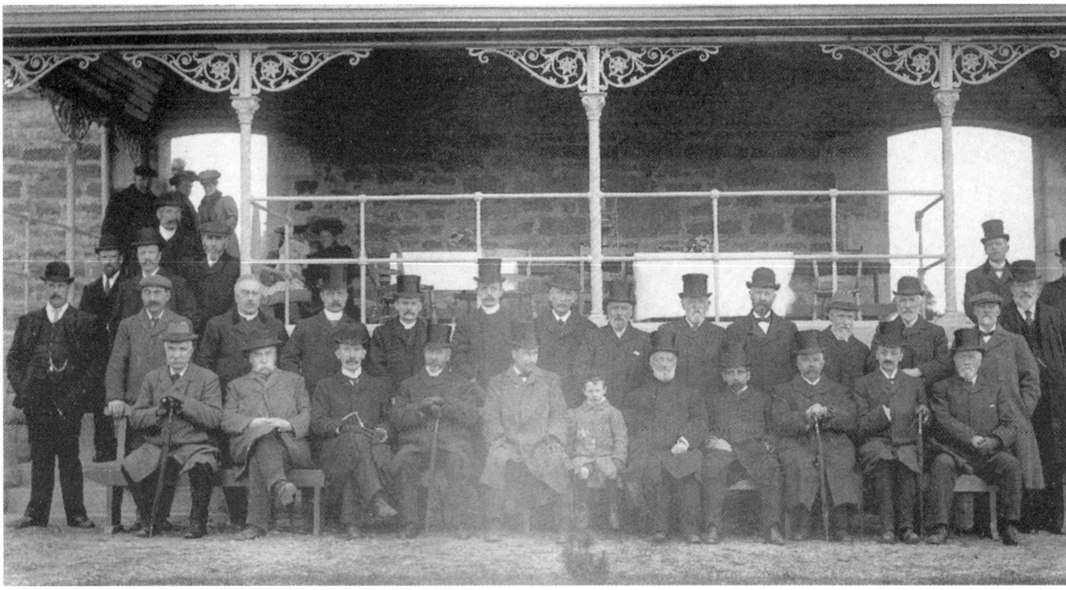

Opening ceremony of the third part of New Elgin cemetery, 1907. The local loons used to play in the sandpits in Jeannie Shaw's wood until the 1 p.m. laundry hooter called them home for lunch. The wood is now an extension of the cemetery and some locals still refer to departed friends as being 'up in Jeannie Shaw's wood'.

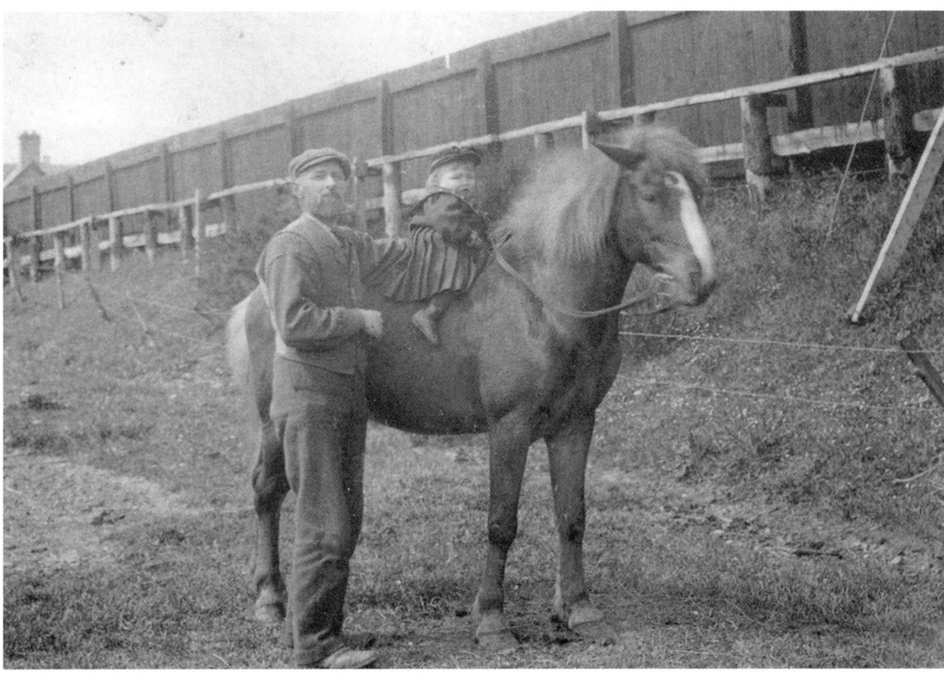

Urqhuart Innes with his grandson at Milnefield football ground, New Elgin, the home of the Ashgrove Warriors. The little boy became the Federal President of the Electrical Trades Union of Australia, retiring in 1965.

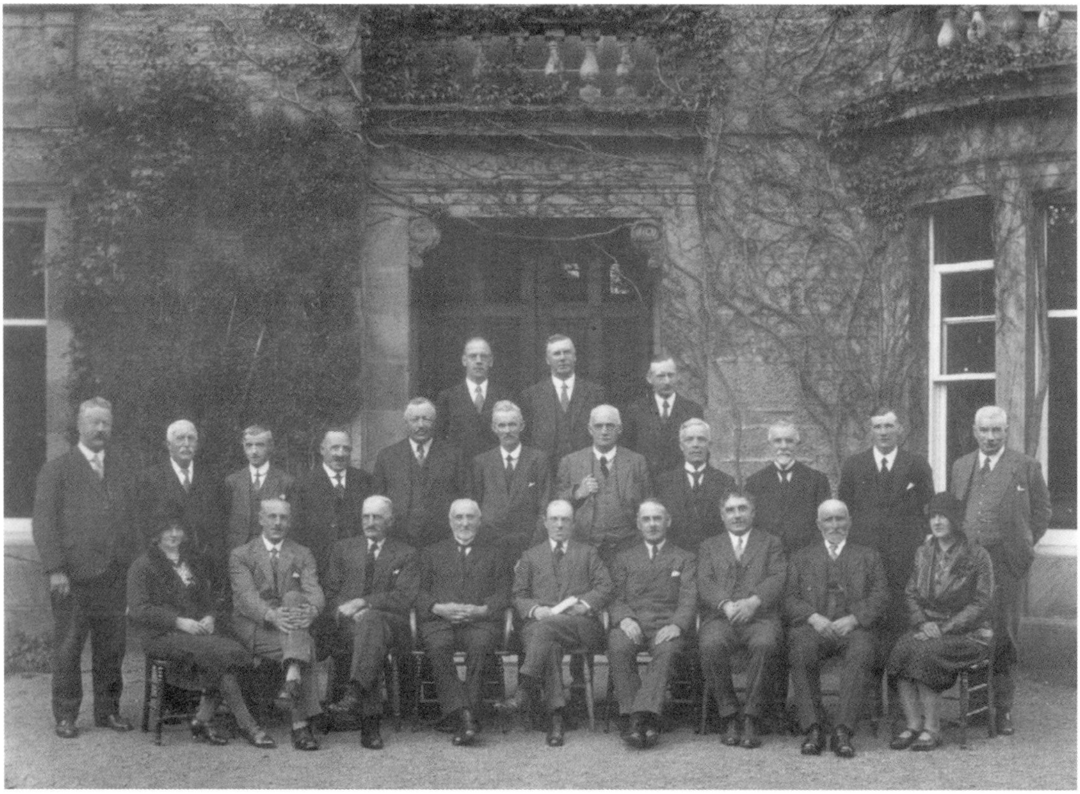

Last meeting of Elgin Parish Council, 1929. This was taken outside Springfield House, opposite the old town hall. Springfield House, now demolished, was used as a private school before it became the Elgin Academy. Back row, left to right: W. B. Cameron, Superintendent of Craigmoray poor house; Henry Savage, solicitor; -?-, Superintendent of the cemetery. Second row: Dr John Taylor; Alexander Andersomn, Heath Cottage, Longmorn; George Robertson, rope works; William Gedds, butcher; Alexander Falconer, contractor; James Keir, draper; William Carrie, grocer; Alexander Lyon, plummer; Peter Dow, schoohnaster; ? Christie, engine driver; John Wittet, architect. Front row, seated: Mrs Brown Grant; A. Hepburn, cabinet-maker; ? Cook, farmer; J. Schiach, grocer; A. D. McCaskie, solicitor; J. W. MacFarlane, inspector of the poor; Frank Anderson, jeweller; John Grant, Mosstowie; Dr Annie MacLeod.

SECTION TEN

TRAINS, TRAVEL, SPECIAL DAYS & LEISURE

The beginning of this century saw major developments in methods of transport. The horse was swiftly replaced by the railway and the petrol engine. The railways opened up the north-east for trade, brought British standard time to the whole country and allowed many people to travel far afield for the first time. In 1852, the quiet town of Elgin was linked to Lossiemouth by 6 miles of railway track. 'There were banners, processions, triumphal arches, banks of flowers and German bands parading the streets.' Flags streamed from every farmhouse, and every ship in Lossiemouth harbour was flying its colours. 'Excisemen and the local colonel set off cannon and there were bread and games for the people.' New forms of transport necessitated changes to the land and buildings. The pace of life altered irrevocably.

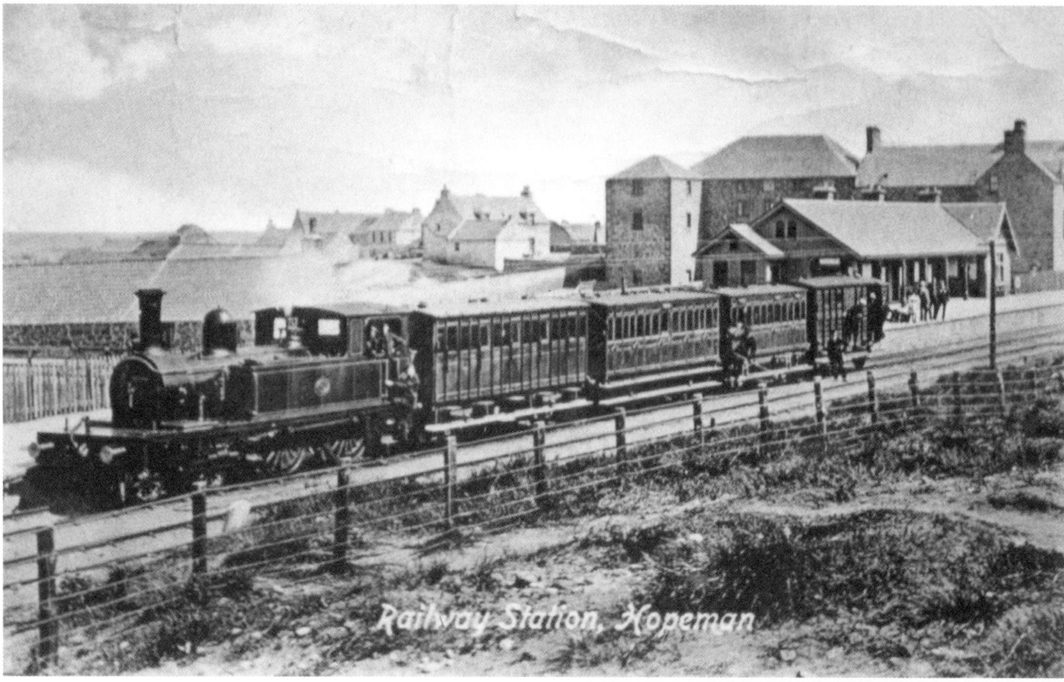

Hopeman station. It was not possible to travel directly from Elgin to Hopeman except by way of Mosstowie, branching off at Alves and through Burghead. Fish and quarry traffic was carried in this way and special precautions had to be taken to cope with the problems of drifting sand. Sand-blowers of iron sheeting, angled towards the track, channelled the wind away and prevented sand being lost.

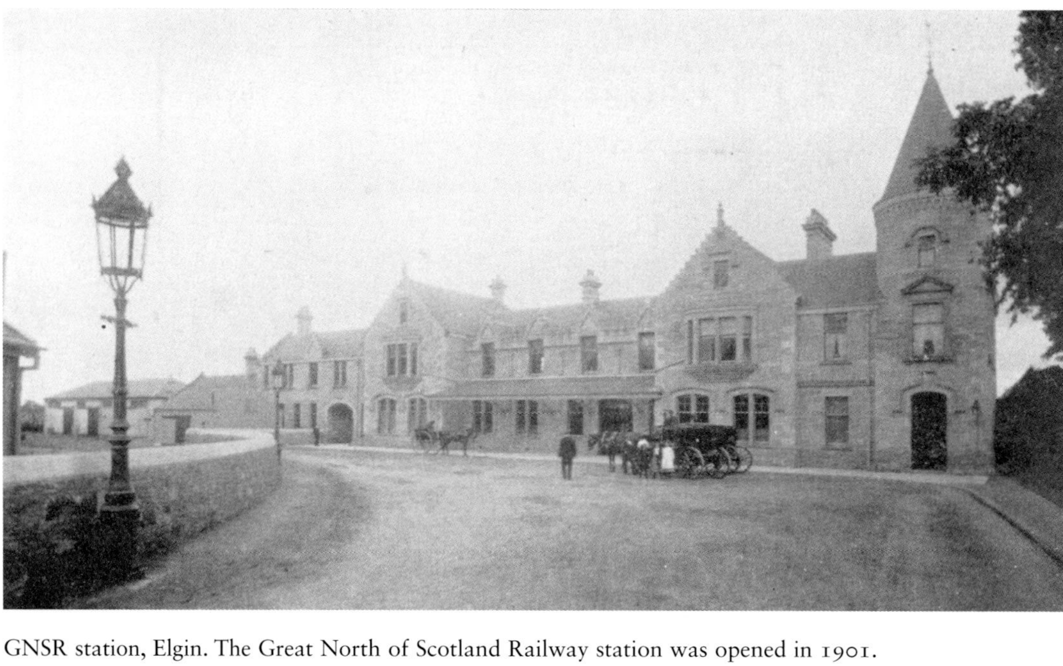

GNSR station, Elgin. The Great North of Scotland Railway station was opened in 1901.

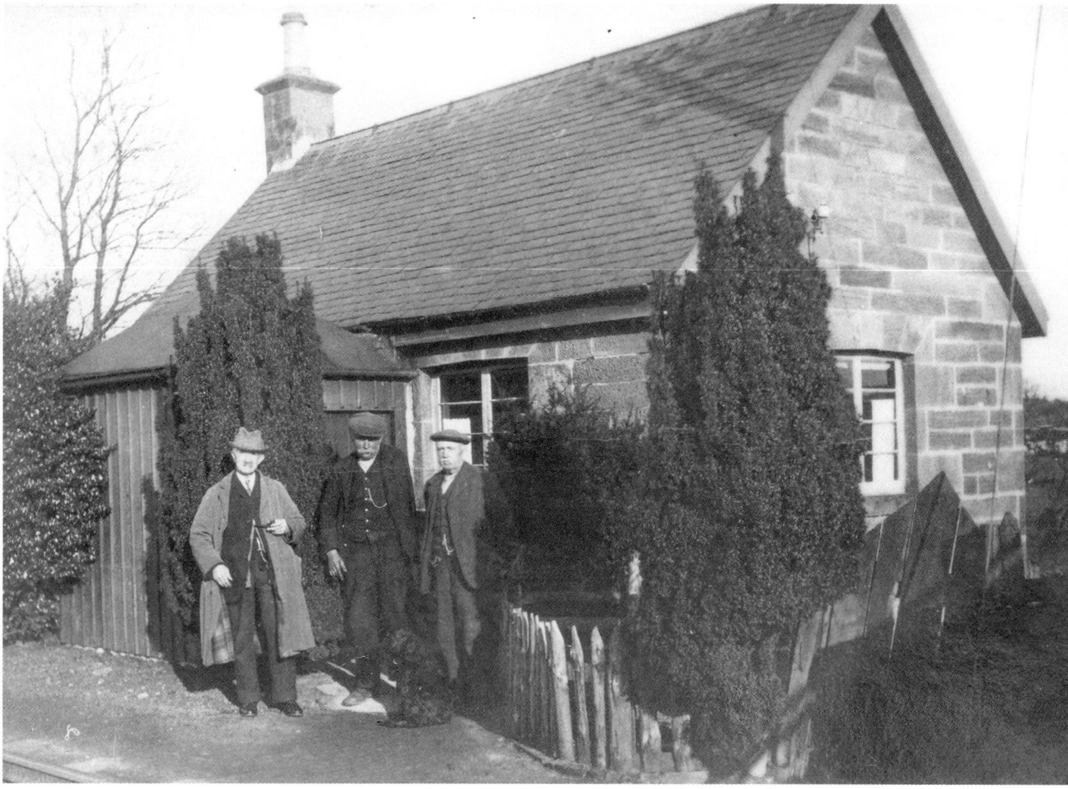

The Railway cottage at Pinefield. The middle man is James McKerron, gatekeeper. He lost an arm in an accident with a train. The dog was called Flossie. Along with James and his wife, seven children lived in the house shown. In 1880 the Morayshire Railway was merged with the GNSR Company and the coast-line section was opened in 1886. The railways employed many people, both during construction and in the maintenance of track. Many people depended directly or indirectly on the railways for their livelihoods. Most of these old railway cottages have now been destroyed and along the old deserted lines old lilac and apple trees are all that remain of the once well-tended railwaymen's gardens.

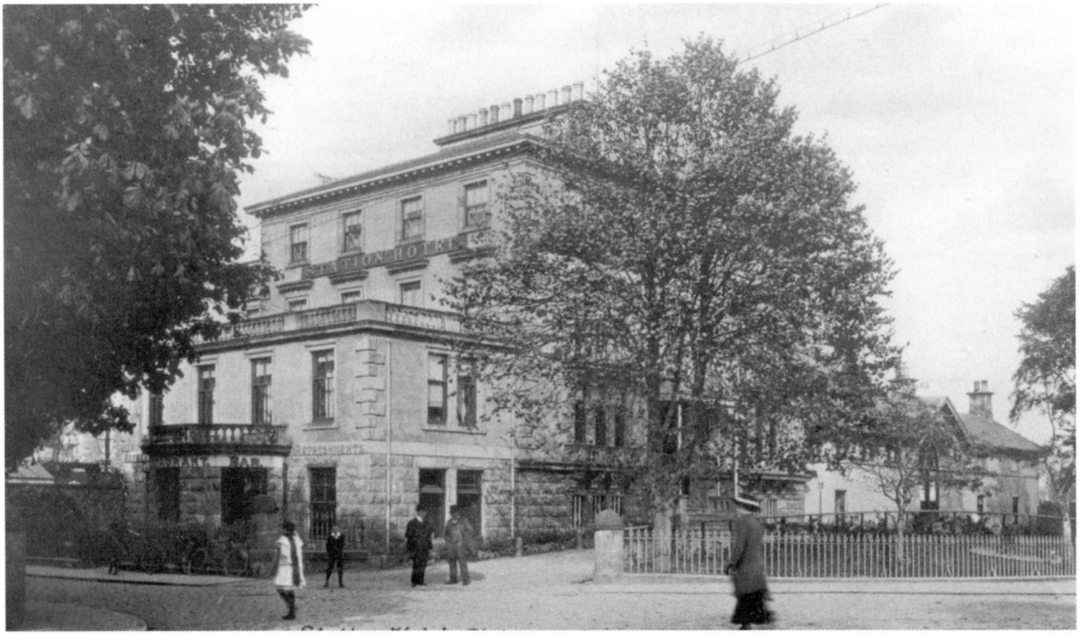

Laichmoray Hotel. This was originally the Railway Hotel, built by the Morayshire Railway Company in 1853. In 1874 it briefly became the Elgin Educational Institute until, closing four years later, it reverted to the Station Hotel. It was renamed in the 1950s.

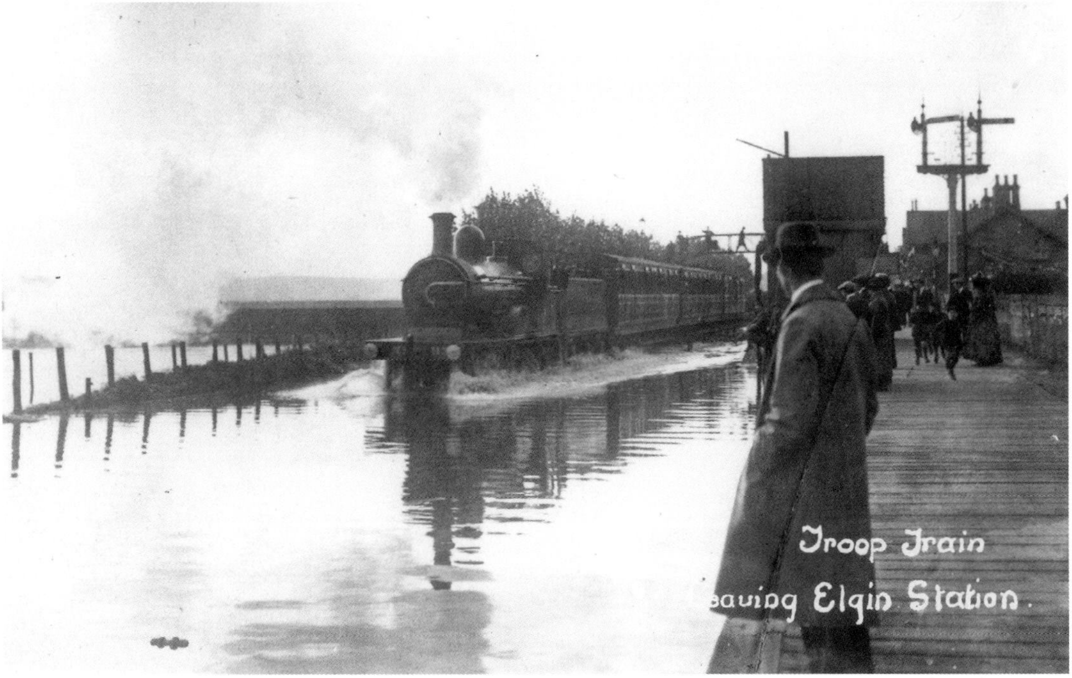

Troop train leaving Elgin in the floods, 1915. For many of the men, on their way to the battlefields of France, this was their last sight of Elgin.

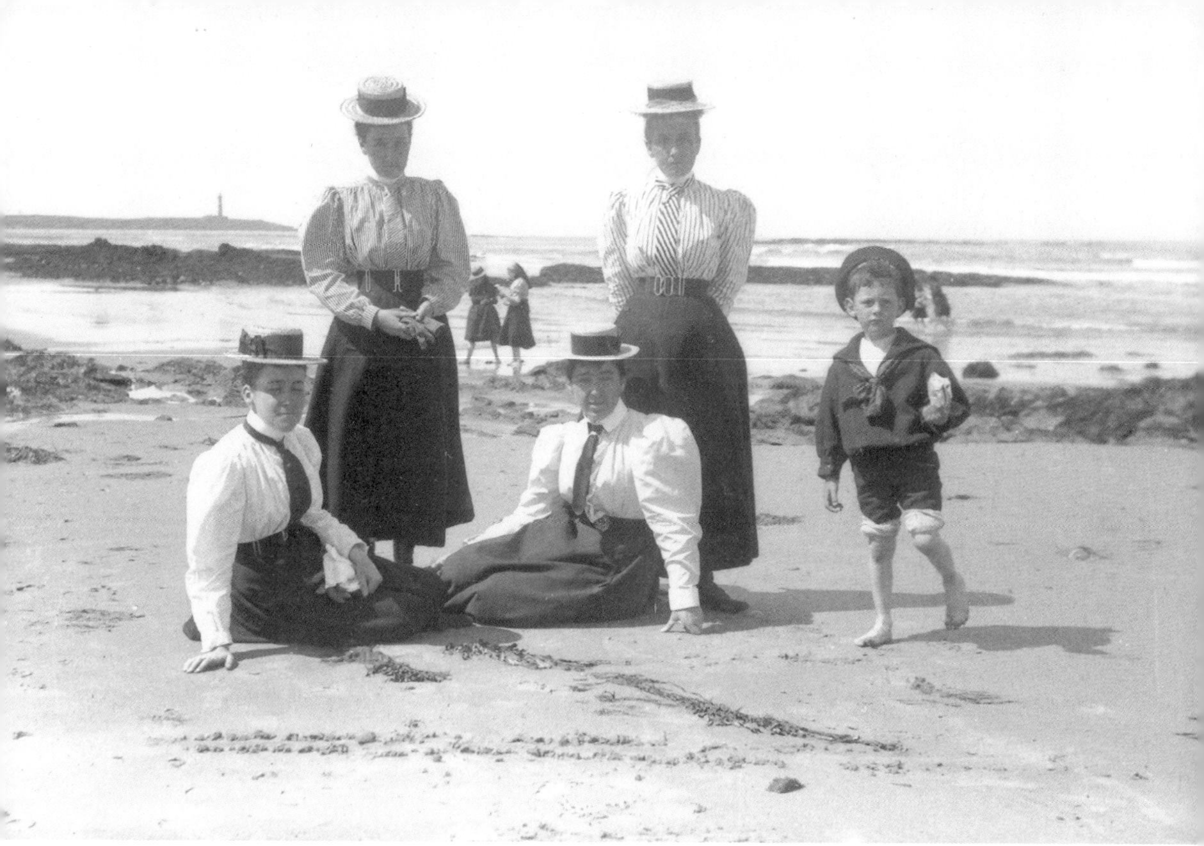

West beach, Lossiemouth. The train enabled Elgin folk to enjoy a day out at the nearby seaside. The Skerries lighthouse, seen in the distance, was designed by Allan Stevenson in 1844.

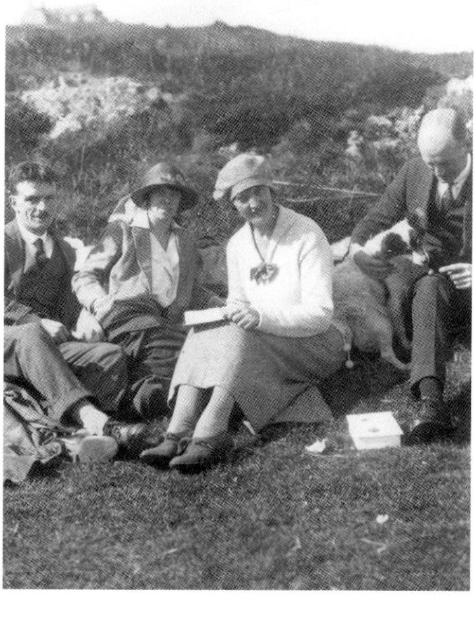

Covesea. This was a popular beauty spot, where Alexander Graham Bell spent his honeymoon in the 1870s.

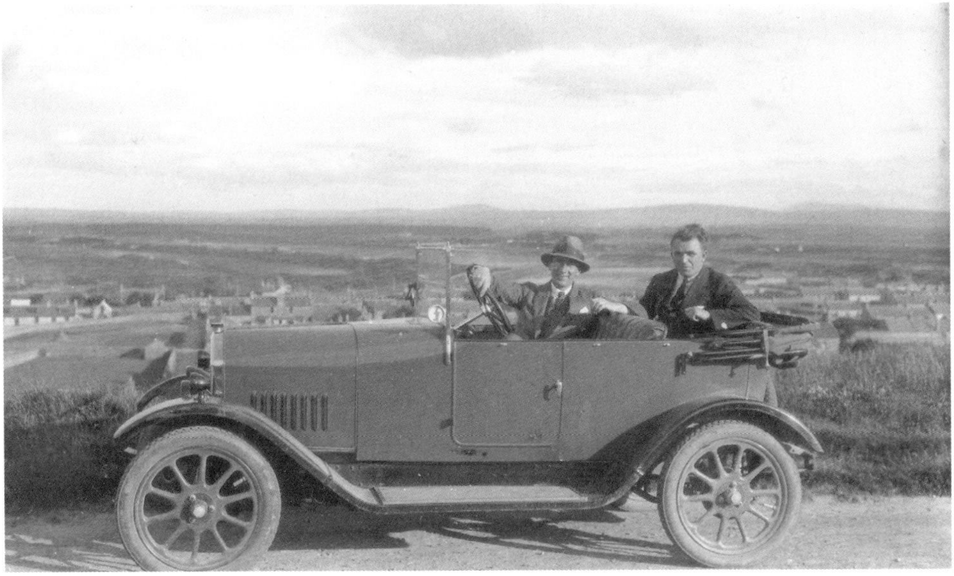

Overlooking Seatown, Lossiemouth, from Prospect Terrace. The advent of the motor car enabled folk to explore the locality and enjoy the views.

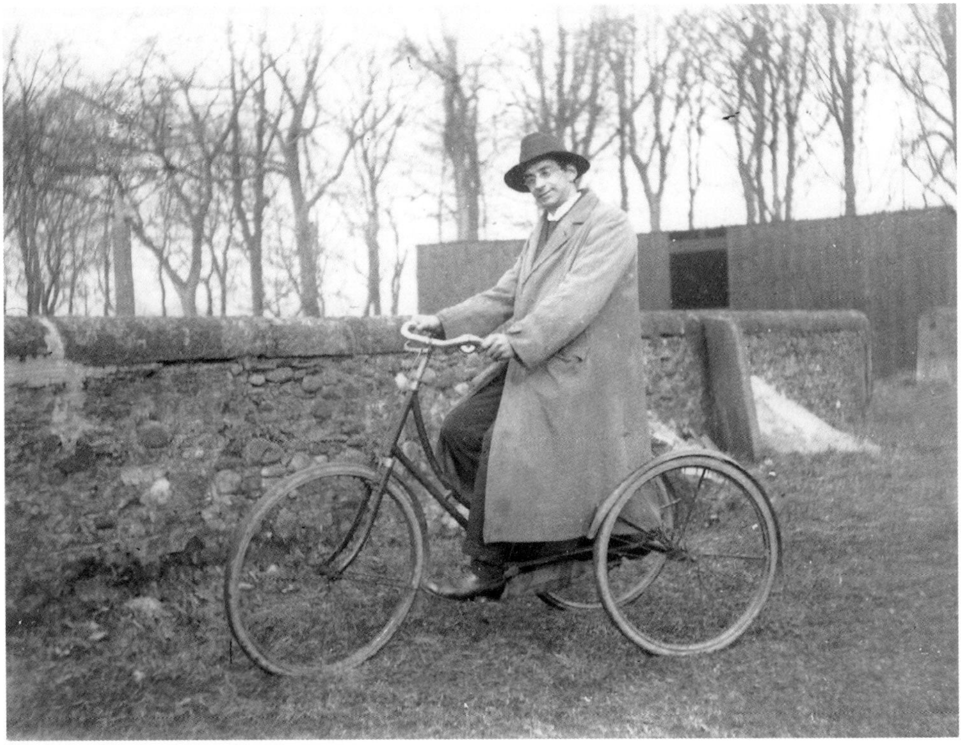

Tricycle. Unafraid of innovation, Elgin folk tried all sorts of modern transportation in the 1930s.

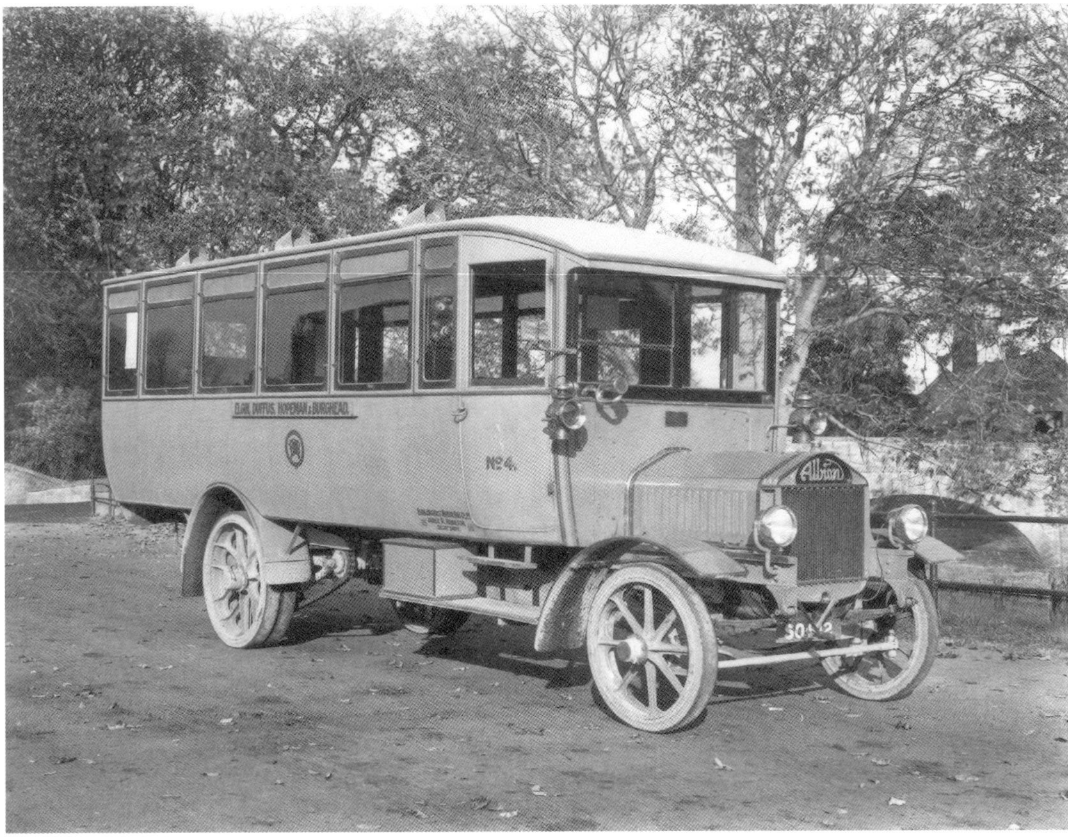

This splendid vehicle is parked by the River Lossie near the Brewery Brig. Without the benefit of modern suspension a long trip would have been quite exhausting, especially if, as was often the case, the seats were wooden-slatted! Note the oil carriage lamps on either side of the windscreen.

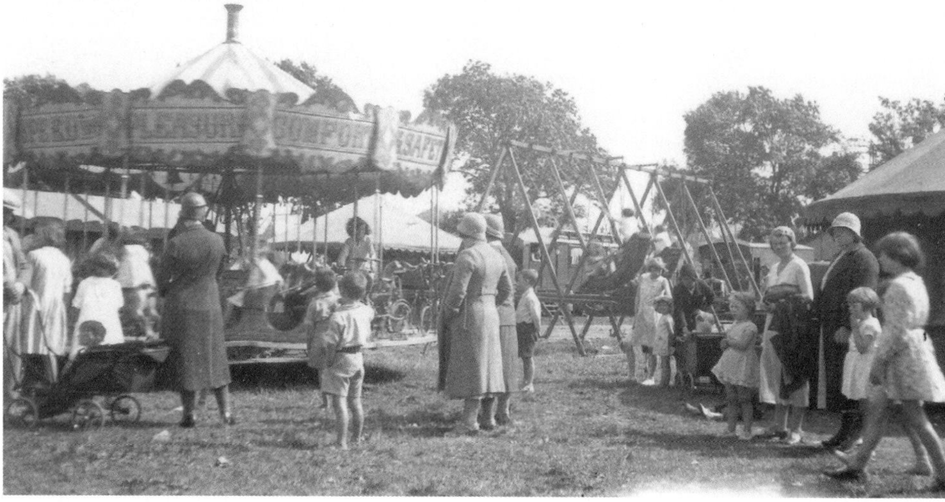

The fair, known as the 'showies', on Lossie Green in the 1930s. The circus also regularly came to town and was held on Lossie Green, Pinefield, or at Milnefield, New Elgin. The 'showies' have been held on Lossie Green since time immemorial — less than ten years ago residents of the new Milnefield housing estate had the dubious pleasure of camels roaring at the bottom of the garden and elephants exercising outside their bedroom windows!

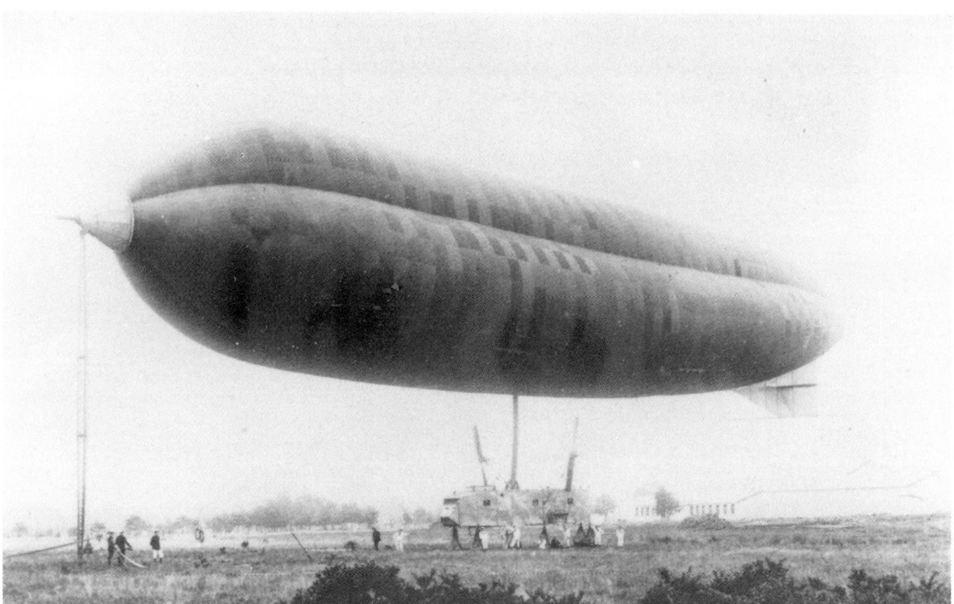

An airship over Elgin, 1920s, also known locally as a "Buchan Soo".

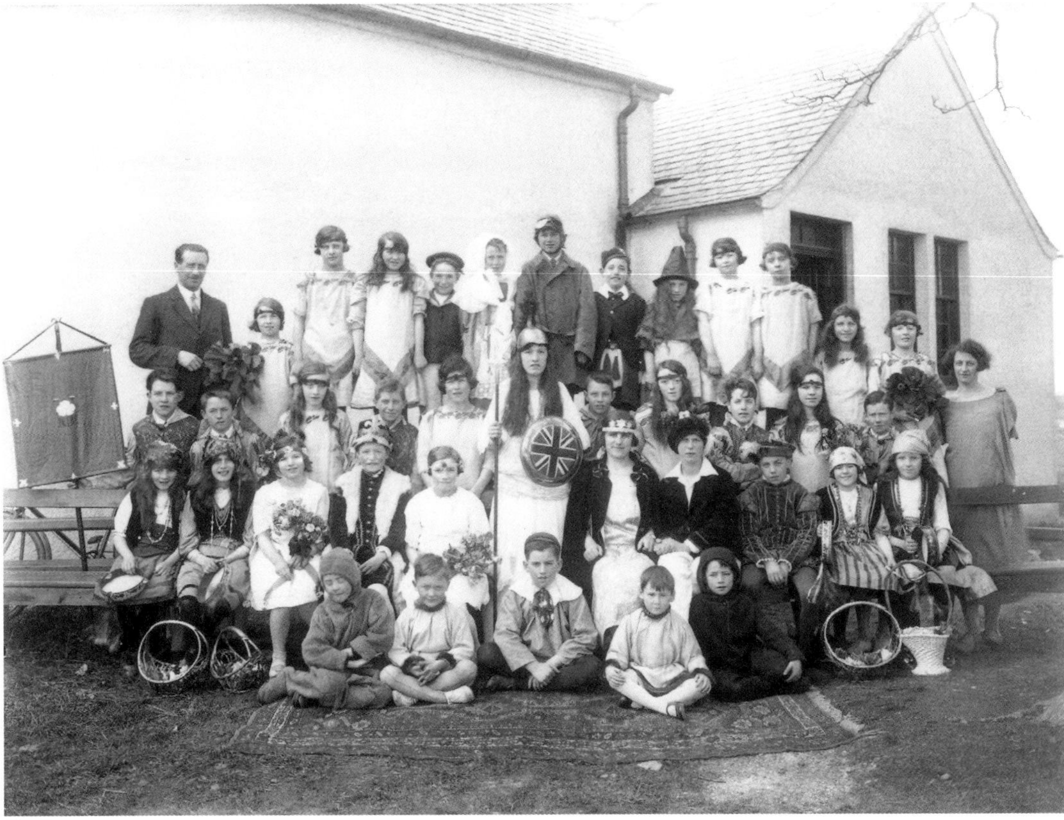

Outside Urquart Parish Hall, built in 1924 by a local mason - Legge. The children from the local school are performing an operetta - "The Princess of Poppyland". At the back, Molly Forsyth is representing Wales and wearing a tall black hat.

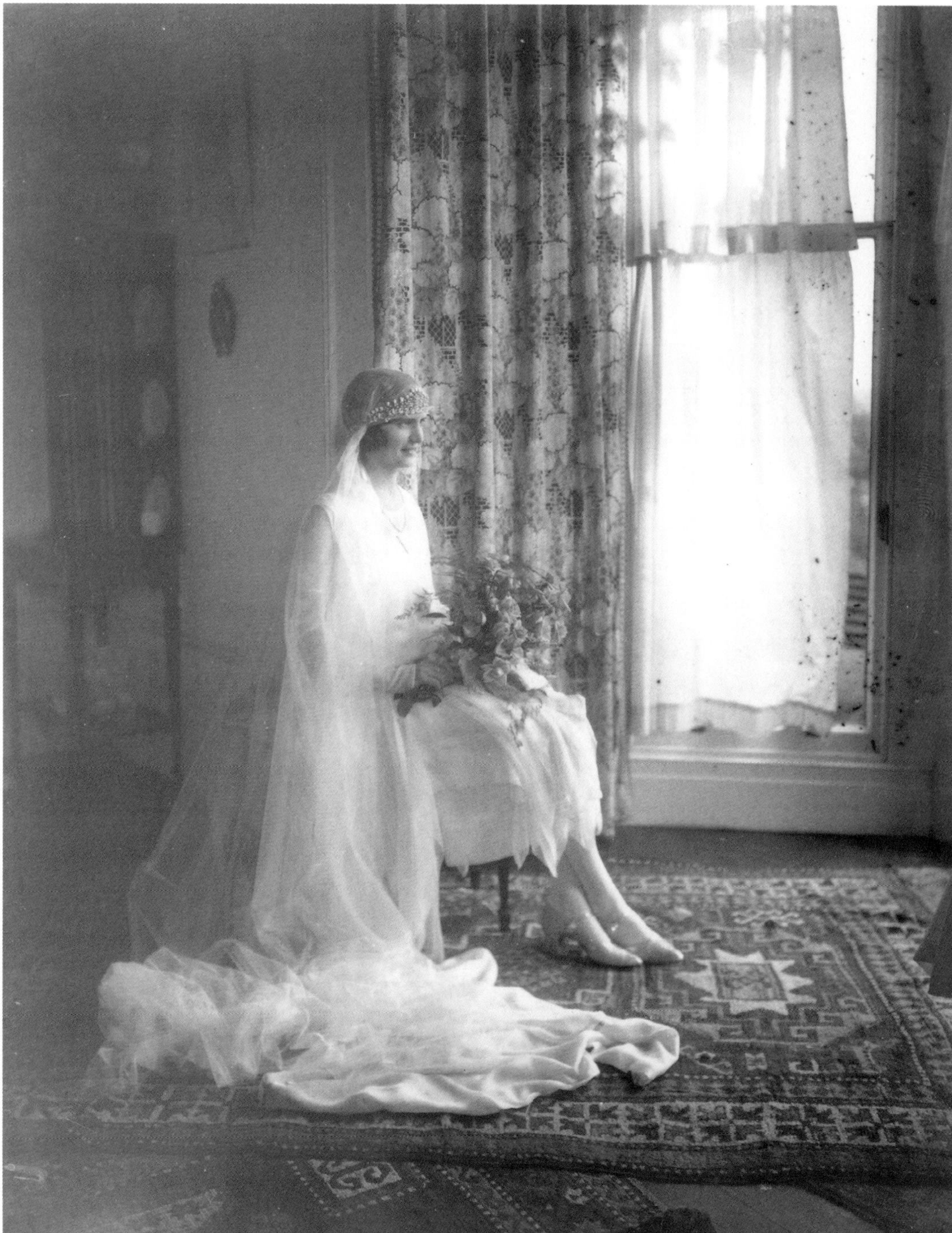

This was a Sellar family wedding showing a 1920s dress and luxurious curtains and carpeting.

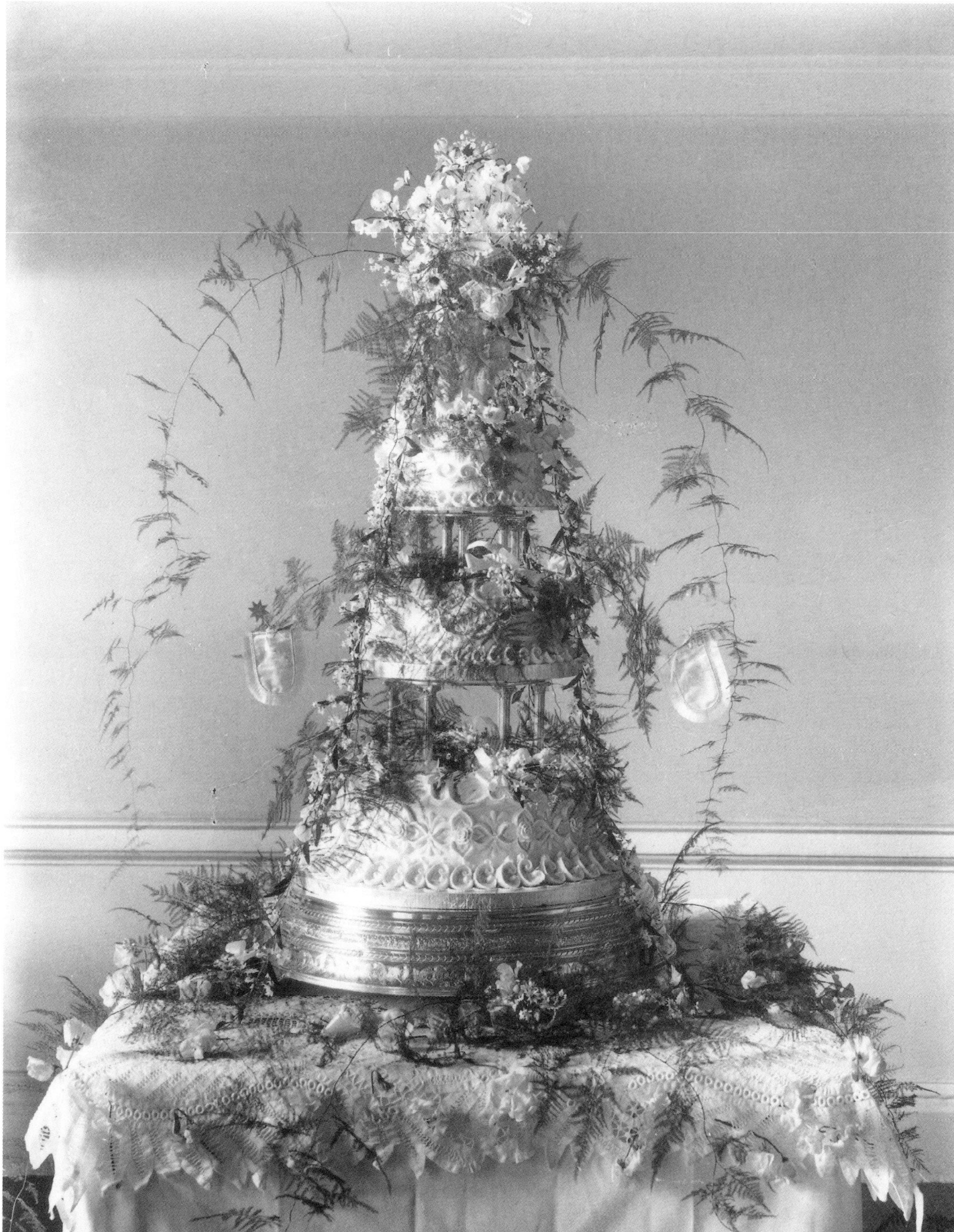

An Austin cake with plenty of bridal 'favours' to present to honoured guests. Alexander Austin, founder of the bakery, died in his late sixties in 1913. His son continued with the business for many years, but now the once famous tea rooms are used as a Masonic hall and function suites.

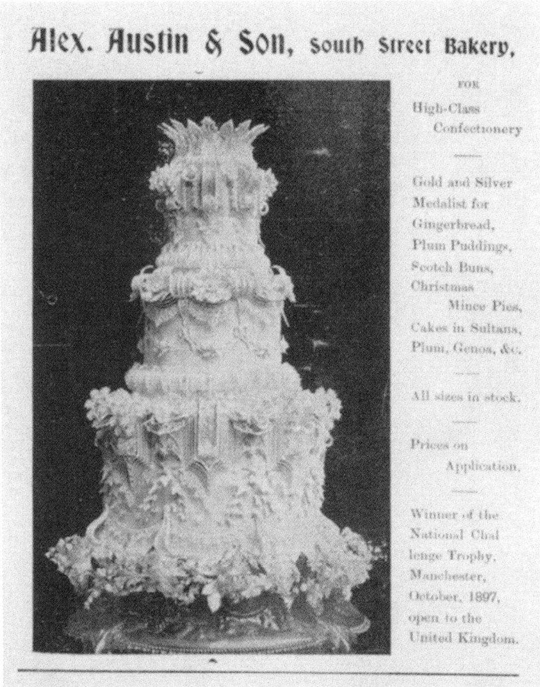

An early advertisement for Austin's bakery and a glimpse of the artist himself at work. Austin's tea rooms are fondly remembered by those who enjoyed the treat of eating in elegant surroundings with crisp white tablecloths and silver cutlery.

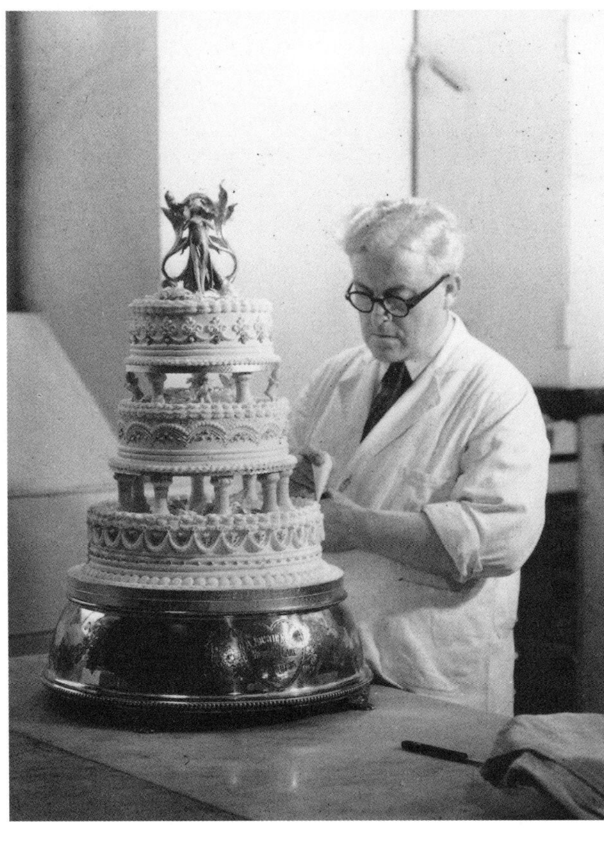

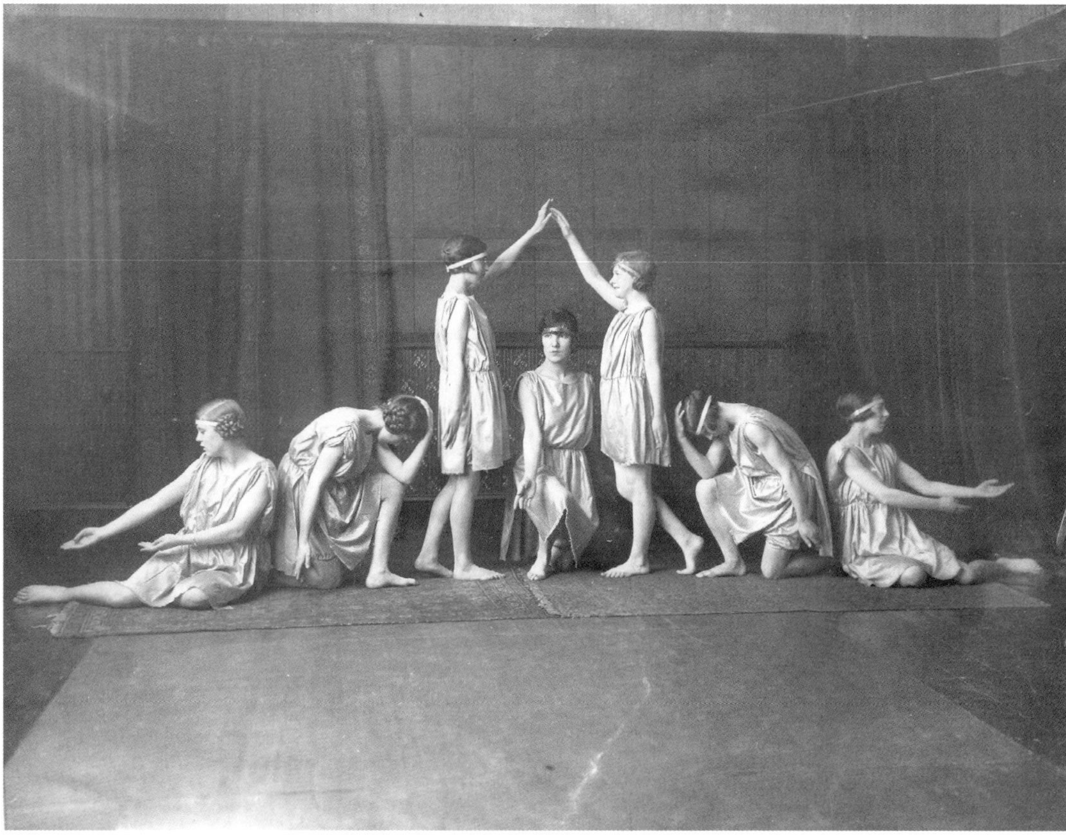

The Graces in Studio Tyrell. Throwing off corsets and dancing as a form of exercise made an enormous difference to women's health and mental attitudes in the early years of this century.

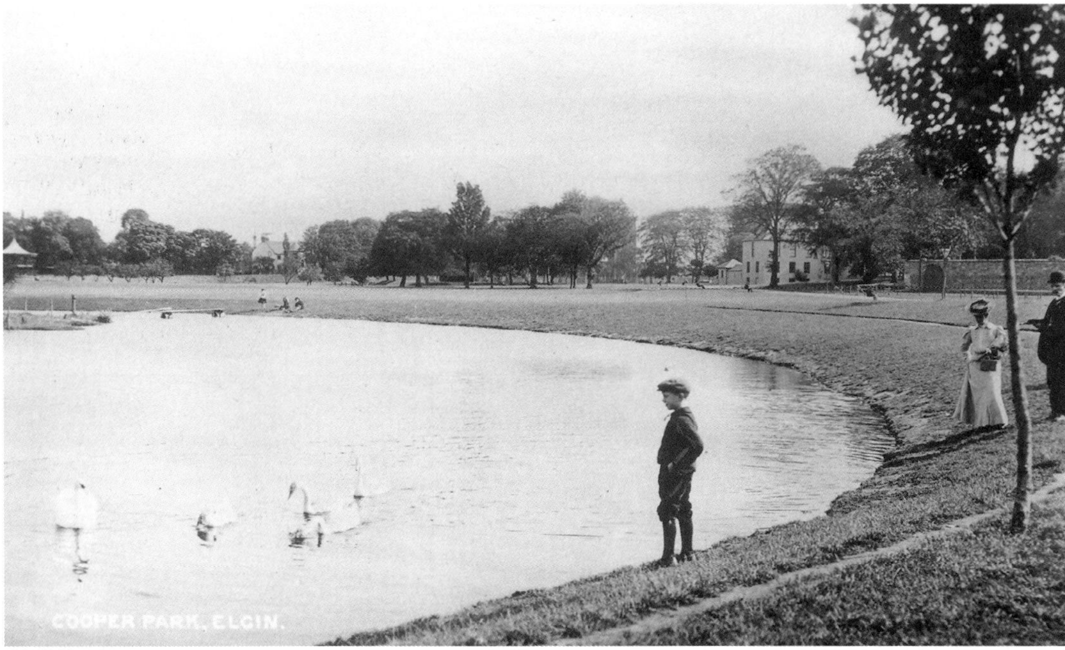

The Pond. The layout of the park was designed by A. Marshall Mackenzie and originally the Cooper Park pond was to be used as a skating rink. Boating began on it in 1923. Grant Lodge and forty acres were given to the town by Sir George Cooper after he had purchased them from the Seafield family. It was opened to the public on 19 August 1903 with much ceremony, and the gates were decorated with banners, flowers and large bunches of heather. The previous town park was a small area at Borough Briggs purchased from the Seafield family in 1888.

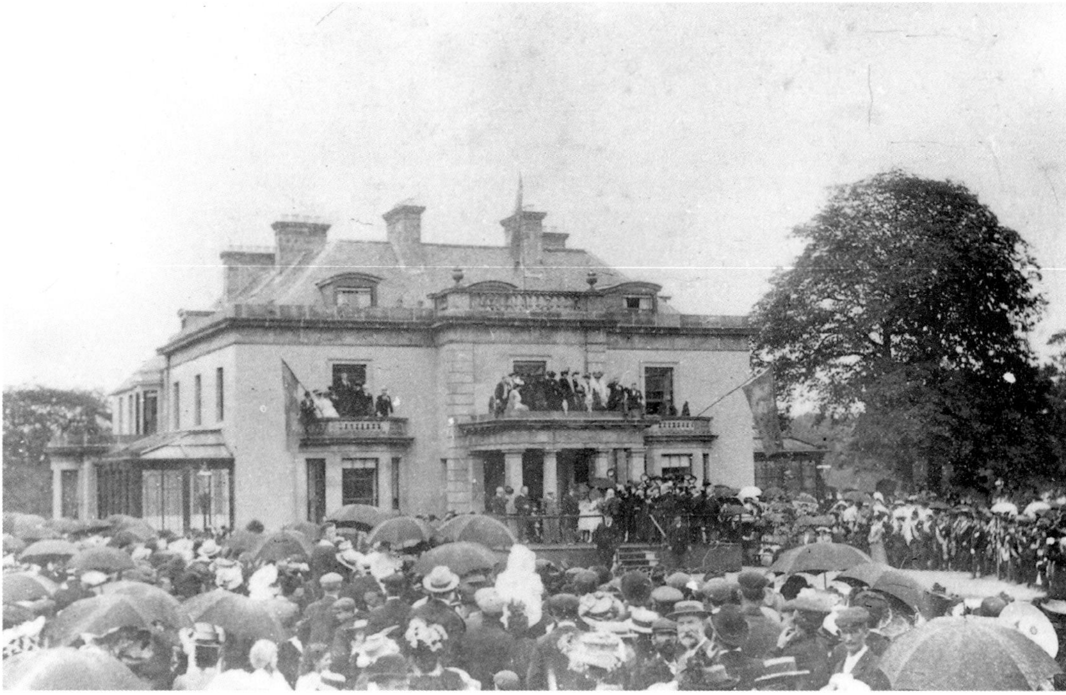

The opening of Grant Lodge, August 1903, after the house and grounds had been gifted to the town by Colonel Cooper in 1902. Grant Lodge was then used as a public library.

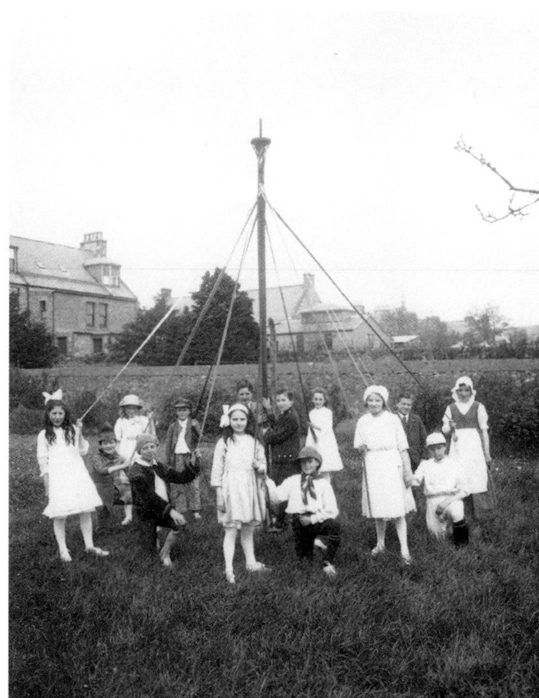

A turn around the maypole, *c.*1900, although maypole dancing was certainly done at East End School 60 years ago. Not a typical Elgin pursuit, presumably the instigators of this activity were unaware of the pagan significance of the maypole. This seems an attempt to introduce a more refined and cultured style to the natives, in contrast to wild eight-some reels and Highland dancing!

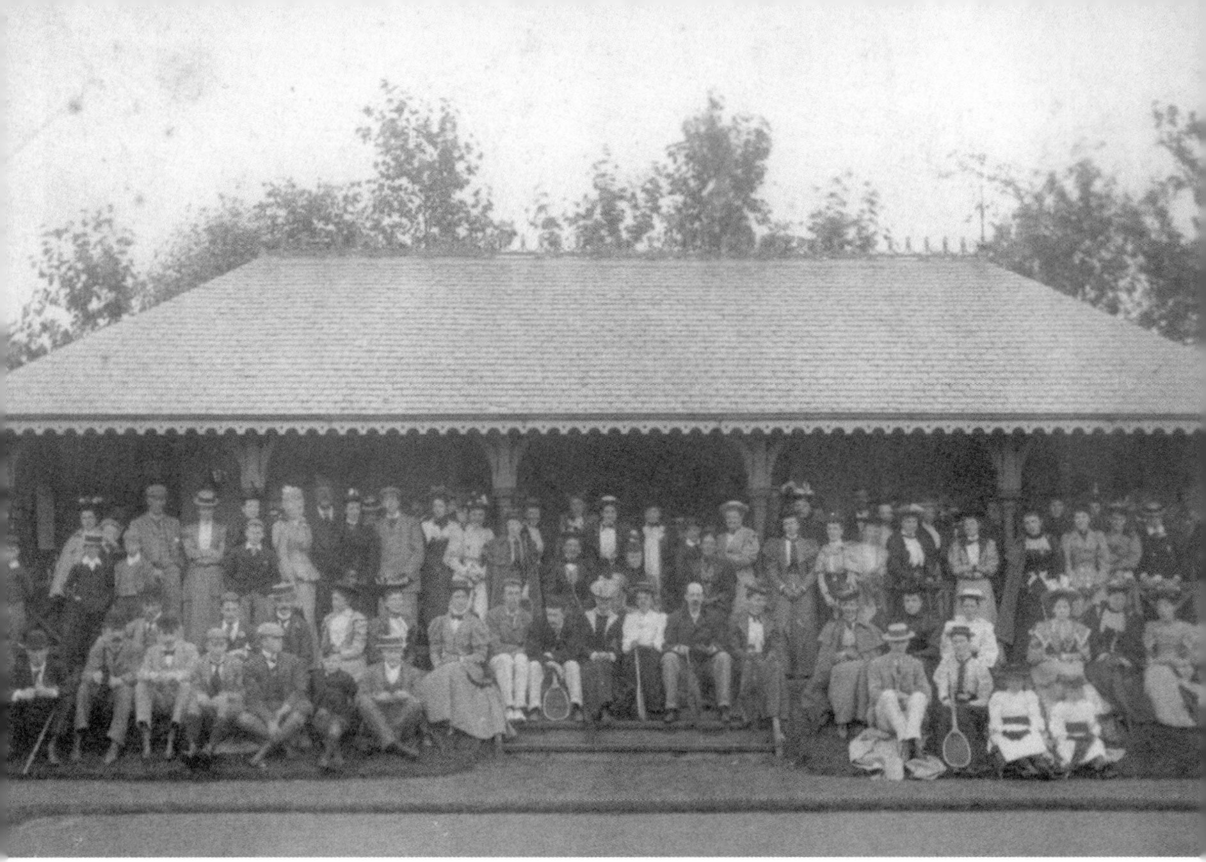

A tournament at Elgin Lawn Tennis Club, 1894. There were two tennis clubs in Elgin — at Marywell and Duff Avenue. The remaining club, at Duff Avenue, celebrated its centenary on 28 April 1989.

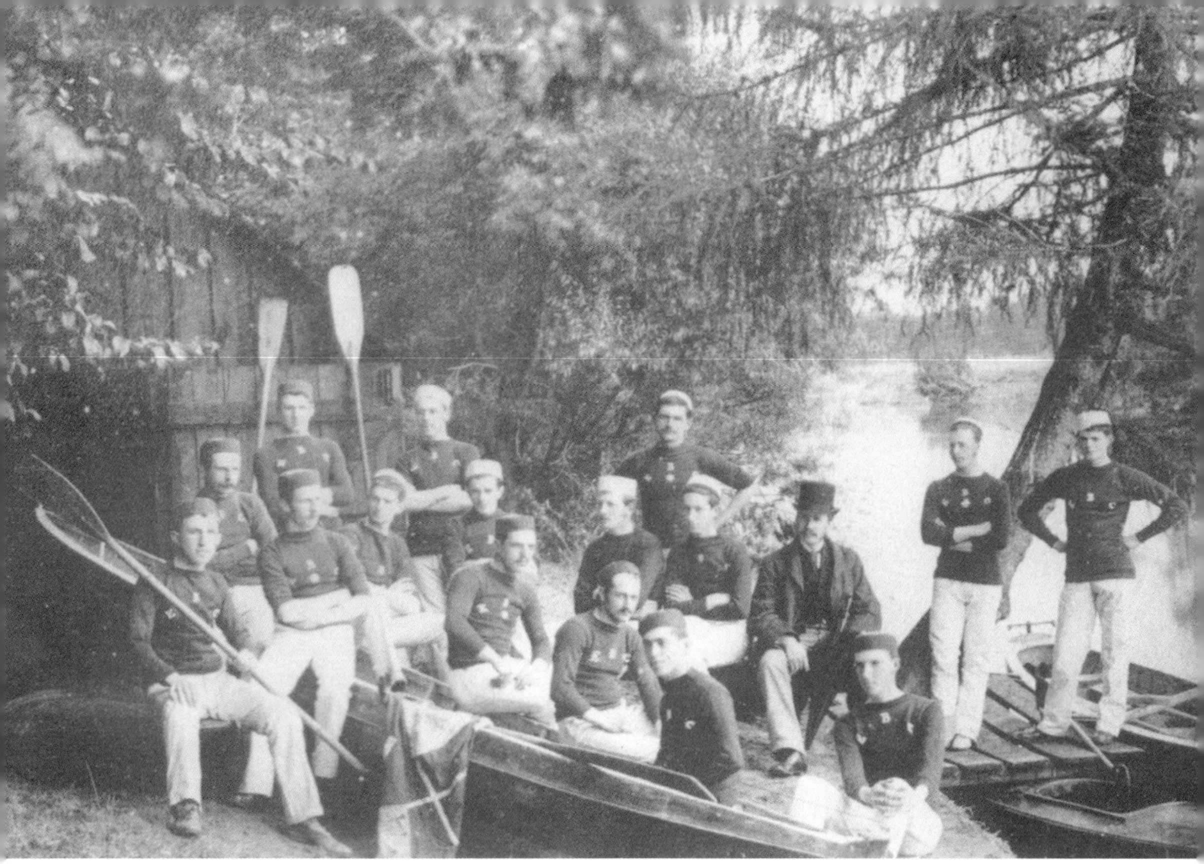

The Elgin Boating Club. This picture, donated by the editor of the *Northern Scot*, was taken in the 1890s on the River Lossie, just above the Bishopmill dam. The club is no longer in existence.

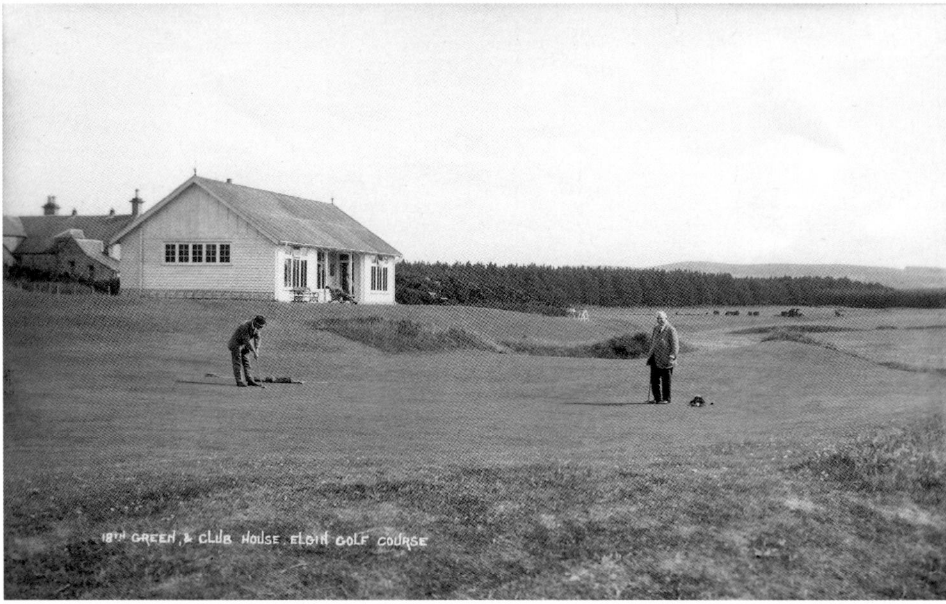

The Elgin Golf Club, opened in 1906, had only six holes and did not acquire eighteen holes until the 1920s. What was once the 18th green is now the 12th, and the 15th green is known as the Lime Kiln. As early as 1652 George Watsone, golf ball-maker, is recorded as being a 'burges of Elgin'. Until 1760 there was a course at Linksfield, between Spynie Palace and the cathedral. Nearby are the ruins of the last of the Elgin lime-kilns.

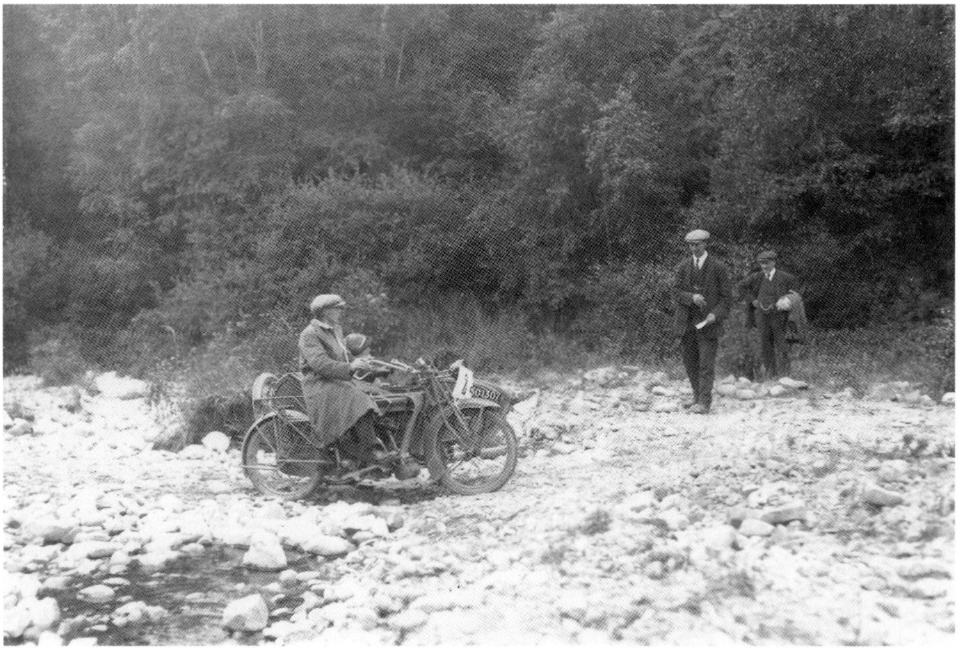

These motorbike trials prove that enthusiasts pushing themselves and their machines to the limit are no new phenomenon!

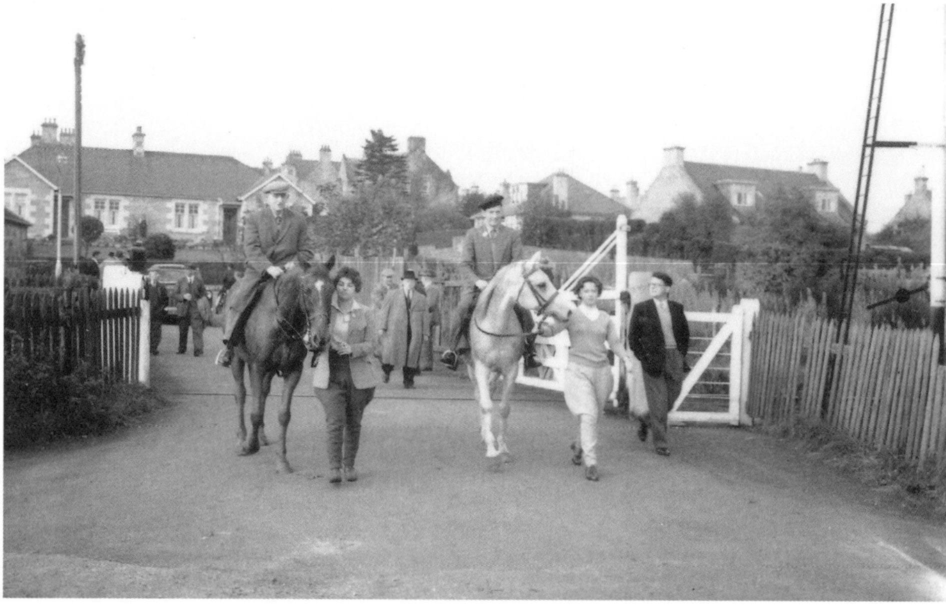

Begun in 1657, the tradition of riding on the Marches is carried out every two years in October, when a new Deacon Convener of the Six Incorporated Trades is installed. This group are passing through the Whitegates and Fred Smith is riding while Francis Kidd is leading one horse. They are heading towards the New Elgin boundry which is now alongside Glen Moray Drive

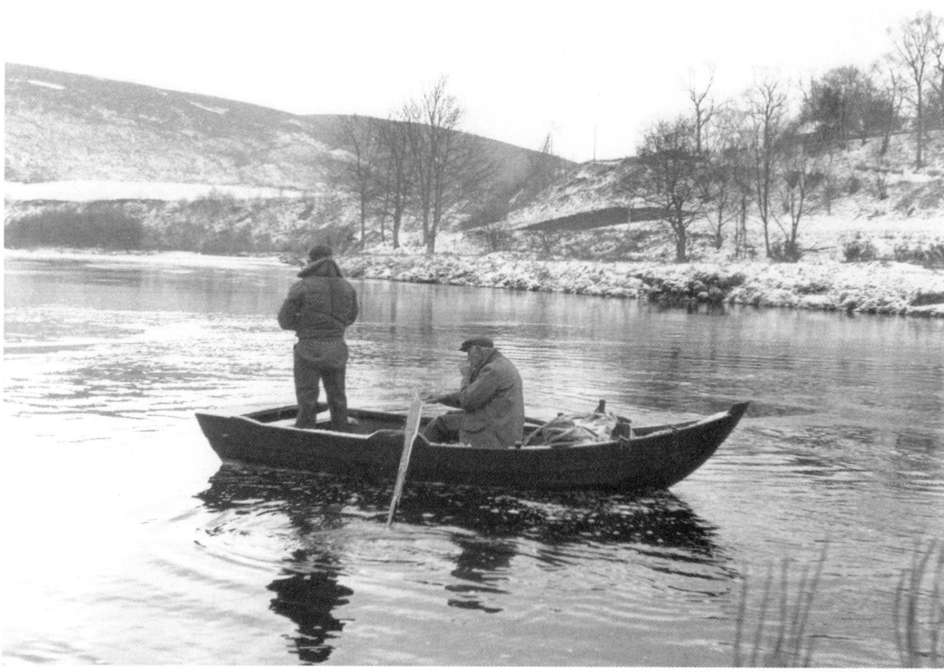

Fishing on the Spey in a typical Spey boat. This picture was taken in February 1960, the ghillie was Ned Ritchie and the fisherman was George Duncan of Gordon Castle, Fochabers.

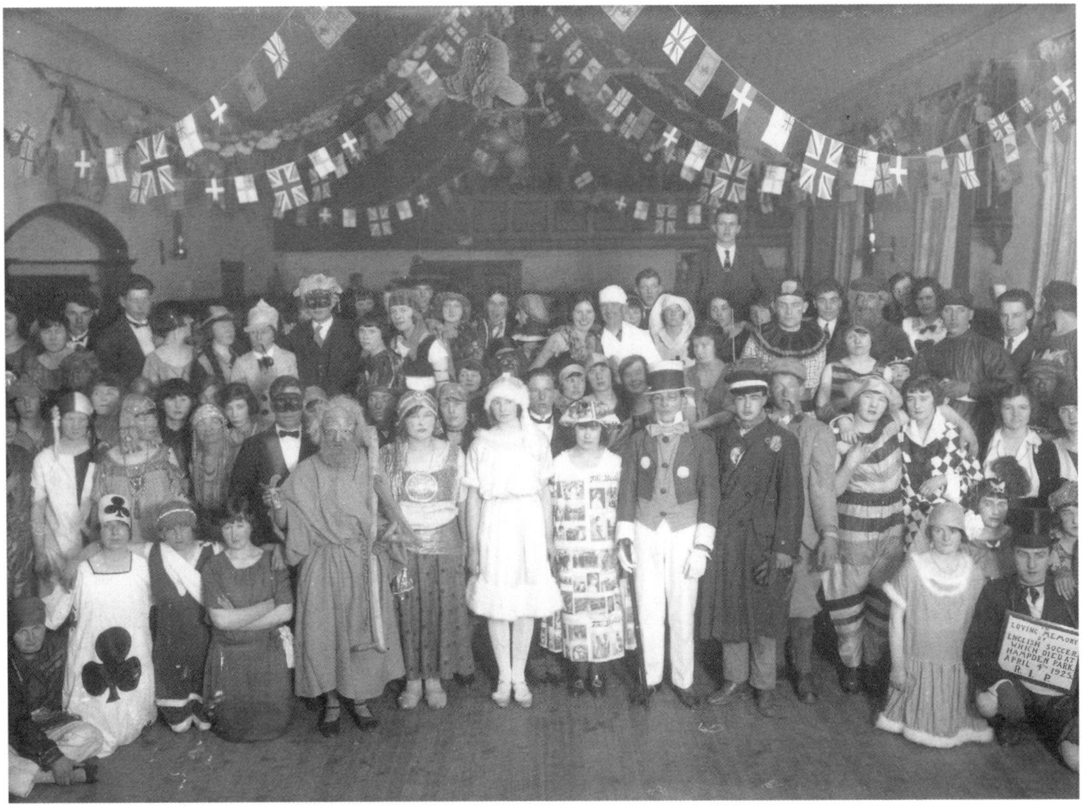

This party is inside the Greyfriars hall, at the top of Moss Street. The placard held by the kneeling figure on the far right states 'RIP English Football 1926'.

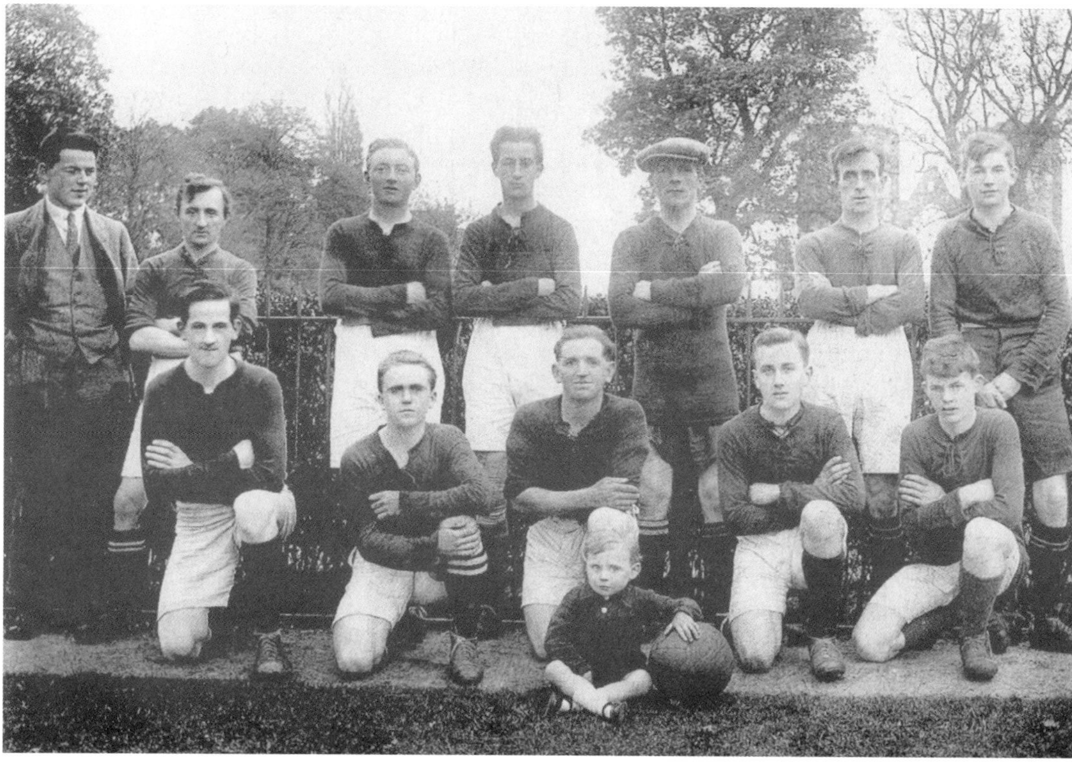

An early photograph of the Bishopmill football team. Among the famous Elgin footballers of the past was the solicitor R. C. Hamilton, proprietor of the net factory in Blackfriars Road who played for Queens Park Rangers and was provost of Elgin. His brother, J. R. Hamilton was a solicitor at Coburn Hamilton & Young and was President of Elgin City football club.

ACKNOWLEDGEMENTS

First and foremost I would like to thank Tony Spring, photographer, without whose forethought and professional skill this book would not be possible. Neither would it have been possible without the help of Susan Bennett, Curator of Elgin Museum, who believed that these photographs should be seen and appreciated instead of lying safely in a drawer.

The support and help of the members of the Moray Society has been invaluable and thanks are due for their photographs to:

Richard Bennett, W. Chalmers, Hamish Dyce, Ian Keillar, George Main, Mrs E. Markes, Jack Woods — and to the editor of the *Northern Scot* for obtaining the photograph on page 123. I am grateful for essential information and practical help from: 'Peem' Anderson, Mary Armitage, Sheila Gow, Hamish Dyce, Jim Inglis, Kerstin and Ian Keiller, Walter and Lydia Riddell, Ken and Ann Ross, Isobel and Margaret Souter, Janet Trythall.

Grateful recognition is also due to H. B. Mackintosh for all the information contained in his book of 1914 - *Elgin Past and Present*, and to the members of the Moray Society who have contributed information over the years in the forms of leaflets, articles and lectures.

I trust any errors there may be are not serious enough to spoil the enjoyment of the book which, it is hoped, will raise a smile now and again and revive a few, warm memories.